The Kids' Book Club Book

PRAISE FOR
THE BOOK CLUB COOKBOOK

"If you're in a book club, you'll savor the stories of the many culturally and ethnically diverse book groups the authors interviewed as much as the recipes."

—*USA Today*

"Part cookbook, part celebration of the written word, the volume illustrates how books and ideas can bring people together. And considering that [there are] an estimated seven million people in America involved in book clubs these days, this should prove to be a popular volume."

—*Publishers Weekly*

"*The Book Club Cookbook* excels at offering book groups new title ideas and a culinary way to spice up their discussions."

—*Library Journal*

"Judy Gelman and Vicki Levy Krupp . . . do an outstanding job of organizing their material so the plot of each book is summarized, the relevant origins and workings of each book group are outlined, and the recipes are clear."

—*The Philadelphia Inquirer*

"If you are searching for the literary equivalent of the power bar to energize your book group discussions, look no further."

—*Women's Lifestyle*

"This book equally inspires you to read, cook, and chew over books and food."

—*The Improper Bostonian*

"This yummy edition features recipes and discussion ideas for book club selections, with intriguing contributions from some of the authors of these favorite reads and fascinating profiles of a wide range of book clubs across the country."

—Santa Rosa *Press Democrat*

Jeremy P. Tarcher / Penguin
a member of **PENGUIN GROUP (USA) INC.** *New York*

THE

Kids' Book Club

BOOK

Reading Ideas, Recipes, Activities,
and Smart Tips for Organizing
Terrific Kids' Book Clubs

Judy Gelman *and*
Vicki Levy Krupp

JEREMY P. TARCHER / PENGUIN
Published by the Penguin Group
Penguin Group (USA) Inc., 375 Hudson Street, New York, New York 10014, USA *
Penguin Group (Canada), 90 Eglinton Avenue East, Suite 700, Toronto, Ontario M4P 2Y3,
Canada (a division of Pearson Penguin Canada Inc.) * Penguin Books Ltd, 80 Strand,
London WC2R 0RL, England * Penguin Ireland, 25 St Stephen's Green, Dublin 2, Ireland
(a division of Penguin Books Ltd) * Penguin Group (Australia), 250 Camberwell Road,
Camberwell, Victoria 3124, Australia (a division of Pearson Australia Group Pty Ltd) *
Penguin Books India Pvt Ltd, 11 Community Centre, Panchsheel Park, New Delhi–110 017,
India * Penguin Group (NZ), 67 Apollo Drive, Rosedale, North Shore 0745, Auckland, New Zealand
(a division of Pearson New Zealand Ltd) * Penguin Books (South Africa) (Pty) Ltd,
24 Sturdee Avenue, Rosebank, Johannesburg 2196, South Africa

Penguin Books Ltd, Registered Offices:
80 Strand, London WC2R 0RL, England

Most Tarcher/Penguin books are available at special quantity discounts for bulk purchase for sales promo-
tions, premiums, fund-raising, and educational needs. Special books or book excerpts also can be created
to fit specific needs. For details, write Penguin Group (USA) Inc. Special Markets, 375 Hudson Street,
New York, New York 10014.

Library of Congress Cataloging-in-Publication Data

Gelman, Judy, date.
The kids' book club book : reading ideas, recipes, activities, and smart tips for
organizing terrific kids' book clubs / Judy Gelman and Vicki Levy Krupp.
p.   cm.
Includes bibliographical references and indices.
ISBN 978-1-58542-559-4
1. Book clubs (Discussion groups).   2. Children—Books and reading.   I. Krupp, Vicki Levy, date.   II. Title.
LC6631.G45   2007   2006101469
028.5'5—dc22

Printed in the United States of America
3   5   7   9   10   8   6   4   2

Book design by Jennifer Ann Daddio

The recipes and activity instructions in this book are to be followed exactly as written. The publisher and
authors are not responsible for specific health or allergy concerns that may require medical supervision. The
publisher and authors are not responsible for any adverse reactions to the recipes or instructions in this book.

While the authors have made every effort to provide accurate telephone numbers and Internet addresses at
the time of publication, neither the publisher nor the authors assume any responsibility for errors, or for
changes that occur after publication. Further, the publisher does not have any control over and does not
assume any responsibility for author or third-party websites or their content.

For Danny and Noah

For Aaron, Ben, and Joanna

Contents

TITLES FOR MIDDLE GRADE READERS (GRADES 4–7)

TITLES FOR YOUNG TEEN READERS (GRADES 6–8)

TITLES FOR OLDER TEEN READERS (GRADES 9 AND UP)

Introduction

The Kids' Book Club Book was born of popular demand. While touring in 2004 to promote our first book, *The Book Club Cookbook: Recipes and Food for Thought from Your Book Club's Favorite Books and Authors* (Tarcher, 2004), a compendium of recipes and discussion ideas for adult book clubs, we met countless adults and children who shared book clubs that met in libraries, schools, and community centers. These book clubs seemed to face many of the same challenges as all-adult book clubs. "When will you write a similar book for kids' book clubs?" was a common refrain. We each have children ages eleven to fifteen and knew that book clubs for children were becoming popular in the Boston suburb where we both reside, so we decided to investigate the popularity of kids' reading groups across the United States. We were excited by what we found. The large and growing number of children and adults participating in book discussion groups in living rooms, libraries, churches, schools, cafés, and bookstores throughout the country persuaded us to make kids' book clubs the focus of our next project, a guide for adult book club facilitators and young adults interested in forming book clubs.

The proliferation of kids' book clubs has been spurred, in part, by a grim reality: Reading rates in the United States drop precipitously after the early elementary school years. Finding a child curled up with a good book has become increasingly rare as high-tech temptations such as video games, wide-screen televisions, and the Internet compete for kids' attention. According to a 2006 report sponsored by Scholastic, Inc., 44 percent of children ages five to eight read a book every day, while by ages fifteen to seventeen, the number drops to 16 percent. The reading habits of young adults between ages eighteen and twenty-four also are in sharp decline, according to a 2004 National Endowment for the Arts study, which found reading in this age group dropped by 28 percent since 1982. The survey also documented a steep decline in the number of adult readers over the past ten years.

The American Library Association, various government agencies, and organizations devoted to improving literacy all have responded to these trends with a number of initiatives, most notably by launching book discussion groups for youth in libraries, community centers, and schools. In addition, the number of private book clubs formed by parents and children continues to grow. Although no one has yet documented with exact figures the growth of kids' book clubs, we noted a marked increase in the number of new clubs reported in our daily searches of media and on the Internet during our eighteen months of research. Children are responding to the surge in the number and variety of children's titles published in recent decades, including multicultural literature, fantasy and science fiction. In addition, an explosion of new titles—books that are not generally assigned as part of school reading—feature topics relevant to the contemporary lives of young adults and teens, and have great appeal to older youth readers.

We heard about many other benefits to these groups as well. A librarian told us her group members are more likely to frequent the library and approach librarians with questions as a result of their library book club experiences. A parent reported that her mother-daughter book club affords the adults an opportunity to talk with their children about difficult issues in a "safe" setting. A teacher told us that the parents in her family book club feel more involved in the school community, and enjoy becoming familiar with quality children's literature. A high school student said she's reading books she would never read on her own, and enjoys discussing them with friends and peers in a relaxed setting. A coordinator of a community-wide reading program reported that the intergenerational discussion of a book on autism helped enhance understanding of the topic and served as a catalyst for positive interactions among community members of all ages. And a leader of a book club for youthful offenders told us the boys in his book discussion group see a dramatic improvement in reading ability, comprehension, and self-esteem.

We set out to create a guide that would help youth and adult facilitators enhance and enliven their book club experiences, and give any adult who reads with a child information that will help both adult and child get the most out of that experience. Because the core of the book club experience is to read good books, we began by asking facilitators of youth book clubs across the country to suggest titles that provoked the most interesting discussions within their groups. One year and five hundred surveys later, our spreadsheet was filled with hundreds of recommended titles. We chose the top fifty titles to feature in *The Kids' Book Club Book*.

From our surveys and telephone interviews, we learned that many book club members enjoy activities and foods related to the theme of the book during their meetings. We also learned that young readers gain a deeper understanding of the book when they connect with a book's author. We decided to ask the living authors of the fifty featured books to contribute activity ideas, recipes, biographical information, or comments related to their work. To our delight, almost all of the authors were excited to participate. Kate DiCamillo suggested an activity for decorating candy wrappers and talking about sadness after reading her book *Because of Winn-Dixie*, in which the characters taste candies that make them feel sad. Pam Muñoz Ryan wrote a recipe for burritos that she enjoyed as a child to pair with her novel *Esperanza Rising*, about the experiences of Mexican immigrants. And Walter Dean Myers explained how his interviews with juvenile offenders informed the writing of *Monster*, about a young man accused of a crime. The contributions of these authors enhance our understanding of their work.

Hundreds of book clubs also offered innovative food and activity ideas to pair with our featured books. Nature journaling, or recording observations about the natural world, when discussing David Almond's *Skellig*, in which a character is a nature artist, was one such idea. Making a "beetloaf" cake for Mary Rodgers's *Freaky Friday*, in which a character mispronounces "meat loaf," was another. In our quest to find foods to complement our featured books, we also turned to restaurants. The Courthouse Café in Monroeville, Alabama, the town where author Harper Lee still resides, serves a cream cheese pound cake from a recipe in a local Monroe County cookbook. Because

Lee based her classic novel *To Kill a Mockingbird* on events, people, and places in her small southern hometown, we thought a typical southern recipe from a favorite Monroeville eatery was a perfect match for her story.

Our year of reading children's literature, and exploring it through recipes and ideas from authors and book clubs, was an exciting, educational odyssey. Our journey introduced us to youth book clubs from coast to coast and to new authors and their work. We enjoyed testing and sampling wonderful new foods and trying our hand at games and crafts. The journey inspired us to delve further into children's, young adult, and teen literature. We hope it inspires you, as well.

What You'll Find in *The Kids' Book Club Book*

Part One is chock-full of ideas for creating a successful book club, or learning how to improve your existing group. We asked book club facilitators how they attract members, run meetings, initiate discussions, choose books, plan activities, and balance the interests of the different generations participating in their groups. While some of the tips apply to all types of clubs, other sections are specifically designated for library, school, or private groups.

Part Two features fifty top reading choices for children in grades one through twelve. Whether you belong to a book club or not, here you will find reading suggestions, information about the author, and suggested activities that will enhance the reading experience you share with children. For each featured book in Part Two, we include a short synopsis of the story line, along with the book's length, genre, and reading level, and any sequels, series, or companion books by the author.

You will find that many of the books featured in our book fall into the middle grade reader category. This reflects the preponderance of middle grade book clubs. Many of these middle grade books can be read and enjoyed by readers in other age categories. A note on the designated reading levels: Some books are aimed at older readers but contain content of interest to younger readers. The content of other titles is geared for younger readers but can also be appreciated and enjoyed by older readers. And, of course, reading skills vary widely from one child to the next. Use our reading level designations as a guide, not as the final word.

For the featured books, you'll find:

Author Scoop. In this section, you will find biographical information and anecdotes about the author that relate to the featured book, often in the author's own words. Book clubs we spoke with were most curious about what inspired authors to write their stories, or whether the authors had experienced situations similar to the ones portrayed in their work. When possible, we asked authors these questions, and tracked down other relevant information about the authors. You might read these short passages aloud at the meeting, or ask group members to read them as a way to stimulate discussion.

Authors Recommend. We asked participating authors to suggest books for further reading, with themes that relate to their work, as well as some of their favorite books. Use their suggestions to help you select the next title for your group, or to give you ideas for further reading outside the group.

Book Bites. We paired most featured books with recipes that relate to the book's plot, theme, setting, or characters. In some cases the recipes come straight from the pages of the book, like the Dump Punch and egg salad sandwiches that characters create for a party in Kate DiCamillo's *Because of Winn-Dixie.* In other cases the recipe is derived from an action or a theme in the book, such as Dirt Pudding with Louis Sachar's *Holes,* in which the characters dig holes in a dry lakebed. You will also find recipes and food ideas contributed by the authors of the featured books, including recipes for Andrew Clements's favorite hot chocolate and an Indian salad from Gloria Whelan to pair with her book, *Homeless Bird,* which is set in India. Many other recipes come from book clubs, such as baklava, to highlight the Greek setting in *The Sisterhood of the Traveling Pants.* Book clubs also gave us ideas for foods to pair with their reading selections, which we feature in sections called "Bites from the Book."

Our recipes range from the very simple—with four or fewer ingredients—to the more challenging. All have been tested and deemed delicious. Some recipes provide opportunities for group participation during book club meetings. For example, kids will enjoy decorating dress-shaped cookies for Eleanor Estes' *The Hundred Dresses,* or twisting New York–style soft pretzels for Gail Carson Levine's *Dave at Night,* set in Harlem. Even if you don't prepare food for your meetings, the recipes you find in these pages can spur a discussion of the book's theme, setting, characters, or author.

Activities. In these sections, denoted by MAKE IT!, TRY IT!, PLAY IT!, TASTE IT!, ASK IT!, and CHECK IT OUT!, you'll find activities ranging from games, puzzles, art projects, and science experiments to suggestions for guest speakers and volunteer projects. All activities relate to the book's setting, or to a central theme, character, or scene in the book. Stephanie Tolan suggests a meditation exercise to accompany her book *Surviving the Applewhites,* in which one character, Aunt Lucy, meditates to relax. A library book club in Lehigh Acres, Florida, contributed their soap-carving activity to accompany Harper Lee's *To Kill a Mockingbird,* in which figures carved of soap are left in the knothole of a tree.

The formats for the activities vary. For some, we describe how a book club has organized a project so its members' ideas can guide you in creating your own activity. For others, we offer lists of materials and step-by-step instructions your group can follow during your meeting. In the THINK ABOUT IT! sections, we describe activities and programs inspired by the featured book that, although more challenging to re-create, can generate excitement, ideas, and discussion in your book club.

Book Links. These sections highlight activity and food ideas contributed by authors.

Topics Discussed. We asked hundreds of book clubs to tell us about their most memorable discussions and compiled the topics most frequently mentioned. Note that these are not suggested discussion questions, but rather common topics of discussions that took place during book club meetings. These ideas offer a preview of how your discussion might unfold, or some topics to chat about during your own meeting.

Ask It! We also asked book clubs about the questions that generated the most interesting discussions. With each featured book, you'll find a sensational question, and a description of the interesting exchange it prompted among members of a book club. These responses give you a sense of the discussion this question might generate in your group, and the direction your discussion could take.

Appendices. A common refrain from book club members during our research was, "Will you share your list of recommended books?" Well, we have! Appendix A lists the top 150 recommended books from our surveys, categorized by genre, theme, and protagonist. Appendix B names major awards that the featured books have won. And Appendix C features a list of resources for book clubs, including books and websites, which offer book recommendations, discussion questions, and more.

Happy Reading!

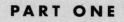

PART ONE

Making It Happen

Creating a Successful
Book Club

Ready, Set, Go: Organizing Your Group

If you picked up this book, chances are you love to read. Book clubs are an excellent way to nurture a lifelong love of reading and to experience the joy of exploring the world of books with others.

Organizing an effective book club requires forethought. What type of club do you want? How will you recruit members? How do you avoid the scheduling pitfalls that discourage or destroy many groups? What settings help set the tone for productive discussions? The more organized and thoughtful you are about setting up your group, the greater the chances for success. This section is designed to guide you through the nitty-gritty of organizing a book club: deciding on the type and size of the club, recruiting members, scheduling meetings, choosing a meeting place, structuring meetings, and locating funding.

What Type of Book Club Should You Create?

Whether you ultimately choose an intergenerational book club, a group for mothers and daughters, or a club for homeschooled kids, the type of club you create or join will be the first, and most important, decision you will have to make. Will you have adult-child pairs? Will you have an adult facilitator, or will young adult members lead the group? What ages will the kids be? What goals do you have for your group? Each type of group has benefits and challenges to consider before you organize. Here is a sampling of some of the most common group arrangements, and what you need to know about each.

To find a book club for a child, contact your local library or school, bookstores, community organizations, churches, temples, museums, and town-wide youth programs. To find an online group, see Appendix C for resources.

Groups for Younger Readers	
WHO JOINS:	Kids in kindergarten through third grade, with or without an adult partner.
WHAT THEY LIKE TO READ:	Picture books or early reading books. Often, the facilitator reads the book aloud, moderates a brief discussion, and organizes a craft or other activity related to the book.
BENEFITS:	Develops positive associations with reading; boosts early academic skills.
CHALLENGES:	Finding books with vocabulary simple enough for young children to understand but with content rich enough to generate discussion; structuring the meeting to help kids maintain focus throughout.

Groups for Middle Grade Readers

WHO JOINS: Tweens, or kids ages eight to twelve, with or without an adult partner.

WHAT THEY LIKE TO READ: All genres.

BENEFITS: Promotes confidence by building on newfound independent reading skills; helps kids develop skills of listening, responding, and taking turns.

CHALLENGES: Finding books that match widely varying reading levels.

The eight-to-twelve-year-old set is a great one for book clubs! The kids are now old enough to read meatier books and can comprehend and discuss themes, inferences, and right versus wrong. They are at an age when they can handle books that don't have happy endings. Tweens take their newfound literary independence seriously, and are extremely enthusiastic with their opinions and analyses. Book clubs are a huge ego boost for kids in their tweens.

—JOELLEN BEAUDET, HOOVER SCHOOL FIFTH GRADE PARENT-CHILD BOOK CLUB
MELROSE, MASSACHUSETTS

Teen Groups

WHO JOINS: Kids ages thirteen to seventeen, generally without, but sometimes with, an adult partner. Some groups have an adult facilitator, while others are facilitated by the teen participants.

WHAT THEY LIKE TO READ: Books belonging to a genre, such as fantasy or historical fiction; edgy, contemporary fiction; or a variety of different genres.

BENEFITS:	Gives teens a safe place to explore difficult issues, such as peer pressure, drugs, or rape; gets them reading books at a time when many other activities compete for their time; and, for library groups, helps teens feel more "at home" in the library.
CHALLENGES:	Getting teens to finish the books and consistently attend meetings.

Gender-Specific Groups

WHO JOINS:	Girls only or boys only, with or without an adult partner.
WHAT THEY LIKE TO READ:	Boys book clubs often choose adventure, fantasy, science fiction, humorous books, and books with male protagonists; girls' groups often enjoy books with female protagonists and strong character development, and books set in faraway locales.
BENEFITS:	Strong camaraderie; provides a setting where kids feel comfortable speaking openly about sensitive issues.

The boys see this book club as something just for them. They're often surprised by the idea that girls can't come. There are plenty of groups geared toward girls, but we're the only organization in our school system geared to boys and boys alone. This is a very liberating experience for them—they know they can say something, and it's "just the guys" hearing it.

—ROB MURPHY, BOYS IN LITERACY INITIATIVE (BILI)
FRANCIS HAMMOND MIDDLE SCHOOL
ALEXANDRIA, VIRGINIA

| CHALLENGES: | Groups lack the diversity of perspectives found in coed groups. |

Coed Groups

WHO JOINS:	Boys and girls of any age, with or without an adult partner.
WHAT THEY LIKE TO READ:	All genres, and especially books with both male and female protagonists.
BENEFITS:	Diverse perspectives of group members.
CHALLENGES:	Balancing book selections to feature both male and female protagonists; moderating discussions to ensure that boys and girls get equal speaking time.

Groups with Adults and Children

WHO JOINS:	Adult-child pairs of any age (the adult could be a parent, grandparent, caregiver, or another adult).
WHAT THEY LIKE TO READ:	All genres.
BENEFITS:	Strengthens the bond between a parent (or another adult) and a child through sharing ideas; fosters communication around issues such as bullying, lying, and sexuality in the context of fictional characters, making it easier for kids to discuss sensitive topics.

CHALLENGES:	Choosing books that both children and adults want to read; ensuring that adults don't dominate the discussion.

Intergenerational Groups

WHO JOINS:	Children or teens, adults, and seniors.
WHERE THEY MEET:	Schools, libraries, community centers, private living rooms, senior centers, and other communal gathering spots.
WHAT THEY LIKE TO READ:	General and historical fiction, especially books set during eras (such as the Great Depression or World War II) that seniors have lived through.
BENEFITS:	Learning about the perspectives of people from different generations; building community.
CHALLENGES:	Ensuring a balanced discussion, in which both seniors and younger members share their life experiences and perspectives.

Community Reading Programs

WHAT IT IS:	An entire community selects a book to explore through discussion, activities, and programming, such as the "One Book" community reading projects organized in states, cities, towns, and schools throughout the country (see Appendix C for related websites).

WHO JOINS:	All members of the community, including children, adults, and seniors.
WHERE THEY MEET:	Schools, libraries, community centers, senior centers, and other communal gathering spots.
WHAT THEY LIKE TO READ:	Books of local or regional interest; books focusing on important national or international issues; or topics the community wants to explore, such as racism, environmental awareness, or physical disabilities.
BENEFITS:	Building community; raising awareness of important social issues.
CHALLENGES:	Reaching and coordinating many different segments of the community; publicizing events.

Online Book Clubs

WHAT IT IS:	Book club discussions in cyberspace, often moderated by an adult.
WHO JOINS:	Middle school and teenage readers with access to a computer.
WHERE THEY MEET:	In cyberspace; some require registration and schedule regular times for online book discussions; others allow postings about the selected title at any time, and have a facilitator who "seeds" the site with provocative questions.

WHAT THEY LIKE TO READ:	All genres.
BENEFITS:	Allows a wide range of participation with no scheduling hassles; offers shy participants a chance to contribute opinions anonymously.
CHALLENGES:	Creating a sense of community in the absence of face-to-face interactions; monitoring and removing inappropriate postings.

What Is the Ideal Size for Your Book Club?

If the goal is to encourage reading and participation in the group, should you limit the size of your group? New members of a growing group can help generate interesting conversation, but the group might also lose its sense of intimacy, and some participants might feel intimidated and be hesitant to share their ideas. To maintain intimacy and encourage participation, many book clubs cap membership. When we asked book club facilitators what they consider to be the optimal number of participants, answers ranged from six to twenty, with the vast majority hovering around ten. For groups involving adult-child partners, four to ten pairs were viewed as ideal. Sherry Rodgers, a teen book club facilitator at the Washington County Library in Fayetteville, Arkansas, says six to eight members is the optimal number for her group: Any more makes her feel like a teacher, but with fewer than six, the group lacks the diversity it needs to stay interesting.

Even larger groups have found ways to maintain a small-group dynamic. When her high school book club swelled to more than twenty members, Paula Cross of Methuen, Massachusetts, found that freshmen members participated less actively in discussions. To address the problem, Cross divided the group in half. After discussions in separate groups, each moderated by a trained library media specialist, the smaller groups reunited with the whole to share ideas.

How Do You Recruit Members?

It is usually easy for private groups to organize, with one or two members asking friends or acquaintances to join. Groups that meet in public places like libraries, schools, and bookstores, however, often need to advertise and spread news of the group by word of mouth and direct contact to attract members. Here are some suggestions from book clubs.

Advertise. David Blaize, who coordinated two youth book clubs at the Pike County Public Library in Petersburg, Indiana, placed full-color advertising, displaying each month's new book, in all three branches of the library, and in school libraries and cafeterias as well. You can also publicize book club meetings in newsletters, local newspapers, or electronic media on library or school websites.

English teacher Kari Healy invited student council members at Dakota Meadows Middle School Book Club in North Mankato, Minnesota, to read the book club selections over the summer and record a thirty-to-sixty-second "book talk"—a short, enthusiastic description of the book—on videotape. She played the videos during advisory periods (when students break into small groups and meet with an assigned teacher) to encourage other students to join. You can publicize your group to parents in a school setting, by announcing the book club at parent-teacher organization meetings, back-to-school nights, and in e-mail notices and newsletters.

Word of mouth. If you have a group already, your members might be your best spokespeople, and can help recruit new participants. Gayl Smith asked members of her Waubonsie Valley High School Book Club in Aurora, Illinois, to staff a booth at the freshmen activity fair, where they fielded questions about the club, gathered

If you have a lot of good theorizers and people who have well-developed ideas and thoughts and can generate good discussion, I say the more the merrier. However, if you have more people who are likely to be disruptive, you may want fewer. For us, the best size is fifteen to twenty members. We can get in good discussion and a few wild tangents without frustrating everyone else in the process.

—AMBER LOWERY, LAKEVIEW'S LEAKY
CAULDRON BOOK CLUB
PEORIA PUBLIC LIBRARY, LAKEVIEW BRANCH
PEORIA, ILLINOIS

Resist the temptation to compose the group based simply on your son's best friends. It's important to choose kids who are good readers (and, ideally, who are willing to talk about what they've read). It's also important to find dads who are self-aware enough to give the kids the space to express themselves and who will be on the lookout for those moments when a shyer member of the group is willing to say something. The dads should mostly facilitate a discussion among the kids.

—RICH MOCHE, FATHER-SON TEEN BOOK GROUP
NEEDHAM, MASSACHUSETTS

names on a sign-up sheet, and later contacted prospective members before the first meeting. Some book clubs elect officers, who have the responsibility to recruit new members.

Partnerships. Terri Snethen, a librarian at Blue Valley North High School in Overland Park, Kansas, partnered with a local public teen librarian to become a Young Adult Library Services Association (YALSA) galley group, in which teens read and review advance copies of forthcoming books for publishers. The participating teens complete a review form with questions about the cover art and their opinions of the book, and their responses are sent directly to the publisher. Snethen says becoming a YALSA galley group boosted attendance. "The kids loved the idea of reading new Young Adult books before anyone else. Also, I've never met a kid who doesn't like getting free stuff. This was a great way to draw kids in," she says. The application for becoming a YALSA galley group, along with eligibility requirements and responsibilities, can be found on the YALSA website (www.ala.org/yalsa).

When Should You Meet?

One of the biggest challenges voiced by the hundreds of book clubs facilitators we surveyed was finding a mutually convenient time for their clubs to meet. Book club meetings often compete with other commitments—sporting events, music lessons, social engagements, jobs, homework, and family obligations. Although finding a good time to meet is a challenge, many book clubs offered ideas to help schedule your meetings.

SCHOOL-BASED GROUPS

The best times: Before or after school, early evening, during lunch or advisory periods (when teachers meet with small groups of student advisees).

Tips: Consider the bus and academic schedules. To include adult group members like parents and teachers, hold a before-school breakfast or early-evening meeting, or consider offering meetings at different times—one in the afternoon and another in the evening. If there are many people who cannot all meet on the same day, consider rotating the day of your meeting each month: Some kids can attend one month, and others can attend the next.

Only a few kids who look at a flyer will take the initiative to join a book club. But if a librarian comes into the school and hands out a flyer, and then a teacher or school librarian follows up in the hallways of school and asks a kid, "Hey, are you going to that meeting?" that's how you get kids to join.

—JOANNA NIGRELLI, YOUNG ADULT! YOUNG
ADULT! (YAYA) BOOK CLUB
AUSTIN PUBLIC LIBRARY WIRED FOR YOUTH
PROGRAM
AUSTIN, TEXAS

LIBRARY-BASED GROUPS

The best times: Evening for teens, afternoons for younger readers.

Tips: Consider where participants are coming from, and give them adequate travel time. Check with other branches about their scheduled events to avoid conflicts—or perhaps hold a joint meeting. If you have limited space, consider holding meetings after library hours.

How Often Should You Meet?

Book clubs typically meet monthly, although if you are meeting during the school day, you might consider weekly meetings and set a target number of chapters to read each week. If parents are involved, you might want to convene your group less frequently.

Scott Morrison says many of the forty or so dads in his Father-Son Book Club at the Park Avenue Elementary School in Mount Gilead, Ohio, need to leave work early to attend meetings. Rather than monthly, Morrison's group meets every nine weeks.

Consider skipping the December and/or summer meetings because of holidays and vacations, or schedule a special holiday gathering with your group.

What Works

The Readers and Writers Review at Gresham Middle School in Birmingham, Alabama, brings together kids and adult community members—including parents, school administrators, a janitor, bus drivers, and teachers—to write and share book reviews. Facilitator Lisa Churchill says the 7:30 a.m. start time for the "Book Breakfast" allows the adult members to attend before heading to work.

When Should You Set the Schedule?

To maximize attendance by helping members plan ahead, you might want to set a schedule at the start of the academic year. Plan around school or conflicting events and avoid using meeting time to discuss when the next meeting should be held.

If you prefer a more flexible schedule, agree on the next meeting date at the end of your discussion, when everyone can be included in the process. Ask members to bring a list of dates that pose potential conflicts to the meeting.

Where Should You Meet?

The physical meeting space you choose can set the tone for conversation—or distract from it. Here are some tips for making your space most conducive to a book discussion.

Find an intimate space. If your group meets privately, the warmth and intimacy of a living room sets an atmosphere ripe for conversation. When hosting a private group in your home, however, take steps to limit distractions that can interfere with the flow of discussion: Ask family members not to interrupt, and try not to answer phone calls.

If you have a library-based group, it can be challenging to find a quiet space that is large enough to accommodate the group but small enough to create a sense of intimacy. Groups have told us they prefer to meet in a back room of the library rather than the library itself, which can feel too big and open for good discussion. Leaders generally set up large rectangular or circular tables—sometimes with food in the center so participants can snack throughout the meeting. Many favor a circle, and if tables are not available, simply sit in a circle on the floor.

If you are meeting in a school, try to find a classroom or school library that is free of distractions. Bookstores can sometimes be noisy and highly trafficked, especially on weekends, so find a quiet corner to meet. "A store setting can be more impersonal, but you can build your own personal space within a public space," says Liz Lacey-Osler, book club coordinator at The Doylestown Book Shop in Doylestown, Pennsylvania. She adds that bookstore meetings offer many benefits: a neutral environment, a central location that everyone knows how to reach, and, in some cases, the opportunity to order coffee and snacks.

Try meeting in a nontraditional space. Carolyn White chose a local coffee shop as the meeting place for her Eighth Grade Book Club at McDougle Middle School in Chapel Hill, North Carolina. She says that the adult atmosphere and "glamour" of this setting generated more participation than meetings held on school grounds. Members enjoyed being able to order coffee and snacks and discuss the book in an "adult" setting. Unlike meetings held at school, however, your group might need to find transportation to get to off-site meetings.

What Works

The Junior Historian Book Club meets at Dallas Heritage Village, a museum dedicated to the history of Texas from 1840 to 1910, and reads historical fiction of that era. When they read *All-of-a-Kind Family* by Sydney Taylor, about an immigrant Jewish family living in New York in the early 1900s, the group toured one of the museum's exhibits, a living history kosher Jewish household, with a museum interpreter. Facilitator Melissa Prycer says the group's access to the museum allowed them to compare Jewish life in Dallas to Jewish life in New York at the turn of the century, helping members make the connection between history and literature.

Connect your meeting space to the reading selection. The Fourth Grade Mother-Daughter Book Club of the Solomon Schechter Day School of Greater Boston generally meets in members' homes, but for *A Single Shard* by Linda Sue Park, about potters in twelfth-century Korea, the group met in the Korean pottery room of the Museum of Fine Arts in Boston. Member Sylvia Fuks Fried says discussing the book in a quiet setting, surrounded by Korean pottery, made for a more meaningful meeting.

Meet off-site. To attract members and avoid a "school-like" feeling in meetings, Christine Durling makes field trips a regular feature of the Ravenous Readers Book Club at Bordentown (New Jersey) Regional High School. "Discussing the latest reads somewhere other than the high school releases the academic tension found in the traditional classroom setting," Durling says. "There are no rules, no rubrics, no right or wrong answers. Students are very free with the critiques of the books we read." Durling also appreciates the opportunity to expose her students to places they might not otherwise visit, such as the historic seaside town of Ocean Grove, New Jersey, and the Princeton University Art Museum.

Wherever you decide to hold meetings, be aware of space constraints or a high noise level that might prevent focused discussion. Members of the Teens 'N Technology Book Club of the Southwest Community Enrichment Center in Philadelphia gather in cafés, but facilitator Christina Dogbey cautions that "choosing a café carefully is key. We go to places that either are well sectioned-off or have outdoor seating." Make sure to check the space in advance to find a quiet area where your group can meet away from the hustle-bustle of a public venue.

How Should You Structure Meetings?

Organizing your meeting time can make the meeting flow more smoothly. While a relaxed and open structure is optimal, you might want to prepare meeting agendas and set informal rules governing meetings.

Getting started. You might begin meetings with a period of socializing and eating, particularly if a meal is served. The parents and boys in Mary Hennessey's East Lansing (Michigan) Public Library Parent-Son Book Group come from various school districts and enjoy time to meet and socialize before the book discussion. Hennessey asks local restaurants to donate meals each month. Group members eat and chat over dinner for twenty minutes or so before diving into discussion. Socializing time helps to reduce extraneous talking during the book discussion.

To begin the meeting, address "housekeeping" details, such as scheduling issues and other announcements. You might distribute the next month's book at this time, and discuss it briefly to get kids excited about it.

Serving food. You can set a casual, fun tone by serving food at the start of your meeting and keeping it available throughout the discussion. Amy Kaplan says the snacks she sets out for the moms and teens in her book club at the Briarcliff Manor (New York) Public Library add to "the fun, 'nonschool' vibe" she likes to create. On the other hand, food can be a distraction: For the younger readers in her My First Book Club, Kaplan offers snacks only at the start of the meeting, and no one may ask for snacks once the discussion is under way. "Seven- to nine-year-old kids are on the verge of being very silly at all times," she explains. "I learned the hard way that it can easily turn into a thirty-minute jokefest about the snacks." If you want to focus intensively on discussion and reduce the chance of distractions, consider supplying food only during a short break, or after discussion has ended.

Group rules. Decide the tone you want to set for your group—should it be fun and relaxed, more structured, or somewhere in between? Danielle King, librarian at the Orlando (Florida) Public Library, points out that with teens it's important to stay positive, and too many rules and guidelines can turn kids off.

But structure can help when it comes to the discussion, ensuring that everyone contributes equally. Amy Kaplan emphasizes that her book club members must simply

The classroom model of discussion, where kids raise their hands, is not something you want to stick with for too many years. An adult-child book club is the perfect place to learn the skills of communicating in a group, with a group, in front of a group. The outspoken kids learn to be better listeners and the shy kids learn to be better contributors. They learn how to respect the flow of a discussion, how to affirm the points of others without getting too far off track, how to jump in with a new question if things are getting too quiet. They learn how to pay attention to the thought processes and communication styles of different people [adults and kids] at the same time, which isn't easy!

—JAN SEERVELD, MOTHER-DAUGHTER BOOK CLUB
SAN CARLOS, CALIFORNIA

respect each other. "I find that sums it up in a nutshell without having a laundry list of rules, such as no interrupting, no negative comments about other people's opinions, or give everyone a chance to speak," she says. Terri Snethen asks students in her Blue Valley North High School Book Club in Overland Park, Kansas, to raise their hands when they have comments so they can be heard by the whole group. Other group leaders encourage members to break away from the habit of raising their hands before speaking because it can give a formal tone to the group and does not allow kids to develop the skills of listening and taking turns.

Some parent-child groups find that adults' enthusiasm for discussion can suppress the children's participation. In other words—they talk too much!

Elaine Hayes believes the teenage girls in her book club at the Laramie County Library in Cheyenne, Wyoming, may be overly influenced by what their mothers say, so she is considering asking the girls to speak before their moms during meetings. Krista Helmboldt, a member of a mother-daughter club in Hopkinton, New Hampshire, recently found another solution to the problem: using an object as a "talking stick." When held, the object designates the speaker in the group. "It's been a great way to give the speaker 'the floor' and help the adults refrain from jumping in too quickly," observes Helmboldt.

When to have activities. You might find that younger readers in your group have a greater attention span when the discussion is held at the beginning of the meeting, while others enjoy warming up with an activity. Stephanie Maroun's Fifth Grade Mother-Daughter Book Club at the Solomon Schechter Day School in Newton, Massachusetts, schedules activities at the start of their meetings that allow the girls to experience firsthand a major component of the plot and make themes more concrete. "This can help them transition into discussion," Maroun says.

Consider the structure that will work best for your group. Tony Carmack begins his Guys Read Book Club at the Ashburn (Virginia) Library with a short activity that latecomers can join, such as watching a video. Carmack saves a physical activity, such as a burlap-sack race, for the end of the meeting, because the boys tend to lose focus after the physical activity. He sandwiches the book discussion in the middle.

Closing the meeting. Use this time to choose the book and date for your next meeting, or simply to socialize and eat, or to distribute copies of the next book, if it has already been selected. This can be a good moment to share information about the author, and generate excitement about reading the next book. David Blaize of the Pike County Public Library in Petersburg, Indiana, says that talking up the next book can boost the kids' interest in it before they even open it.

Keep Them Coming Back

Here are some quick strategies facilitators can use to encourage regular attendance by helping kids remember and feel positive about the book club experience.

- Maintain contact with book club members between meetings.
  - Talk to members of the group before and after meetings, and encourage them to contact you with any questions or ideas.
  - Make a reminder call or send a reminder e-mail a week before the meeting, and then again the day before the meeting.
  - Send "We missed you" notes to members who fail to show up for a meeting.
- If possible, provide a copy of the book for participants to keep. Distribute copies of the next month's book at the meetings so participants are encouraged to attend in order to receive their copy.
- Give out favors as a reminder of the experience, or give kids stickers to decorate something used during the book club (for example, a stand-up name tag), so kids can keep track of how many discussions they have attended.

How Can You Fund Your Book Club?

If you're hosting a private group, you'll likely be expected to cover the costs of the meeting, including food and any art supplies needed for projects. Contact group members in advance to ask them to contribute if a project will be costly. Choosing paperback books can help reduce the cost, as can book club discounts offered at local bookstores. If several members of your group plan to borrow books from the same library, request the book well in advance so librarians have time to gather copies from other libraries. Consider providing your local bookstore and the library with your reading list for the entire year, if possible.

What Works

Two pizza parlors in Petersburg, Indiana, agreed to donate pizzas to middle and high school book clubs at the Pike County Public Library. In return, group facilitator David Blaize includes the sponsors on any advertising he does for the club.

For school, library, and other groups, the costs of running a group can include snacks, art supplies for activities or projects, and, in some cases, purchasing books.

Funding Your Club

Below is a sampling of the many strategies that school and library clubs have used to meet the costs of running a book club.

- **Charge a fee.** Some groups charge a mandatory or optional fee to help pay the costs of running a group.
- **Ask parents.** Parents understand the value of book clubs and are often willing to contribute to their costs. To reduce the strain on your budget, ask parents to provide snacks. Sometimes parents have access to corporate funding resources that can significantly help with costs.
- **Approach local businesses.** When asked, many businesses—including bookstores, restaurants, and craft stores—are quite willing to support book club activities.
- **Hold special events.** School book clubs engage in a wide range of fundraising efforts for their groups, from silent auctions to empty-printer-ink-cartridge return programs to craft sales during book fairs. Many of the groups with these ideas are committed to providing books for participants to keep, and the funds they raise help to meet this goal.

2

Novel Ideas:
Choosing the Right Books

As a facilitator, one of your greatest challenges will be to find engaging books that stimulate discussion and match the interests of your group. Here are some strategies for finding the right books for your group.

Who Should Select the Books for Your Group?

Involve your group in selecting books, but remember that adults and kids often have very different ideas about what should be on the reading list. Adults tend to prefer books that are educational or teach what they consider to be valuable lessons. Parents, in particular, can become focused on getting their children to read difficult or complex books, turning the book club experience into a vehicle for self-improvement rather than an opportunity to share ideas and the joy of reading.

Carol Bell of Cody, Wyoming, says that initially it was tricky for her mother-daughter book club to choose books that everyone would read. The mothers wanted to read classics like Charlotte Brontë's *Jane Eyre* (1847) to nudge their children beyond their school reading requirements. The girls were more interested in reading mainstream fiction, such as Alice Sebold's *The Lovely Bones* (Little, Brown, 2002) or Yann Martel's *Life of Pi* (Harcourt, 2002). The kids wanted the book club to be different from school. "They are active, busy girls, and it takes time to read many of the classics. We didn't want it to feel like homework," says Bell. According to Bell, now the girls choose most of the titles.

Amy Hewes of San Luis Obispo, California, agrees that the "power struggle" over choosing books can be a pitfall. Her mother-daughter group voted on the books, which often pitted the girls' choices against those of the moms. Now the mother-and-daughter pair that hosts the next meeting selects the book.

Sara Stevenson, a middle school librarian who runs book clubs in Austin, Texas, also emphasizes that children and adults may make very different choices when it comes to books. "You can't be a snob," says Stevenson. Some of the titles her girls' book clubs have chosen are not well reviewed in library journals, focusing on themes like gossip and girls being mean to each other. For Stevenson, these are topics the girls are interested in exploring. "I want to read what they want to read," she adds.

Consider choosing the books for the first few meetings, before getting the group involved.

Suggestions from Book Clubs

Following are methods to consider when your group selects books:

- Members take turns bringing several books of interest to meetings for a group vote.
- The facilitator selects an assortment of books from which the group votes for its favorites.
- Each member or adult-child pair take turns selecting books for the group.
- The group brainstorms together to create a reading list.

When it comes to soliciting input from your members, here are some strategies to help you get started.

Hold a "book party." Rosemary Pugliese sponsors a quarterly "book bash" for the

Graphic novels are not just comic books anymore: They have complex themes and deep character development. Looking at a sizable chapter book can be daunting for many kids, especially if you are dealing with reluctant readers. Kids see a "comic-like book" and the format draws them in. Before they know it, they've read a great story that has as much to offer as traditional novels.

—NICOLE CHASE-IVERSON,
FAMILY LITERACY PROGRAM (FLiP)
SULLIVAN FREE LIBRARY
CHITTENANGO, NEW YORK

youth book groups that meet at Quail Ridge Books & Music in Raleigh, North Carolina. She displays a variety of books she has chosen, and asks kids to contribute titles as well. Pugliese then "book talks" the book, describing each title before the group votes on which books to read in the future.

Take a poll. At the start of each school year, teacher Rob Murphy in Alexandria, Virginia, takes an "interest inventory" among boys in his middle school book club. He then chooses books each month based on themes—such as sports, hip-hop, and adventure—that emerge from the boys' "inventory" of interests.

Solicit recommendations. Janet Edwards of Kirkwood, Missouri, says her mother-daughter book club only chooses books that have been read and recommended by at least one group member. "Both the moms and daughters in our group are avid readers, so recommendations seem to come naturally," says Edwards.

Although chewing over book possibilities can be a fun and interesting part of a book club meeting, you might prefer to avoid regular extended discussions about what to read next, and the conflicts or lobbying that might ensue. You can simplify things by creating a reading list for the year, leaving a few spots open for new books of interest to the group.

What Types of Books Should You Select?

Although some groups focus on a single genre such as fantasy or science fiction, many groups see an eclectic mix as an opportunity to introduce and explore new genres. Most youth book clubs favor fiction—out of the fifty recommended titles featured in this book, only two are nonfiction—and give diverse reasons: Because the message or moral in fictional stories is often ambiguous, or because issues frequently are not resolved easily in fictional stories, they present great fodder for discussion.

What Factors Should You Consider When Selecting Books?

Take into account the reading level of your group, the nature of the themes in the book, and whether the book presents interesting and relevant discussion points.

Reading level. The reading level of the books selected should match the reading skills of your group, although you might also try varying the difficulty level of the books you read. Amy Hewes says her mother-daughter group mixes up the reading levels of their selections. If one book has been more challenging, the next month's selection might be less difficult. "We look at the long time frame," says Hewes.

While you might select some titles that challenge readers, most books should not be beyond the reading level of the participants. Ramona Demme, a daughter in a mother-daughter group in Nyack, New York, says her group made the mistake of tackling books such as Virginia Woolf's *Mrs. Dalloway* (1925) and Franz Kafka's *Metamorphosis* (1915) before the daughters were ready to appreciate them fully. Demme says these books went right over the kids' heads and probably should have been saved for a time when the girls could have better appreciated them.

I look for books that have a lot of "soul." These are books that have multiple themes where both child and parent can relate to the characters and share similar experiences. I want everyone to have a deep appreciation for the story I have chosen. This makes for a rich book club experience for anyone at any age.

—KIRSTEN CONSIDINE, HOFFMAN SCHOOL PARENT-CHILD BOOK DISCUSSION GROUP GLENVIEW, ILLINOIS

Subject matter. All groups grapple with whether to choose books with themes that are serious or light. Many groups look for lighter themes and try to avoid selecting too many books that deal with topics like family dysfunction or death, especially when younger readers are involved. "It is easy to overdose on message books about adolescent angst," says Rich Moche, a parent member of a father–teenage son book group. Moche

I try to avoid having too many selections that are overly grim and serious. We don't avoid meaningful issues and relevant topics. We just try to include some books that don't read like the six-o'clock news. We use fables, fantasy, humor, historical fiction, and more to challenge our young readers to think, to exercise their imaginations, and to simply enjoy reading.

—JACK VOELKER
SUMMER YOUNG READERS PROGRAM
CHAUTAUQUA INSTITUTION
CHAUTAUQUA, NEW YORK

says his group has had success with books such as Gary Paulsen's *Winterdance: The Fine Madness of Running the Iditarod* (Harcourt, 1994), which not only transcends age but also is an exciting, compelling story with adventure, comedy, and themes that were fun to discuss together.

Other groups aim for books that address serious issues relevant to group members. The Teens 'N Technology program, a book group for urban adolescents sponsored by the Southwest Community Enrichment Center in Philadelphia, tackles books about gangs, peer pressure, school, and family issues, along with books that offer a broader social commentary. Kirsten Hansen, a high school senior who participates in the Groton (Massachusetts) Public Library's Oreos and Talk High School Book Discussion Group, says the books her group selects need to have "substance that goes beyond just the plot or the characters to real issues that real teens want to discuss." Hansen looks for books that inspire discussion on such details as the quality of the writing, on how the literature connects to real life, and on questions of ethics it raises.

Adults should provide guidance to children selecting books to ensure the titles are appropriate for their age group. If possible, an adult facilitator should read all books under consideration in advance to determine if the books are suitable. Elise Sheppard of the Harris County Public Library in Cypress, Texas, says that when teens sign up for book clubs, she always tells both the parents and the teens to review the books to decide together which discussions they would like to participate in.

While many teen book groups seek books of interest to teens, some parents do not want their teenagers exposed to topics like sex and drugs. Elementary-level book clubs are also cautious in choosing books. Leaders of book clubs for younger readers emphasize that you should have a good understanding of the book before suggesting it to your group. Dorothy Distefano runs several elementary-school book groups in Hilton, New York. She says the most important part of choosing books is reading every single book cover to cover before choosing it. "I was dismayed at how many books that have great story lines include items that may be objectionable, presumably for shock value," says Distefano. The group's age mix should also be considered when selecting appropriate books.

Elaine Hayes of the Laramie County Library in Cheyenne, Wyoming, found it surprisingly hard to get the younger girls in her mother-daughter book group to discuss Laurie Halse Anderson's *Speak* (Farrar, Straus & Giroux, 1999). "The mothers in the group were more vocal on *Speak* than the girls," says Hayes, who believes the younger teens found it hard to discuss the topic of rape explored in the book.

Points for discussion. Judging whether a title is meaty enough for discussion can be tricky but crucial to the success of the discussion. As Connie Mathews of the Girls Night Out Book Club in Pittsburgh describes: "When I

We want to encourage students to read by introducing them to material that includes some of their reality. Many of the students I encounter say they don't like to read because books are boring. I believe that what they are really saying is that they don't see themselves in the books they are being asked to read in their English classes, therefore they find it hard to relate to the characters, the conflicts and the resolutions. Beyond placing a literary lens on their reality, we also use each book as a teaching tool in getting students to think about how they would seek positive solutions to similar situations in their own lives. Once we get them into reading "contemporary" books, it's not that long of a journey to reading the classics. The proof is in the pudding. They just finished reading George Orwell's *1984*, and they loved every word of it.

—CHRISTINA DOGBEY, TEENS 'N TECHNOLOGY BOOK CLUB SOUTHWEST COMMUNITY ENRICHMENT CENTER, PHILADELPHIA

look for a book for our group, the most important element is discussability. If I can't get ten juicy questions out of it, I won't use it." It is important to remember that many popular books may not provoke the most interesting discussions.

Book length. Choose books that the entire group has time to read, but that still offer interesting discussion points. "Since we all are busy with school and other activities, we can't be reading seven-hundred-page books," says Zoe Cordes Selbin, a teenage member of a mother-daughter book group in Georgetown, Texas. On the other hand, she explains, "a short book often means a very straightforward and simple plot, which doesn't make for an amazing conversation." For groups that meet every four

I look for books that will stir controversy and promote thought. A book that asks the reader to think about the impact of new scientific discoveries like human cloning and test-tube babies will be much more valuable than a "beach book," with simple characters and a happy ending, that never forces the reader to take a closer look at life.

—ALLYSON SHAW, STUDENT, BLUE VALLEY
NORTH HIGH SCHOOL BOOK CLUB
OVERLAND PARK, KANSAS

to six weeks, Cordes Selbin recommends books under 350 pages, so members realistically have time to finish before the next meeting.

Suggestions from Book Clubs

- Review classroom readings lists and choose books that the kids will not be reading in school.
- Try a book that is the basis for a recent or upcoming film adaptation.
- Consider books that might introduce new genres to your group (for example, a scary book for Halloween, or poetry for poetry month), or select a single topic to explore in depth over several months.
- Pick lesser-known titles by popular authors who are already familiar to group members.

I try to go back and forth along the continuum of self and world in terms of themes. A book like Kate DiCamillo's *Because of Winn-Dixie* [Candlewick Press, 2000] falls at the "self" end: All my kids can easily relate to the main character, Opal, and her life as a nine-year-old, trying to make friends in a new town. But Kashmira Sheth's *Blue Jasmine* [Hyperion, 2004], about a young girl who moves from India to the United States with her family, falls more toward the global end: It exposes kids to life in India and the experience of an Indian girl coming to America.

—ANDREW SPENO, CINCINNATI COUNTRY DAY SCHOOL
OPPORTUNITY, APPRECIATION AND KNOWLEDGE (OAK) BOOK CLUB (GRADES 4–5)
CINCINNATI

3

Talk It Up: Running Dynamic Discussions

Terrific questions, supplemental information relevant to the book, and a facilitator who can draw participants into the discussion all contribute to lively and interesting discussions. Your group might opt for a more casual, free-flowing exchange, where members are encouraged to explore interesting tangents, or you may prefer a more structured discussion where you stick to an agenda or questions formulated in advance.

Most youth book clubs have a facilitator to guide the discussion and ensure that the meetings run smoothly. You might have a single facilitator or rotate the position. Remember that older children and teens can take turns facilitating the discussion.

What Types of Questions Should You Ask?

If you're the facilitator, do your homework. Come up with discussion questions in advance of the meeting and prepare background material. You can write down discussion questions as you read the book, or find discussion questions on publishers' websites, reading group websites (see addresses in Appendix C), and in the back of the book selection. Also, see our ASK IT! sections throughout Part Two. Here are some

The discussion should be *student*-led and *adult*-facilitated. The adults should do as little talking as possible. However, this takes time to build because students need to feel comfortable enough to talk and place themselves in the role of owning the book club. Scheduling frequent meetings and making sure you get to know the students and help them understand that they have a social and intellectual support network from the facilitators and fellow book club members are key.

—CHRISTINA DOGBEY, TEENS 'N
TECHNOLOGY BOOK CLUB
SOUTHWEST COMMUNITY ENRICHMENT
CENTER, PHILADELPHIA

tips from book clubs for stimulating lively discussions and encouraging members to actively participate.

Even if members are asked to bring questions, make sure to have your own on hand. Jackie Hemond, of the Simsbury (Connecticut) Public Library, asks club members to bring their own questions but prepares general questions in case the discussion lags or the members assigned to bring questions cannot attend. General questions might include: Do you know anyone who is like a certain character in the book? What do you think of the artwork on the cover of the book? Were you happy with the ending of the book, or would you rewrite it? A good question can launch an invigorating twenty-minute conversation, while other questions might fall flat. After some time, most facilitators get to know the types of questions that work best in their group.

Ask questions that are factual. Facilitators can sometimes get members to talk by asking simple questions related to the plot. If the book is historical, ask when and where the story takes place and what group members know about that time period. This helps participants review the basic story line and warms them up for discussion.

Ask questions that are opinion-based. What was your favorite scene? Did you like the book? Questions that solicit each kid's opinion involve members in the conversation right away. Nancy Zimble of Los Angeles devises open-ended questions for her private mother-daughter group. She urges the girls to defend their positions. Zimble often plays devil's advocate. "I ask for explanations and/or examples of any position they take, even if it means taking a position myself that I might not really believe."

Ask questions that relate to the participants. Kids become more engaged when questions relate to their own lives. When talking about setting or time period, ask members how the setting compares with where they live, suggests Kitty Felde, host of Book

Club of the Air, a televised youth book club in Los Angeles. Felde also recommends asking kids if the situation in the book reminds them of something similar at school or whether a conflict between characters rings true. Joanna Nigrelli of Austin, Texas, tries to bring the questions back to the participants' lives: "Have you ever been misjudged by someone? How did that make you feel?" and "The main character has dreams of doing something. What are your dreams?"

Eighth-grader Talia Greenberg, who participates in Solomon Schechter Day School's Mother-Daughter Book Club in Newton, Massachusetts, agrees that discussions flourish when members can relate to characters in the book. "In our book club we have great discussions about how characters change throughout the book, why characters act and say the things they do, what we would have done in the character's position and why, and if any of the events in the character's life have also happened to us," she says.

Be very prepared. Discussion facilitators should read the book twice, if possible, and have discussion questions and information about the author available. Also be a good listener so you can pick up the small comments that will lead you into the next issue.

—ELAINE HAYES, MOTHER-DAUGHTER BOOK CLUB LARAMIE COUNTY LIBRARY CHEYENNE, WYOMING

Pose questions that help members identify key elements of the story. Ask club members to play detective to uncover the author's hidden messages. In their parent-child book groups, Lawrence and Nancy Goldstone, the authors of *Deconstructing Penguins: Parents, Kids, and the Bond of Reading* (Ballantine, 2005), guide members in identifying the plot, character, point of view, and conflict in the book. "We begin with incidents in the book, often in a passage where there is conflict between key characters, and follow it through until the group has unearthed whatever moral issue is at play." They recommend that facilitators "steer away from questions or answers that lead only to dead ends of superficial observation, and manage the discussion in such a way as to make steady identifiable progress that the children can follow."

Ask participants if they can find similarities to or differences from other books they may have read. "Kids are particularly good at comparing the book with previous books they've read and explaining why," says Kitty Felde. She says the middle school

> The questions that prompt the most heated discussions are the ones involving morality and touchy issues. Last year we read a nonfiction book on politics, and those with very strong opinions raised their voices and argued for an hour.
>
> —KATHRYN WEAVER, STUDENT, BLUE VALLEY NORTH HIGH SCHOOL BOOK CLUB OVERLAND PARK, KANSAS

students in her club have referred to both William Shakespeare's *Hamlet* and the *Star Wars* series while discussing *The Eagle of the Ninth* by Rosemary Sutcliff (Oxford University Press, 1987). Lisa Hughes says many of the members of her Oregon, Wisconsin, mother-daughter group have been inspired to read sequels of books they enjoyed, such as *The People of Sparks* (Random House, 2004), Jeanne DuPrau's sequel to *The City of Ember* (Random House, 2003; see p. 133).

Reading the sequel allowed the group to compare details of the books, including the cover art, and analyze the characters common to both books more fully.

What Other Kinds of Information Should You Bring to the Meeting?

Bring outside materials to the meeting that can enhance your group's understanding and enjoyment of the literature. Here are a few ideas from book clubs.

Information about the author. Many book clubs enjoy learning about the author, particularly biographical information that relates to the reading selection or what inspired the author to write the book. Rosemary Pugliese shares information about the author's childhood with her bookstore book clubs in Raleigh, North Carolina. "It reinforces to children that authors are real people," says Pugliese, "and when there's drama in the author's life or something unusual happens, the kids begin to think about how it might have affected the author." When her group read *The Haunting of Granite Falls* (Dutton, 2004), which refers to World War II, they learned that author Eva Ibbotson had left Austria as a child during the Holocaust, and discussed what it might be like to be forced to leave your home and be unable to return.

Details about the book's time period, subject, or setting. Understanding the time period, setting, or themes of the book can broaden the discussion. Jill Dean of the Wardsboro (Vermont) Public Library asks members to bring a fact related to the book to the club's meeting. For example, when reading Frances Hodgson Burnett's *The Secret Garden* (1909), in which the main character sails from India to England, the boys in the club gathered facts about England, and the girls about India. Sharing this information sparked a discussion about what it would be like to live in each of the cultures. The group then traced the character's voyage from India to England on a globe, and discussed her life after she arrived in England.

How Can You Encourage Participation?

Some members of your group are likely to be more reticent than others. To ensure that everyone gets an opportunity to talk, take note of who has not participated and encourage their involvement in the conversation. Use the techniques suggested by book clubs below to guide you.

Notice who is participating. All members won't participate equally, and for many book clubs, the more vocal members can easily dominate the quieter members. "For a facilitator, it is important to be attuned to those moments when a shy kid is willing to speak up, and to act quickly to protect that kid's opportunity to speak," says Rich Moche, who participates in a father-son teen book group in Needham, Massachusetts. "Sometimes getting kids to participate ten percent feels like success."

Ask group members to devise questions. Assigning responsibility for coming up with questions gives members a stake in the discussion and will

I led the discussion for *Tess of the D'Urbervilles, East of Eden,* and *Gone With the Wind.* Getting everyone involved in a discussion can be hard, especially if they haven't read the book. If I notice that someone is not involved, I sometimes ask that person a specific question. I think we get most excited while talking about the characters, and having many questions about the characters is always good.

—SASHA THALHEIMER, AGE SIXTEEN,
TEEN HOMESCHOOLERS BOOK CLUB
CONCORD, NEW HAMPSHIRE

force some level of participation. In Janet Edwards's Kirkwood, Missouri, mother-daughter book group, each girl develops discussion questions to share with the group.

Keep journals. Encourage all club members to keep a journal in which they record before the meeting why they did or did not like the book, explain a favorite part of the book, or even sketch some illustrations. Jotting down notes helps members prepare for the discussion and easily allows everyone to participate in the beginning of the meeting. Nancy Zimble of Los Angeles says journals were especially important during the early days of her mother-daughter book club when some girls dominated discussions. Using journals gave the quieter girls opportunities to get more involved. "Not everyone could think or remember on the spot. Journals are a tool to help that process," says Zimble.

Try a group synopsis. Ask members to take turns telling parts of the story. "Telling the story as a group is a good way to review the plotline," says Claudia Jiménez, whose parent-child book group in Vero Beach, Florida, begins with a group synopsis. "It also leads to discussions about specific characters and conflicts."

Rate the book. Rating the book on a common scale at each meeting can encourage group members who do not participate actively to start talking. The members of Amy Hewes's San Luis Obispo, California, book club rate the book from one to ten at the beginning of the group meeting, each member explains her vote, and then they rate the book again at the end of the discussion. "It's fun to see how people's opinions change through the discussion," says Hewes.

Distribute tasks before the meeting. You can involve multiple members in the conversation from the start by assigning research tasks. At the Simsbury (Connecticut) Public Library, facilitator Jackie Hemond employs a discussion format she calls her "bible" (see below). Hemond assigns jobs to her girls' book club members before the meeting, each of which requires some thought and preparation. Hemond says shy girls can be assigned the task of bringing food that is connected to the theme of the book, but she asks them to explain why they chose the snacks they did.

Jackie Hemond's Discussion Tasks

Members of the Simsbury (Connecticut) Public Library's Girls' Book Club volunteer for these tasks before each meeting:

- *Feeders of the Hungry* bring food associated with the book.
- *The Word Wizard* looks up and shares meanings of new vocabulary words.
- *The Illuminator* pulls out the Big Ideas.
- *The Connector* compares ideas in the book to other books and/or movies.
- *The Questioner* comes up with open-ended questions (a maximum of five) to ask the other kids.
- *The Character Shrink* chooses one character to "psychoanalyze."
- *The Stateswoman* finds facts about the setting of the book.
- *The Game Warden* develops a short, fun activity connected with the book.
- *The Gossip* tells a little something about the author.

Read parts of the book aloud. Every member can take a turn reading or acting as a character. Jill Dean prints quotations from the book's characters on slips of paper. She asks her middle school book club members in Wardsboro, Vermont, to draw the slips from a basket, and to use what they imagine to be the "voice" of the character while reading the quotations. Members then take turns guessing which character is being portrayed. "This prompts the kids to discuss what is happening in the story at that time and how the characters relate to each other," says Dean. She then follows up with questions: "What do you think the character meant by that?" and "What do you think the character was feeling?"

What Are Some Other Ways to Enhance Your Discussion?

Good literature has many dimensions, and sometimes moving beyond discussion alone can help your group explore the books more fully. Consider these suggestions from book clubs:

Invite an author. Invigorate your discussion by chatting with an author. Many authors are available to speak to book clubs in person, or by telephone if you have access to a speakerphone. Visit our website (www.bookclubcookbook.com) for a listing of authors who will speak to your book club, or visit individual publishers' and authors' websites.

Invite an outside speaker. Community members can enhance your appreciation of a story by sharing personal experiences or expertise on a topic related to your reading. Sherry Rodgers invited a Native American storyteller to her Fayetteville, Arkansas, teen book group meeting when they read several Native American stories. Lisa Churchill's Birmingham, Alabama, middle school book club invited a band director to explain the drumbeats mentioned in Jordan Sonnenblick's *Drums, Girls & Dangerous Pie* (Scholastic, 2004).

Try an icebreaker. These questions or activities are designed to "warm up" a group and help book club members relax before the discussion, or help new members get to know one another. For some clubs, an icebreaker is a craft or game of charades, while other groups simply ask questions to draw out new members.

Connie Mathews of the Mt. Lebanon Public Library in Pittsburgh asks her mother-daughter book club members to tell two truths and one lie about themselves. Everyone talks together to try to figure out which statement is the lie. "When the lies are revealed, more conversation is usually generated," says Mathews. "Everyone always has fun with this activity, and members gain a new level of familiarity with each other."

Dawn Rutherford, a facilitator of teen book groups in Bellevue, Washington, tries "to create questions that everyone will have an answer to, so right off the bat they feel that they have something to contribute." Before discussing Michael Chabon's *Summerland* (Miramax, 2002), in which the main character considers himself to be a terrible baseball player but unexpectedly finds himself recruited to help fairies compete against their foes on the field, she asked: "What is the most unexpected thing that happened to you this summer?" Questions like this can give teens a voice, attention, and respect, all within the first five minutes of the meeting, says Rutherford.

Deb Grimmett of the Abington (Massachusetts) Public Library asked members of the Cliffhanger Club Parent-Child Book Discussion Group to bring family photographs when they discussed Patricia Reilly Giff's *Pictures of Hollis Woods* (Wendy Lamb, 2002). It was the group's first discussion of the year and many new members were in attendance. "Bringing a picture of family fit so well with the book, in which the main character draws pictures of the family she wishes for," says Grimmett. "It was a good way to help everyone feel comfortable talking to each other."

Create a "book review" club. You can form young adult and teen book clubs in which members read different books and review them for the group. This type of discussion often generates considerable interest in and introduces members to new books.

Kimberly Paone of the Elizabeth (New Jersey) Public Library says one benefit of reading different books is that kids can attend meetings when they are able, and not feel as if they have missed out. "If we all read the same book, and someone is unable to make a meeting, they might feel like they missed out on the opportunity to hear what their peers had to say about that book and the opportunity to throw their opinions out there as well," says Paone. "By reading whatever they like, they can talk about what they've read at any meeting and hear from others about a variety of books."

Renee Nichols of the Akron–Summit County Public Library in Ohio facilitates a book club where teens read different books, covering a variety of characters and plots but all focused on the same general theme. Nichols chooses the theme, such as school violence, and offers a short list of books from which participants can choose. If you do not have a common theme, you can introduce a focus for the discussion, such as a character that stands out, a particular point of view, or the importance of setting, says Sally Leahey of the Best Books for Young Adults Book Group at McArthur Public Library in Biddeford, Maine. Leahey minimizes conversation about plot summary and emphasizes qualitative comments and explanations of opinions.

Francisca Goldsmith's Earphone English Book Club members at the Berkeley (California) Public Library and Berkeley High School listen to different books on audiotape. Goldsmith begins the discussion with a round robin about what excited the members most in their audio reading during the week. "That generally forces a theme into the discussion and we then trace it to different books," says Goldsmith. "These might include unreliable narrators, character-driven stories, humor, or point of view."

Discussion Tips from Book Clubs

- Be flexible. Be prepared to jettison your scripted questions to talk about what the group finds interesting, even if it is not a main point in the book.
- Initiate and guide the discussion, but do not ask all of the questions.
- Do not be afraid of occasional periods of silence during the discussion— that is thinking time.
- Welcome opposing viewpoints. Differences of opinion can lead to some of the most interesting discussions.
- Keep a list of books you discuss and record the group's opinions of each title.
- Relax and have fun!

4

Get a Jump Start: Energizing Your Book Club Meeting

Discussion might be the only agenda item for your club, or you might want to include activities—from simple games to organized field trips—to add fun to the meeting and encourage members to think creatively. By exploring various dimensions of literature through art, science, music, or sports, book club members find new ways to connect with their reading. Kids enjoy watching film or stage adaptations of books they have read, locating the book's setting on a map, bringing stories to life by performing skits from the book, participating in trivia contests, and making models and crafts connected to their reading. These activities can also cater to different strengths and interests of members, some of whom may be more physically active, or scientifically or artistically inclined, than others.

What Types of Activities Work Well?

Here are some general ideas for broadening the horizons of your book club, with examples from book clubs across the country. In the featured-books sections of *The Kids'*

Book Club Book, we describe hundreds of other terrific ideas from book clubs that relate directly to our featured books.

Arts, crafts, and construction. Focus on the book's central theme, its principal setting, or the culture portrayed in the book, and design a craft project to make this aspect of the book come alive. For example, make clothespin dolls using scraps of old material for clothes as you discuss Mildred Taylor's *Roll of Thunder, Hear My Cry* (Dial, 1976), in which poor characters' clothes were made from scraps; make elfish pottery with clay, as described in Gail Carson Levine's *Ella Enchanted* (HarperCollins, 1997), in which elves make pottery; or fold origami cranes while discussing Eleanor Coerr's Japan-based *Sadako and the Thousand Paper Cranes* (Putnam, 1977).

Create games. You can adapt a favorite board game to the theme of the book or ask group members to design a game in advance. Board games work well with books involving a journey or quest. For example, you can create a board game where players travel the path of the Iditarod for your meeting about *Balto and the Great Race* (Random House, 1999) by Elizabeth Cody Kimmel. Games that focus on word definitions, vocabulary, or wordplay are also popular among book clubs. You might play Balderdash, a word game that rewards a wild imagination, as part of your book club's discussion of Rodman Philbrick's *Freak the Mighty* (Scholastic, 1993), which features one character who makes up his own creative definitions for words.

Field trips. Take advantage of local opportunities to connect with a book's characters, themes, or settings. Try meeting at an arboretum that reflects the setting of Frances Hodgson Burnett's *The Secret Garden* (1909); rock climb at a local gym to hone your outdoor survival skills with Gary Paulsen's *Hatchet* (Macmillan, 1987); or visit a museum and speak to the security guard about E. L. Konigsburg's *From the Mixed-up Files of Mrs. Basil E. Frankweiler* (Macmillan, 1967), in which a brother and sister breach security in an art museum.

In general, plot means more to boys than character, and boys seem to be moved by action relationships. Boys enjoy physical connections with the book, so we always break our discussions with movement. When boys are moving and engaged in an activity, they're more likely to be engaged in a book.

—EDE MARQUISSEE
SUMMIT MIDDLE SCHOOL
STRONG WILD ACTION TEAM (SWAT)
FORT WAYNE, INDIANA

Dress up. Dressing as a character from the book encourages kids to pay attention to details about the characters as they bring them to life through clothing and props—and it is just plain fun! Amelie Welden's *Girls Who Rocked the World: Heroines from Sacagawea to Sheryl Swoopes* (Gareth Stevens, 1999) offers a range of characters to choose from. Or encourage girls to dress up as pioneers with Laura Ingalls Wilder's *On the Banks of Plum Creek* (Harper, 1953).

Re-create scenes from the book. Simple objects like a roll of tape or a piece of cardboard can help simulate scenes from the book. For example, you can tape a circle on the floor the diameter of the tree described in Jean Craighead George's *My Side of the Mountain* (Dutton, 1959), to see how it might feel to live in a tree; pack items in an imagi-

Maps and timelines provide visual ways to talk about history. We always pull out a map of the United States or the world and locate where the book takes place, and if travel is involved we plot the route and discuss modes of transportation available and routes that would have been used. When we read Cornelia Funke's *The Thief Lord* [Chicken House, 2002], the family hosting had a map of Italy with details of the characters' journey/adventure. We digressed and discussed the sites in Italy and many of the mothers had travel memories to share. I often give the girls index cards with events on them, such as the first transatlantic plane ride, slavery, the invention of computers, or the birth of someone's grandmother, and ask them to create timelines on a long sheet of butcher paper.

—NANCY ZIMBLE, READING MANIACS
LOS ANGELES

nary wagon outlined with tape on the floor for Gary Paulsen's *Mr. Tucket* (Delacorte, 1994), a story about traveling on the Oregon Trail; or have group members climb through a cardboard cutout the size of the window used by a character to escape from jail in Betsy Byars's *The Not-Just-Anybody Family* (Delacorte, 1986).

Explore intriguing aspects of the book. Pull your group into the book by trying activities mentioned in or related to the story. You might card sheep's wool when discussing Elizabeth George Speare's *The Witch of Blackbird Pond* (Houghton Mifflin, 1958), a story about a girl growing up in Puritan New England; try fingerprinting while discussing Louise Fitzhugh's *Harriet the Spy* (Delacorte, 1964); or determine your "mood" with mood rings for Megan McDonald's *Judy Moody Predicts the Future* (Candlewick, 2003), a story in which Judy finds a mood ring.

Community service. You can contribute to a charity or do volunteer work on a book-related theme. For example, you could plan a public service project at a school for autistic students as part of your reading of Cynthia Lord's *Rules* (Scholastic, 2006), a story about a girl whose younger brother is autistic.

Recreation. Try some of the outdoor sports activities you read about in your group. Exploring recreational references in the book is a particularly good activity for high-energy book groups. For example, you can play a game of Wiffle ball with John Ritter's *The Boy Who Saved Baseball* (Philomel, 2003); or hold sack races in conjunction with Richard Chase's *The Jack Tales* (Houghton Mifflin, 2003), a collection of Appalachian folktales, in which one of the characters has a magical burlap sack.

Should You Serve Food?

"Feed them and they will come," one librarian told us. Most youth book club leaders agree that refreshments are an integral part of their get-togethers. Snacks draw kids to meetings and can also add fun, creativity, and meaning, especially when book clubs experiment with foods that complement the reading selection.

Consider whether you want to serve healthy snacks, sugary treats, or a meal. Book clubs that serve meals commonly choose sandwiches or pizza—foods especially popular with teen groups that meet at the dinner hour. Breakfast book clubs, often held at schools, enjoy bagels, muffins, and juice. For all meetings where food is involved, be sure to ask members about food allergies and provide alternatives.

Food can play a leading role in a book by setting a novel in its time or place, or conveying other important details about the story. You might enjoy pairing food and literature by preparing foods mentioned in the pages of the book, serving dishes derived from the ethnic theme of the book, or choosing foods that represent some aspect of the book's plot or theme. Remember to ask members to guess the connection between the food and the book. Here are some strategies for pairing foods with your reading selections.

Find a food in the book's pages. Serve a food referenced in the pages of the book, especially one that might be new or intriguing to the group. You might try watercress-garlic soup for Kate DiCamillo's *The Tale of Despereaux* (Candlewick, 2003) or snickerdoodles with Jerry Spinelli's *Loser* (Joanna Cotler, 2002). The food need not be elaborate or fancy. In fact, book clubs sent us hundreds of clever ideas for foods mentioned in stories they read that they purchased or prepared easily, such as the pancakes Ramona's parents make in Beverly Cleary's *Ramona and Her Mother* (HarperCollins, 1979); the cake and milk Harriet enjoys after

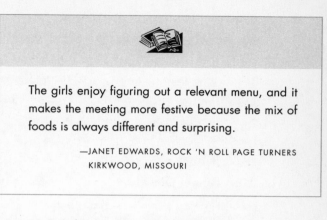

The girls enjoy figuring out a relevant menu, and it makes the meeting more festive because the mix of foods is always different and surprising.

—JANET EDWARDS, ROCK 'N ROLL PAGE TURNERS
KIRKWOOD, MISSOURI

school every day in Louise Fitzhugh's *Harriet the Spy* (Delacorte, 1964); and the egg cream Hannah's grandfather makes in Mindy Warshaw Skolsky's *Love from Your Friend, Hannah* (DK Children, 1998).

Serve food drawn from the book's culture or setting. Food offers the group an opportunity to explore a new ethnic culture or geographic setting. Some simple ideas include serving sushi for Eleanor Coerr's *Sadako and the Thousand Paper Cranes* (Putnam, 1977), set in Japan; or Italian cookies with Cornelia Funke's *The Thief Lord* (Chicken House, 2002), set in Venice.

Be inventive. Let a scene, character, or theme in the book inspire your culinary creativity. Serve angel food and devil's food cupcakes with Lynne Reid Banks's *Angela and Diabola* (Avon, 1997), a story about good and evil twins; foods shaped like trees and dirt in a wiggly Jell-O base with Joe Cottonwood's *Quake!* (Scholastic, 1995), a fictionalized account of the 1989 Loma Prieta earthquake in northern California; or a carved watermelon—complete with star-shaped fruit—to symbolize Mr. Grin, the crocodile from Dave Barry and Ridley Pearson's *Peter and the Starcatchers* (Hyperion, 2004).

A cake can offer an edible canvas ready to be decorated to reflect the book's theme. Decorate a cake as a newspaper from Andrew Clements's *The Landry News* (Simon & Schuster, 1999) about a girl who creates a newspaper, or make a sheet cake and decorate it with plastic skiers and white frosting mounded in the shape of hills to depict Sharon Creech's *Bloomability* (Joanna Cotler, 1998), partially set in a Swiss ski area.

Checklist for a Book Club Meeting

Beyond the book your group is discussing, here are some items you might bring to your book club meeting:

✓ Notes on the reading selection	✓ Supplies and materials for activities
✓ Journal	✓ Information about the author
✓ Pens or pencils	✓ Book selections for future meetings
✓ Colored pencils or markers for sketching	✓ Food
✓ Dictionary	✓ Calendar for scheduling future meetings
✓ Map related to the book's setting	✓ Books on a related theme

Now it's time to put these ideas into action. In Part Two, we feature the fifty books most highly recommended by the hundreds of book clubs we surveyed. These were the books that facilitators told us their groups found engaging and fun, taught them about other cultures, and challenged them to examine their values, question their assumptions about the world, and deepen their understanding of issues affecting their lives. These books have sparked great conversation among adults and children. We hope they will do the same for you.

PART TWO

A Bumper Crop of Books

Fifty Top Titles
Recommended by
Book Clubs

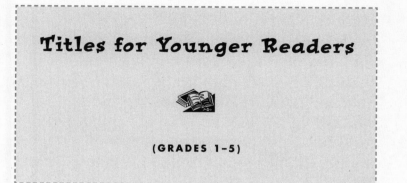

Titles for Younger Readers

(GRADES 1–5)

The Boxcar Children by Gertrude Chandler Warner

The Hundred Dresses by Eleanor Estes

Sarah, Plain and Tall by Patricia MacLachlan

Because of Winn-Dixie by Kate DiCamillo

Half Magic by Edward Eager

Charlie and the Chocolate Factory by Roald Dahl

Frindle by Andrew Clements

Maniac Magee by Jerry Spinelli

The Lion, the Witch and the Wardrobe by C. S. Lewis

The Phantom Tollbooth by Norton Juster

The Boxcar Children

Gertrude Chandler Warner

Rand McNally, 1924; Scott Foresman, 1942 (revised)
Available in paperback from Albert Whitman
256 pages
Fiction/Mystery

Series: *Surprise Island* (Scott Foresman, 1949); *The Yellow House Mystery* (1953; this and all the following titles: Albert Whitman); *Mystery Ranch* (1958); *Mike's Mystery* (1960); *The Blue Bay Mystery* (1961); *The Woodshed Mystery* (1962); *The Lighthouse Mystery* (1963); *Mountain Top Mystery* (1964); *Schoolhouse Mystery* (1965); *Caboose Mystery* (1966); *Houseboat Mystery* (1967); *Snowbound Mystery* (1968); *Tree House Mystery* (1969); *Bicycle Mystery* (1970); *Mystery in the Sand* (1971); *Mystery Behind the Wall* (1973); *Bus Station Mystery* (1974); *Benny Uncovers a Mystery* (1976)

The four Alden children's parents have died. To avoid the guardianship of their grandfather, a wealthy but seemingly cross old man, Henry, Jessie, Violet, and Benny run away, taking shelter in an abandoned boxcar in the woods. With resourcefulness, hard work, and good humor, the children furnish the boxcar with "treasures" they find at a local dump, and support themselves doing yard work for a local resident, Dr. Moore. If their identities are discovered, though, the children know their pleasant existence in the boxcar may come to an end.

- Gertrude Chandler Warner grew up in Putnam, Connecticut, across the street from a train station. As a child, she and her siblings enjoyed watching and waving to trains as the cars headed to Boston and New York City. Sometimes Warner would glance inside the caboose of a train and imagine what it would be like to live inside.

- In 1918, during a wartime teacher shortage, Warner was hired to teach first grade, a position she held for thirty years. She wrote *The Boxcar Children* in 1924 while home from school recuperating from bronchitis. "I decided to write a book just to suit myself," she has written. "What would I like to do? Well, I would like to live in a freight car, or a caboose. I would hang my wash out on the little back piazza and cook my stew on the little rusty stove found in the caboose."

- Some of Warner's students were poor readers or were just learning English. In an effort to reach these readers, Warner rewrote *The Boxcar Children* using simpler language. This version, published in 1942, is the one readers are familiar with today.

- Warner claims that *The Boxcar Children* met with alarm from some adults when it was first published. She said in an interview:

  Perhaps you know that the original Boxcar Children . . . *raised a storm of protest from librarians who thought the children were having too good a time without any parental control! That is exactly why children like it! Most of my own childhood exploits . . . received very little cooperation from my parents.*

- Although more than fifty *Boxcar Children* books have been published, Warner wrote only the first nineteen books in the series. The remaining books were penned after Warner's death by authors who were faithful to her vision.

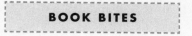
Cherry Dumplings

After the Boxcar Children help Dr. Moore pick cherries from his orchard, Mary, his cook, bakes the fruit into sweet cherry dumplings.

Unlike savory dumplings (soft balls of dough boiled in stew or soup), dessert dumplings consist of fruit filling baked inside sweet dough. Our cherry dumpling recipe calls for pie dough and cherry pie filling, and is loosely adapted from the cherry dumpling recipe in *The Boxcar Children Cookbook* by Diane Blain (Albert Whitman, 1991). It's simple enough for younger children to make, or help an adult make, and is sure to prompt the same excitement Benny expressed when Mary approached with a bowl of fresh dumplings: "I can smell something good!"

These are delicious served warm.

NOTE: Make sure to buy refrigerated—not frozen—piecrusts. Unlike frozen piecrusts, which generally come preformed in a pie tin, refrigerated piecrusts come rolled in a box. Allow the refrigerated piecrusts to sit at room temperature for 10–15 minutes before unrolling.

1 (21-ounce) can cherry pie filling

1 teaspoon fresh lemon juice

1½ teaspoons grated lemon peel

1 (15-ounce) package refrigerated piecrusts (see note)

1 egg yolk

1 tablespoon milk

½ teaspoon ground cinnamon

1 tablespoon sugar

1. Preheat oven to 425° F.
2. In a medium bowl, combine the cherry pie filling, lemon juice, and lemon peel.
3. On a lightly floured surface, unroll one piecrust (it should be 12 inches in diameter, about ⅛ inch in thickness. If necessary, roll dough to these dimensions.) With

a cookie cutter or sharp knife, cut out six 4½-inch circles. Repeat with second crust.

4. In a small bowl, combine the egg yolk and milk. In another small bowl, combine the cinnamon and sugar.

5. Spoon 1 tablespoon of the cherry pie filling onto one side of each pastry circle. Brush edges of the pastry with egg yolk mixture. Fold the pastry in half, and press on edges firmly to seal. With a fork, press on sealed edges to make decorative design, being careful not to pierce the dough.

6. Place the dumplings on an ungreased baking sheet. Brush the tops with the egg yolk mixture. Sprinkle with the cinnamon and sugar.

7. Bake 15–20 minutes, or until dumplings are golden. Remove dumplings to a wire rack to cool.

YIELD: 12 DUMPLINGS

BOOK BITES

Chocolate Boxcars

Paula Owens, member of the Tween Book Club at the B. J. Chain Public Library in Olive Branch, Mississippi, served chocolate boxcars when her group discussed *The Boxcar Children*. She bought Wilton Candy Melts, which are chocolate discs that melt easily, and a mold in the shape of trains and boxcars from a cake-supply store. Owens set the finished boxcars on top of cupcakes and served the extra boxcars on a tray.

NOTE: Owens cautions that Wilton Candy Melts harden quickly and do not mold well when remelted, so she suggests melting the chocolate in small amounts until you are sure how much you need to fill the molds.

MATERIALS

Chocolate candy discs (see note)   *Molds in the shape of boxcars*

1. Melt the chocolate in the top pot of a double boiler or in a microwave oven. To microwave: Melt chocolate in a glass bowl on Half or Defrost power 30 seconds and stir. Continue to melt in 15-second intervals, stirring after each interval, until chocolate is completely melted.
2. Pour melted chocolate into the molds, and refrigerate 20–25 minutes. Unmold the boxcars and repeat.

Suitcases for Survival

The Boxcar Children's travels are a good opportunity for your group to talk about packing for a trip—and what objects are necessary for survival. In this activity, give participants templates of suitcases and ask them to create suitcases that "open" out of construction paper. Then, ask them to find or draw pictures of three items they deem most necessary for survival on a long trip. Finally, ask them to share the reasons for their choices with the group.

This activity works well after reading the first two chapters of *The Boxcar Children*, when the children have just left home, but can be done at any stage of the book.

NOTE: The suitcase template should be a simple, two-dimensional drawing of a suitcase cut from card stock. You can draw one yourself or find a suitcase pattern in a craft book. Make sure to provide at least one template for every two to three children in the group.

MATERIALS

Construction paper	*Scissors*
Suitcase templates cut from card stock (see note)	*Markers*
	Magazines
Pencil	*Glue*

1. Fold construction paper in half. Place suitcase template on construction paper so that the bottom edge of the suitcase aligns with the folded edge of the paper (so the suitcase can "open"). Trace and cut out the suitcase.
2. Decide what three items you would take if leaving home. Draw pictures inside your suitcase, or cut out pictures from magazines and paste them inside.
3. If there's time, decorate the outside of your suitcase.
4. Share your choices—and the reason for your choices—with the group.

TRY IT!

Turn Junk into Treasure

The Boxcar Children turn a tin cup and stick into a ladle and a tin can into a dinner bell. What creative uses can your group think of for everyday objects? After placing "junk" (e.g., coffee can, rubber band, mason jar, napkin, zip-lock plastic bag, paper clip, straw, small matchbox, paper plate, plastic cup, or toilet-paper roll) in a large bag, ask each participant to pull an object from the bag without looking. Then, ask participants to write down as many uses for the object as possible and share their ideas with the group. See how creative and innovative they can be.

Topics Discussed

- Which items you would bring if you left home and needed to survive on your own
- In what ways the Boxcar Children used familiar objects for unfamiliar purposes
- Why the Boxcar Children ran away from their grandfather before getting to know him
- Why families are important

Why do the Boxcar Children run away from their grandfather?

We discussed how the Boxcar Children were reluctant to get to know their grandfather because they thought he would not be supportive of them, and would split them up. We talked about how you need to get to know people before making judgments, and give people a chance.

—SUSAN PESHECK, RIVER FALLS READS BOOK DISCUSSION (GRADES 1–2)
RIVER FALLS PUBLIC LIBRARY
RIVER FALLS, WISCONSIN

The Hundred Dresses

Eleanor Estes

1944
Available in paperback from Harcourt
96 pages
Fiction

Wanda Petronski is different from her classmates: She has a long, strange last name, lives in a run-down part of town, and wears the same blue dress to school every day. Yet she insists she has one hundred dresses all lined up in her closet at home—a statement that brings taunts from the girls at school, who don't believe her. One day, when Wanda fails to show up at school, her classmates learn the truth about the hundred dresses—and some important lessons about tolerance and acceptance.

AUTHOR SCOOP

- Eleanor Estes grew up in West Haven, Connecticut. After graduating from high school, Estes worked as a children's librarian, first at the nearby New

Haven Public Library, and later at the New York Public Library, until her first book was published in 1941.

- With its themes of childhood prejudice and persecution, *The Hundred Dresses* is more serious in tone than Estes' other books, many of which are based on happy memories of childhood spent growing up in a poor but loving family—most notably, her humorous four-book series about the Moffat family, who live in Cranbury, Connecticut, a town based on Estes' West Haven childhood home.
- Estes has been praised for her ability to write honestly and empathically from the perspective of a child. She has said, "In my writing, I like to feel that I am holding up a mirror, and I hope that what is reflected in it is a true image of childhood."

BOOK BITES

Decorated Dress Cookies

The five moms and daughters of the Mother-Daughter Book Club in Westborough, Massachusetts, discussed *The Hundred Dresses* at their first meeting, when the girls were in second grade. "Although the girls were very young, they really understood the themes of this book and could discuss them," says Linda Rice, a mother in the group.

For an activity and a snack, the hostess, Sharon Britton, baked sugar cookies in the shape of dresses for the girls to decorate. Britton set out tinted frosting and sprinkles in various shapes and colors, and the girls created "a hundred dresses" with the supplies.

Fellow member Judy Martin found a dress-shaped cookie cutter, about 5 inches tall and 2¾ inches wide, on the Internet. The cookie cutter produced large, easy-to-decorate shapes, and if you use this size, one cookie per person is plenty.

The following recipes for sugar cookies and butter frosting are adapted from *Kids' Party Cook Book*, edited by Mary Jo Plutt (Meredith, 1985).

NOTE: To make this a stiffer frosting, which is preferable for piped designs, add more confectioners' sugar. To thin the frosting, add a few drops of water.

To tint the frosting, use food coloring paste (available at party-supply stores) rather than liquid food coloring, as liquid will thin the frosting. Use the tip of a wooden toothpick to add small amounts of the paste, blend, and add more if necessary to achieve desired tint.

FOR THE COOKIES

2¼ cups all-purpose flour

2 teaspoons baking powder

½ teaspoon salt

½ cup (1 stick) unsalted butter, softened

1 cup sugar

1 large egg

2 tablespoons milk

½ teaspoon vanilla extract

FOR THE FROSTING

3 tablespoons butter, softened

2¼ to 2½ cups sifted confectioners' sugar

2 tablespoons milk, plus additional if needed

¼ teaspoon vanilla extract

1. To make the cookies: In a small bowl, mix the flour, baking powder, and salt.
2. In a large bowl, cream the butter and sugar with an electric mixer on medium speed until fluffy. Add the egg, milk, and vanilla, blending well. Gradually add the flour mixture and beat until well blended. Cover and chill the dough 1 hour.
3. Preheat oven to 375° F. Divide the dough in half. Roll out one half of dough on a lightly floured surface to about ¼-inch thickness. Cut into desired shapes with cookie cutters or knife, rerolling dough as necessary. Transfer cutouts to ungreased cookie sheets.
4. Bake 8–10 minutes, or until cookies are light brown around edges. Remove cookies to a wire rack and let cool completely.
5. To make the frosting: In a small bowl, beat butter with an electric mixer on medium speed until light and fluffy. Gradually add about half of the confectioners' sugar, blending well.
6. Beat in the milk and vanilla. Gradually beat in the remaining sugar. Then beat in additional milk, if necessary, to make frosting spreadable.

YIELD: ABOUT 1 DOZEN (5-INCH) DRESS COOKIES (NUMBER VARIES WITH SIZE OF COOKIE CUTTER) AND 1 CUP FROSTING

Dressy Stick People

The moms and daughters of The Hoffman School Parent-Child Book Discussion Group in Glenview, Illinois, made stick dolls with dresses when they met to discuss *The Hundred Dresses*. Coordinator Kirsten Considine set out tongue depressor sticks (from the school nurse), and embroidery floss for the dolls' hair for the third-graders and their mothers to use, and asked them to be creative. "Each girl and mom designed and created their own dress, and some girls made cheerleading outfits," says Considine. "They loved it!"

Considine read about the doll craft in *Bright Ideas: From Girls, For Girls!* by American Girl Library (Pleasant Company, 1997).

MATERIALS

Tongue depressors

Googly eyes

Fine-tip markers

Embroidery floss

Felt scraps

Fabric scraps

Fabric glue

Create a face and hair for your doll using googly eyes, markers, and embroidery floss. Use felt and fabric scraps to design a dress, and glue it in place. Enjoy!

TRY IT!

Design a Dress

In advance of her book club's second meeting, when they planned to discuss *The Hundred Dresses*, mother Cathy Holberg sent letters asking the daughters and moms in her York, Pennsylvania, group to design dresses for each other, and bring their rough sketches to the meeting. "Clothing reflects personal style and taste," Holberg explains. "My aim was to find out how well we know our daughters, and how accurately our daughters perceive our style and taste." Holberg adds that the mothers were genuinely impressed with the clothing choices their daughters made for them.

Donate a Dress

For their discussion of *The Hundred Dresses,* Nancy Zimble asked members of the Reading Maniacs in Los Angeles to bring an article of clothing to contribute to a women's shelter or other needy organization. Donating clothing was appropriate, says Zimble, because the book depicted a girl so embarrassed by her lack of clothing, she lied about the hundred dresses. "I think we are all concerned with setting a good example for our children," says Zimble, who thought they could "help someone feel better about themselves with a new dress."

Topics Discussed

- How Wanda was treated differently from the other girls because of her differences
- How Wanda might have felt when she was teased
- If you have ever had feelings of not fitting in or of being an outsider
- If you have ever witnessed teasing and not stepped in to stop it

Have you ever had an experience similar to
Wanda's that you would like to share?

As a facilitator at the time, I brought up my own experience as a kid being bullied, and I encouraged moms to tell their experiences. If one of the girls in our group was inclined to gang up on other kids, this helped her to understand what it might feel like to be a victim, and to develop empathy in that situation. Or, if one of the girls had been a victim of bullying, she was given an opportunity to talk about the problem and learn that she was not alone. The moms loved it; they felt it was an opportunity to talk about things that are normally difficult to talk about.

—LIZ LACEY-OSLER, MOTHER-DAUGHTER BOOK CLUB (AGES 9–11)
THE DOYLESTOWN BOOKSHOP
DOYLESTOWN, PENNSYLVANIA

Sarah, Plain and Tall

Patricia MacLachlan

Joanna Cotler, 1985

Available in paperback from HarperTrophy

64 pages

Historical Fiction

Sequels: *Skylark* (Joanna Cotler, 1994); *Caleb's Story* (Joanna Cotler, 2001); *More Perfect than the Moon* (Joanna Cotler, 2004)

In the late nineteenth century, a widower raising his two children on the prairie posts a newspaper advertisement for a bride. A young woman from Maine, Sarah Wheaton, responds with a letter, and soon arrives by train to spend a month with the small family before deciding if she will stay. As Sarah adjusts to life on the prairie, she shares reminiscences of her beloved home in Maine—the ocean, the roses, the wind, and the colors. The children embrace Sarah for her warmth and energy, even as they fear she may decide to leave them.

- The character of Sarah Wheaton was inspired by a story that Patricia MacLachlan's mother related, about an ancestor who was a mail-order bride and came to the prairie from the coast of Maine.

- MacLachlan has strong ties to the prairie, the setting for *Sarah, Plain and Tall*. Her parents were native westerners, and MacLachlan was born in Wyoming. Everywhere she goes, MacLachlan carries with her a small bag of prairie dirt because "it keeps me centered and reminds me where I began, and why I write," she has said.

- Before MacLachlan's children left for college, MacLachlan's parents took her family on a cross-country trip to the prairie. This trip "home" profoundly moved MacLachlan, and finally prompted her to write about Sarah, a character she'd long thought about. She said in her Newbery Medal acceptance speech:

   It was a gift for all of us, for the children to see a land they had never seen, to know family they had never met, to stand on the vast North Dakota farm where my father had been born in a sod house and, as Anna observes, "the prairie reached out and touched the places where the sky came down." Maya Angelou said recently that when Thomas Wolfe said you can't go home again, he was right. But he was also wrong, for you can't really ever leave, either.

- During the family trip west, MacLachlan's mother, who was suffering from Alzheimer's disease, was losing her memory. Looking back, MacLachlan recognizes that she wrote *Sarah, Plain and Tall* as a tribute to her mother's memories, and that she wanted to "wrap the land and the people as tightly as I could and hand this small piece of my mother's past to her in a package as perfect as Anna's sea stone, as Sarah's sea."

- MacLachlan's favorite passage in her book is: "My brother William is a fisherman, and he tells me that when he is in the middle of a fog-bound sea the water is a color for which there is no name." MacLachlan thinks Sarah's comment demonstrates that "words are limiting," and that silences sometimes express ideas and thoughts that words cannot. "It is often what is left unsaid that shapes and empowers a moment, an experience, a book," she says.

Film adaptations:
Sarah, Plain and Tall (Random House Video, 1988), 30 minutes
Sarah, Plain and Tall (Hallmark Hall of Fame Productions, Inc., 1991),
   rated PG, 99 minutes

BOOK BITES

Baking Powder Biscuits

In America, biscuits are soft, thick, scone-like breads leavened with baking powder or baking soda. Pioneers prized biscuits for their quick and simple preparation and the ease with which they could be carried and stored. Nineteenth-century prairie dwellers, like Anna and her family, likely mixed the fat drippings from meat with flour and bicarbonate of soda to make biscuits for a hot breakfast or accompaniment to supper.

These light, sweet biscuits, adapted from *The Fannie Farmer Cookbook* by Marion Cunningham (Knopf, 1987), are best served warm with butter and jelly.

NOTE: The texture of biscuits should be light and tender. Although in the story Anna stirs and stirs the dough as she listens anxiously to Sarah's admissions of homesickness, the dough should be minimally stirred and kneaded to ensure a flaky crumb.

2 cups all-purpose flour
½ teaspoon salt
4 teaspoons baking powder
½ teaspoon cream of tartar

1½ tablespoons sugar
½ cup (1 stick) butter, or ½ cup vegetable shortening
⅔ cup milk

1. Preheat oven to 425° F. Lightly grease two 8-inch round cake pans.
2. In a medium bowl, mix the flour, salt, baking powder, cream of tartar, and sugar.

Cut the butter into the flour with two knives held together or a pastry blender until the mixture resembles coarse cornmeal. Make a well in the center of the flour mixture. Add the milk all at once and stir quickly and lightly with a fork 30 seconds, just until the dough forms a ball around it.

3. Turn the dough onto a lightly floured surface and knead 14 times. Pat to a ½-inch thickness. Cut into rounds with a 2-inch cookie cutter. (An empty 6-ounce tomato paste can also works well.)

4. Place touching each other in the prepared cake pans, about 9 rounds of dough per pan. Bake 15–18 minutes, or until golden brown. Serve warm.

YIELD: 1½ DOZEN (2-INCH) BISCUITS

MAKE IT!

Tissue Paper Flowers

Sarah's reminiscences about the blooms she admired in Maine—roses, dahlias, columbines, and "nasturtiums the color of the sun when it sets"—prompted Sharon Coppola to organize a flower craft when her Mother and Daughter Book Club at the St. Petersburg (Florida) Public Library discussed *Sarah, Plain and Tall*. Coppola began by showing the group pictures of wildflowers Sarah might have seen in New England, as well as wildflowers native to Florida. She then asked members to create flowers of their own.

MATERIALS (FOR ONE TISSUE-PAPER FLOWER)

4–6 tissue-paper squares of various dimensions (3, 4, 5, and 6 inches), in a variety of colors

Crimping shears (optional)

1–2 long pipe cleaners

Scissors

1. Choose up to 6 squares of various sizes and colors. Stack the squares in order of size, with the largest on the bottom. If desired, you may cut the edges of the tissue paper with crimping shears to give the petals a jagged look.

2. Fold the squares in accordion pleats. Tie a pipe cleaner around the middle of the accordion, tight enough so that the pleats stay together but loose enough so that the tissue paper can move a little bit.

3. Pull the tissue paper up on each side. Gently separate the tissue-paper squares one at a time, starting from the inside and working out, until it resembles a flower. If desired, make a center for the flower with a smaller piece of pipe cleaner.

Draw with Ocean and Prairie Colors

Sarah enjoys drawing pictures to send to her brother in Maine, and describes her favorite colors as "the colors of the sea, blue and gray and green."

Starting with a full set of colored pencils, Nancy Zimble of Los Angeles separated out the grays, blues, and greens and placed them in a basket. She set the remaining colored pencils in a separate basket, noting that, after removing Sarah's favorite colors representing Maine and the ocean, what remained were "the warm colors of the prairie." Zimble then asked the mothers and daughters of her Reading Maniacs Book Club to draw pictures using both baskets of colors, and to contrast the feelings of the two different groups of drawings.

PLAY IT!

A Drawing Game

The girls and moms of the Secret Readers in Oregon, Wisconsin, played their own version of Pictionary, a game where players take turns drawing words while others try to guess the answer, using key words from *Sarah, Plain and Tall*. Lisa Hughes, the group's facilitator, selected the words and asked the girls to take turns drawing them, while the other girls guessed what the drawings were. "The words that we had the most fun with were names of colors and feelings," says Hughes. "At first the girls found it difficult to draw a color, but soon they found ways to get the idea across."

MAKE IT!

A Collage

When they read *Sarah, Plain and Tall*, Nancy Zimble of the Reading Maniacs asked the second-grade girls in her Los Angeles group to bring something to the meeting that reminded them of the book, and that could be made into a collage. At the meeting, the girls explained why they chose their objects—including flowers, seashells, sand, horse and cat figurines, and pictures of wildflowers—and why it was important to the book and/or to the reader. As a background for the collage, Zimble provided a United States map with train tracks drawn between Maine and Kansas, and the girls glued their objects to the map. Zimble says choosing the objects provided a wonderful lesson in symbolism and in understanding that the pieces put together made a pictorial view of the novel.

Topics Discussed

- What Anna and Caleb asked Sarah in their letters, and what you might have asked Sarah
- The items, such as shells and flowers, that are important to Sarah, and what items are important to you
- What Maggie meant when she said, "There are always things to miss, no matter where you are"
- The colors Sarah used to describe the ocean, and which colors you would use to describe where you live

Have you ever been homesick? Can you explain how Sarah might feel?

The children talked about feeling homesick when they slept at a friend's house when they were younger, or went away to camp. I mentioned that Sarah said the house she had lived in with her brother no longer felt the same to her because her brother had gotten married and now the house belonged to another woman, her sister-in-law. Sarah wanted a place of her own, and a husband of her own, and that's why she had come such a long way. And although she was lonely, she had a new family who loved her, and who tried their best to make her feel comfortable in their home. I asked the children how they knew whether Sarah was going to stay or go back to Maine, and they mentioned that she had left Seal, her cat, behind, so she had to come back.

—SHARON COPPOLA, MOTHER AND DAUGHTER BOOK CLUB (GRADES 1–4)
ST. PETERSBURG PUBLIC LIBRARY
ST. PETERSBURG, FLORIDA

Because of Winn-Dixie

Kate DiCamillo

Candlewick, 2000
Available in paperback from Candlewick
184 pages
Fiction

Ten-year-old India Opal Buloni and her father are newcomers to Naomi, Florida. Opal struggles with feelings of loneliness and longing—for her mother, who left the family, and for new friends—until the day she meets Winn-Dixie, a stray dog with a goofy smile. Winn-Dixie helps Opal connect with the strange but warmhearted collection of folks, young and old, that populate her new town.

AUTHOR SCOOP

- As a child, Kate DiCamillo owned a black standard poodle named Nanette, whom she liked to dress up in costumes, including but not limited to a green ballet tutu. Although not currently a dog owner, DiCamillo is the proud aunt of a terrier-poodle named Henry.

- Born in Philadelphia and now living in Minneapolis, DiCamillo grew up in Clermont, a small town in central Florida similar to the fictional Naomi. She says her southern roots partially inspired the writing of *Because of Winn-Dixie*:

> *Because of Winn-Dixie owes a lot to my childhood in the South. I wrote the book during the worst winter on record in Minnesota, where I live now. I was homesick for the South: the warmth, the southern cadences of speech. Also, for the first time in my life, I was without a dog and I desperately wanted one. Because of Winn-Dixie is a product of those two longings: for the South and for a dog.*

- DiCamillo's constant early childhood illnesses prompted her parents to move to the warmer climate of central Florida, where she first encountered the southern speech patterns and small-town ways of life depicted in *Because of Winn-Dixie*. "I did not know it at the time," DiCamillo says, "but Florida, and pneumonia, gave me a great gift: a voice in which to tell my stories."

Author website: www.katedicamillo.com
Film adaptation:
Because of Winn-Dixie (Twentieth Century–Fox, 2005), rated PG, 106 minutes
Kate DiCamillo recommends:
Becoming Naomi León by Pam Muñoz Ryan (Scholastic, 2004)
Love, Ruby Lavender by Deborah Wiles (Gulliver, 2001)

Dump Punch

Opal and her friend Gloria Dump throw a grand party fashioned after the Twelve Oaks barbecue depicted in *Gone With the Wind*. Their menu? Peanut butter sandwiches, egg salad sandwiches, pickles, and Gloria's specialty, Dump Punch.

Wayne County Public Library manager Teresa Jager sent us the recipe for the Dump Punch she served to her Book Snacks Book Group in Dalton, Ohio. The group festooned the room with pink, orange, and yellow streamers as in the book and posted dog pictures on the walls.

NOTE: We reduced the amount of grapefruit juice to avoid bitterness, but you can adjust the amount to the taste of the group.

2 cups orange juice

1 cup grapefruit juice (see note)

2 cups club soda, seltzer, or ginger ale

Orange slices

In a large punch bowl, mix the orange juice, grapefruit juice, and soda. Float orange slices on top. Serve chilled.

YIELD: 10 (4-OUNCE) SERVINGS

Egg Salad Sandwiches

Kate DiCamillo tells us she thought egg salad would be something Gloria Dump would especially like because egg salad sandwiches are comforting and familiar.

Sharon Coppola, a librarian with the St. Petersburg (Florida) Public Library, served this deliciously tangy egg salad to the participants of her Mother and Daughter Book Club when they discussed *Because of Winn-Dixie*. Although she had participants make their own sandwiches, she strongly recommends making the sandwiches in advance with a larger group "so that chaos does not ensue."

If you want to be true to the story, make sure to cut off the crusts, and don't forget the "little toothpicks with frilly tops."

7 large eggs, hard-cooked and peeled	*¼ teaspoon ground pepper*
½ cup diced celery	*3 tablespoons mayonnaise*
½ cup diced sweet pickles	*8 slices sandwich bread*
½ teaspoon salt	

1. Slice the eggs in half. Remove three of the yolks and set aside.
2. In a medium bowl, chop the remaining whites and yolks into small pieces. Add celery, sweet pickles, salt, and pepper.
3. In a small bowl, mash the three yolks with a fork. Add the mayonnaise and mix until creamy. Add the egg-mayonnaise dressing to the chopped egg mixture. Stir to combine.
4. Scoop some egg salad onto a slice of bread, cover with another slice, and cut into triangles. Repeat with remaining bread.

YIELD: 4 FULL SANDWICHES

MAKE IT!

Book Link: An Idea from Kate DiCamillo

LITTMUS LOZENGE CANDY WRAPPERS

Kate DiCamillo suggests book club members design their own Littmus Lozenge candy wrappers and share how it makes them feel.

Miss Franny Block, the librarian in *Because of Winn-Dixie,* tells of her great-grandfather Littmus, who, after returning from the Civil War, found that all his family members had died. Determined to find happiness again, he created a candy full of sweetness—and sorrow. "That's the secret," says Miss Franny of her great-grandfather's recipe. "He manufactured a piece of candy that tasted sweet and sad at the same time."

Markers or colored pencils

Squares of thin paper, about 2 x 2½ inches, 2 or 3 per member

Butterscotch candies, unwrapped, 2 or 3 per member

Use markers to design one or more Littmus Lozenge candy wrapper(s). Wrap them around the candies. Share your wrapper(s) and talk about what kinds of sadness you feel.

THINK ABOUT IT!

An Insider's View of an Animal Shelter

Kirsten Considine, coordinator of The Hoffman School Parent-Child Book Discussion Group in Glenview, Illinois, invited a worker from a local animal shelter to speak to the group's third-grade girls and moms when they discussed *Because of Winn-Dixie.* Considine says not all homeless animals are as fortunate as Winn-Dixie, who finds a loving caretaker in Opal. "I wanted to give the children and their parents an opportunity to better understand what actually happens when animals are abandoned or given up," Considine says. Group members were surprised to learn that animals are often left at the front door of the shelter at night, with no identifying information. They had a lengthy discussion about commitment and responsibility, specifically related to children who beg their parents for a pet, only to decide several months later they no longer want to care for it. The group agreed that Opal's behavior toward Winn-Dixie did not follow this pattern. "The dog in this story plays an integral role in the family life, even helping to mend broken hearts," Considine says.

Topics Discussed

- Judging new people quickly, and then developing compassion for them
- Connecting the ten facts about Opal's mother to themes and other characters in the novel, especially Gloria Dump
- Whether or not Opal's father had failed her
- The benefits and disadvantages of holding on to sad memories

Who was your favorite character?

This question is so well suited to this book because the characterizations are incredible. Everyone in the group had a different favorite character.

—DEBORAH GRIMMETT, JUNIOR CLIFFHANGER CLUB (GRADES 2–3)
ABINGTON PUBLIC LIBRARY
ABINGTON, MASSACHUSETTS

Half Magic

Edward Eager

Harcourt, 1954
Available in paperback from Harcourt
208 pages
Fantasy

Sequel: *Magic by the Lake* (Harcourt, 1957)

When siblings Mark, Katharine, Jane, and Martha find a magical coin that grants wishes, it appears their summer boredom is over. The children soon discover the magical token delivers only partial magic, granting half of any wish: When they wish to be whisked away to a desert island, the children land in the desert—with no island. The four take turns making wishes, eventually doubling their requests to make them "whole," with unpredictable results. As their misadventures continue, the children learn to appreciate the maxim "Be careful what you wish for."

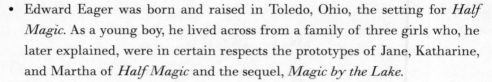
- Edward Eager was born and raised in Toledo, Ohio, the setting for *Half Magic*. As a young boy, he lived across from a family of three girls who, he later explained, were in certain respects the prototypes of Jane, Katharine, and Martha of *Half Magic* and the sequel, *Magic by the Lake*.

- Eager was a lyricist and playwright before turning to children's books. He began writing when he could not find stories he wanted to read to his own young son, Fritz. Through reading to Fritz, Eager discovered the books of British author E. Nesbit, whom he considered to be the greatest author of children's books in the world. According to Eager, Nesbit's books have strongly influenced his own work, a debt Eager has often acknowledged in writing. Although Eager missed reading Nesbit's books as a child, he claims he became a "second-generation Nesbitian" when he discovered a second-hand copy of Nesbit's *Wet Magic*. "I have not got over the effects of that discovery yet, nor, I hope, will I ever," wrote Eager.

- In the introduction to the fiftieth-anniversary edition of *Half Magic*, author Jack Gantos suggests that Eager chose to set *Half Magic* in the 1920s to escape his current world of 1954, when television brought images of events such as atomic bomb tests into American homes. Gantos concludes that Eager set *Half Magic* "in a distant, simpler time—the 1920s . . . to sidestep the packaged visual world being defined by popular culture, and also he wanted to separate out and protect the joys of childhood."

BOOK BITES

Toledo Hot Fudge "Dope"

Mark, Jane, Katharine, and Martha decide to take a break from their wild adventures to enjoy an outing in downtown Toledo, including lunch at an old-fashioned soda fountain where Mark orders a "double hot fudge dope." We were intrigued by the reference to "dope" in Mark's order, and contacted Toledo ice creameries to learn more about the term.

Marcia Helman has served ice cream at Lickity Split in Toledo's South End for twenty-five years, and says that in the Toledo of Edward Eager's day, "dope" meant ice cream topped with sauce, but without whipped cream, nuts, or cherries. "My mother used the word 'dope' to describe ice cream with sauce, and she's the last person I've heard call it that," says Helman. Mark's order for "double hot fudge dope," Helman says, is two scoops of ice cream with hot fudge sauce. We think Mark made a good decision at the soda fountain; you'll find this sweet treat—one of our favorite hot fudge sauce recipes—purely magical. Make yours a double and pour it over two scoops!

2 ounces unsweetened dark chocolate	*1 cup sugar*
¼ cup (½ stick) butter	*¼ cup milk*
⅛ cup unsweetened cocoa powder	*¼ cup heavy cream*

1. Melt the chocolate and butter in the top pot of a double boiler. Add the cocoa powder and stir until dissolved. Gradually stir in the sugar, and cook for 10 minutes, stirring.
2. Add the milk and cream. Cook, stirring occasionally for 10 minutes. Serve warm over ice cream.

YIELD: 1½ CUPS

TASTE IT!

Bites from the Book

The Reading Maniacs of Los Angeles munched on snacks that the children in *Half Magic* enjoyed: cake, celery soda, potato salad, watermelon, popped corn, and saltwater taffy.

Because things were always changing in *Half Magic,* says Cathy Holberg, members of her York, Pennsylvania, mother-daughter book club brought "foods that change" to snack on during their meeting. Their evolving foods included raisins (grapes to raisins), orange juice (oranges to orange juice), taco chips and dip (corn to corn chips and tomatoes to salsa). Holberg says it was challenging for the girls to think of so many changeable snack ideas, but they all agreed the exercise was clever and fun.

TRY IT!

Make a Wish

Dorothy Distefano distributed foil-wrapped chocolate gold coins to her parent-child book club in Hilton, New York, and asked all the members to state what they would wish for on their coin—and how they would phrase their wish. The group considered the possible outcomes of their wishes and examined how the results could go awry, depending on the words they chose when doubling a wish to get "whole" magic. For example, when one member wished for a million dollars—"twice"—the group pointed out that he might end up with two million dollars, but with the bills cut in half.

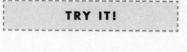

Make Magic

To highlight the magic theme of *Half Magic*, each child in Cathy Holberg's mother-daughter book club in York, Pennsylvania, performed a magic trick with or without her mother's assistance. Card tricks were most popular, says Holberg, whose daughter performed a disappearing coin trick.

Parcheesi

In Los Angeles, the mothers and daughters of the Reading Maniacs played two simultaneous games of Parcheesi, the board game the children play in *Half Magic*. One of the earliest patented American games, Parcheesi is played with two dice and colored pawns. "Playing board games is old-fashioned and slow-paced compared to the action-packed bells and whistles of video games that this generation seems to like," says mother and member Nancy Zimble.

Topics Discussed

- The dilemmas the children experienced because the coin only provided "half magic"
- The lessons or morals each adventure taught the children
- The meaning of the two different *Half Magic* book covers (half knight/half girl and a shattered knight with four children)
- Your favorite historical setting in the book, and why

When do you think Half Magic *was written?*

All of the children in our group thought the book was written recently and were surprised when I explained that it was written over fifty years ago. The children were also surprised to have a working mother as a character in a story written so long ago. They thought J. K. Rowling created the idea of writing about magic, but I introduced other books about magic written long ago, such as the works of E. Nesbit, the author Eager credits in his book.

—CLAIRE SCARBOROUGH, BOOK TALK (GRADES 4–5)
BURBANK PUBLIC LIBRARY, BUENA VISTA BRANCH,
BURBANK, CALIFORNIA

Charlie and the Chocolate Factory

Roald Dahl

Alfred A. Knopf, 1964
Available in paperback from Puffin
176 pages
Fiction

Sequel: *Charlie and the Great Glass Elevator* (Alfred A. Knopf, 1972)

The reclusive candy inventor Willy Wonka closed the doors to his chocolate factory more than a decade ago. Now Wonka has announced that he will once again open his factory to the five lucky recipients of Golden Tickets that are hidden in ordinary Wonka candy bars around the world. Young Charlie Bucket, living in poverty in a ramshackle house with his mother and four grandparents, is astonished when he uncovers the last of Mr. Wonka's Golden Tickets. Charlie's tour around Mr. Wonka's mysterious chocolate factory will change his life forever.

AUTHOR SCOOP

- In his autobiography, *Boy: Tales of Childhood* (Farrar, Straus & Giroux, 1984), Roald Dahl writes of a favorite childhood candy store, the sweetshop in Llandaff, Wales, which Dahl says for him and his friends was the "very centre of our lives." "Sweets were our life-blood," writes Dahl, who shares detailed recollections of candies he adored at the shop, including licorice bootlaces, sherbet suckers, and gobstoppers.

- In contrast to today's modern "chocolate-guzzling" society, Roald Dahl recalls, only a few chocolate bars were available when he was growing up in the 1920s.

> *When I was young, there was Cadbury's Bournville and Dairy Milk. There was the Dairy Milk Flake (the only great invention so far) and Whipped Cream Walnut, and there were also four different flavours of chocolate-coated Marshmallow Bar (vanilla, coffee, rose, lemon). Consequently, we were much more inclined to spend our money on sweets and toffees or on sherbet-suckers, gobstoppers, liquorice bootlaces and aniseed balls—we did not mind that the liquorice was made from rats' blood and the sherbet from sawdust. They were cheap and to us, they tasted good.*

- At Repton, a private boarding school in Derbyshire, England, Dahl and his classmates frequently received boxes containing a variety of new candy bars to be sampled and critiqued from the nearby Cadbury chocolate company. Dahl and his friends would taste the bars and send comments on the new candy inventions back to Cadbury. In *Boy*, Dahl describes his fantasies that he would one day work in the inventing room of a factory and create a fabulous new candy bar. He traces the origins of *Charlie and the Chocolate Factory* to his chocolate-tasting experiences at boarding school.

> *For me the importance of all this was that I began to realize that the large chocolate companies actually did possess inventing rooms and they took their inventing very seriously. I used to picture a long white room like a laboratory with pots of chocolate and fudge and all sorts of other delicious fillings bubbling away on the stoves, while men and women in white coats moved between the bubbling pots, tasting and mixing and concocting their*

wonderful new inventions. I used to imagine myself working in one of these labs and suddenly, I would come up with something so absolutely unbearably delicious that I would grab it in my hand and go rushing out of the lab and along the corridor and right into the office of the great Mr. Cadbury himself. . . .

It was lovely dreaming those dreams, and I have no doubt at all that, thirty-five years later, when I was looking for a plot for my second book for children, I remembered those little cardboard boxes and the newly invented chocolates inside them, and I began to write a book called Charlie and the Chocolate Factory.

- In an early draft of *Charlie and the Chocolate Factory* Dahl wrote of ten Golden Tickets and winners, and Charlie found a Ticket on his first attempt. In each subsequent draft, the number of Ticket winners was gradually reduced.

- In the original published version of *Charlie and the Chocolate Factory,* the Oompa-Loompas were black pygmies from Africa; the characterization resulted in public disapproval of the book's racist stereotypes, including the exploitation of the Oompa-Loompas and their "childishness and dependency on whites," a criticism made by writer Lois Kalb Bouchard. Dahl was initially surprised by the attacks, and emphasized that he intended the Oompa-Loompas to be seen as "fantasy creatures," but in 1973 Dahl revised the story, turning the workers into white pygmies with long hair from an island called Loompaland. In his response to the criticism, Dahl claimed, "it didn't occur to me that my depiction of the Oompa-Loompas was racist, but it did occur to others."

- Before Dahl's death in 1990, he and his wife, Felicity, were planning to write a cookbook for children based on foods that appear in his books. Dahl thought the idea was daunting, but he had carefully listed every food in his works for Felicity to turn into recipes. Felicity Dahl's creations fill two volumes, *Roald Dahl's Revolting Recipes* (Viking, 1994) and *Roald Dahl's Even More Revolting Recipes* (Viking, 2001).

Author website: www.roalddahl.com

Film adaptations:

Willy Wonka & the Chocolate Factory (Warner, 1971), rated G, 98 minutes

Charlie and the Chocolate Factory (Warner, 2005), rated PG, 115 minutes

---

BOOK BITES

Wonka's Whipple-Scrumptious Fudgemallow Delight

Charlie and the Chocolate Factory is filled with descriptions of fantastic sweets, but perhaps none is as central to the book's plot as Wonka's Whipple-Scrumptious Fudgemallow Delight, the candy bar Charlie receives on his birthday and that his Grandpa George says is "the best of them all!" When Charlie is starving from lack of food, he finds a dollar in the street, buys a Fudgemallow Delight, and wolfs it down. The candy bar leaves him so "marvelously, extraordinarily happy" that he buys another with his remaining coins—and finds Willy Wonka's Golden Ticket inside.

Dahl and his wife, Felicity, created a delicious ice cream topping with the ingredients in Wonka's Whipple-Scrumptious Fudgemallow Delight for *Roald Dahl's Even More Revolting Recipes* (Viking, 2001). We think it will make you feel as if you've won a Golden Ticket!

NOTE: This dessert is very sweet, so you might want to add fewer marshmallows, depending on your preferences. You can keep any leftover sauce in the refrigerator and reheat it in the microwave.

FOR THE TOPPING

2 ounces dark chocolate

*1 (1.4-ounce) English toffee-
flavored candy bar, such as Heath*

¼ cup (½ stick) unsalted butter

¼ cup firmly packed dark brown sugar

⅔ cup heavy cream

8 large marshmallows (see note)

Your favorite ice cream (enough for 4 people)

1. Break the chocolate and the candy bar into large chunks. Set aside.
2. In a medium saucepan, melt the butter with the sugar and cream over low heat. Stir until the sugar has dissolved. Increase the heat to medium and continue stirring 10 minutes, or until the mixture has thickened slightly. (Be careful, as the mixture gets very hot and splutters. Use a very long wooden spoon, or have a tall adult with a long arm do the stirring.) Reduce the heat to low.
3. Scoop the ice cream into four individual bowls. Put the marshmallows, chocolate, and candy bar chunks into the saucepan and stir once. Spoon the sauce over ice cream.

YIELD: 4 SERVINGS

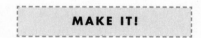

MAKE IT!

Candy Inventions—Imaginary and Real

Members of LeAnn Kunz's Book-by-Book club at the Washington (Iowa) Public Library felt as clever as Willy Wonka when they invented "imaginary" candy bars at their *Charlie and the Chocolate Factory* discussion. After coming up with ideas for the perfect candy, the candy creators designed paper candy-bar wrappers, which they decorated with crayons and markers and wrapped around foil-covered cardboard to create the look of a candy bar.

The group also wrote and performed commercials to promote their candy creations. "The kids liked using their imagination to create candy, especially after reading about the crazy candy in the book," says Kunz. The results were magical: Some members dreamed up candy bars that make you smarter or taller. One commercial was set in an airport and the candy bar was said to transport you to any location if you took a bite, says Kunz.

Although her group imagined the candy bars, Kunz says a book group could easily create real candy bars with some basic ingredients and then hold a taste test and vote on the tastiest confection.

Follow these instructions below for creating candy bars with your group.

NOTE: Use shaved or finely chopped chocolate, chocolate morsels, or chocolate discs. Candy-bar molds are available at party-supply or arts and crafts stores. If you prefer, you may combine the melted chocolate and mix-ins in a small bowl and spread the mixture into the mold for a chunkier candy bar.

MATERIALS

Semisweet or milk chocolate for melting (see note)

A variety of ingredients to mix with chocolate, such as chocolate morsels, candy-coated chocolate pieces, mini-marshmallows, peanut butter, honey, cereal, nuts, and candy flavorings, placed in separate containers with spoons

Microwave-safe bowl or saucepan for melting chocolate

Large spoon

Plastic spoons and knives

Candy-bar molds, one per member (see note)

1. Melt the chocolate in the top pot of a double boiler, uncovered, over low heat. Or microwave on high power for 1 minute, check chocolate, stir, and place back in the microwave for another minute. Repeat until the chocolate has melted.
2. Spoon a small amount of the melted chocolate into a mold (leaving room for additional ingredients). Spread the chocolate evenly with a plastic knife. Gently tap the bottom of the mold to remove any air bubbles.

3. Select mixing ingredients for candy bars and place them on top of the chocolate. Cover with additional melted chocolate and spread until smooth.

4. Let the chocolate cool slightly, and place the mold in refrigerator or freezer to harden, 5 to 30 minutes, depending on the thickness of the chocolate. When the chocolate begins to separate slightly from the mold, and the mold is no longer warm to the touch, remove the chocolate. If necessary, gently dip the bottom of the mold in warm water to loosen chocolate.

PLAY IT!

Candy Bar Guessing Game

The candy makers in LeAnn Kunz's Book-by-Book middle school club at the Washington (Iowa) Public Library had a chance to test their knowledge of chocolate with a "guess the candy bar" game. Kunz sliced eight different commercial candy bars and placed the small pieces under cups. The children took turns being blindfolded, tasting the candy, and guessing which candy bar they had tasted.

Topics Discussed

- If you think the Golden Ticket winners deserved to be on the tour of the candy factory
- If you think each of the Golden Ticket winners changed after their visit, and if so, how they changed
- If you have ever been tempted to eat something you weren't supposed to eat
- If you have ever had a close relationship with a relative, as Charlie does with Grandpa Joe

How did greed play a role in each child's experience at the chocolate factory?

The members noted that other than Charlie, the characters were quite greedy, because they didn't listen to Willy Wonka when he warned them about eating certain things that could be dangerous. Kids are very motivated by food and they understand the characters' urges to eat these fabulous creations at the chocolate factory. We discussed whether we've ever been tempted to eat something we weren't supposed to eat. While they know greed is not a good thing, they could partially sympathize with the characters.

—LeANN KUNZ, BOOK-BY-BOOK (GRADES 6–9)
WASHINGTON PUBLIC LIBRARY
WASHINGTON, IOWA

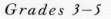

Frindle

Andrew Clements

Simon & Schuster, 1996
Also available in paperback from Simon & Schuster
112 pages
Fiction

Nick Allen has a reputation for making mischief. When his no-nonsense teacher, Mrs. Granger, asks him to research the origin of words, Nick schemes to invent a new word by calling a pen "frindle." Nick's fellow fifth-graders embrace the idea, and use of the word quickly spreads beyond the classroom. When Mrs. Granger, who worships the dictionary, protests, a battle of wills ensues.

AUTHOR SCOOP

- The idea for *Frindle* was born when author Andrew Clements discussed how words work with a class of first-graders. The students were surprised when he explained that ordinary people make up new words in the dictionary. Clements recalls his discussion with the students:

Pulling a pen from my pocket I said, "For example, if all of us right here to-day said we would never call this thing a pen again, and that from now on we would call it a . . . frindle." I just made up the word frindle, *and they all laughed because it sounded funny. And then I said, "No, really—if enough other people start to use our new word, then in five or ten years, frindle could be a real word in the dictionary."*

- Clements, a former teacher, describes Mrs. Granger as a composite of many teachers he has known, including himself. "When I was a fourth-grade teacher kids would come up to me and ask, 'Mr. Clements, how do you spell *pancakes*?'" says Clements, "and I would say, 'Go look it up in the diction-ary!' Mrs. Granger in *Frindle* says that a lot. So in a way, Mrs. Granger is sort of like me."

- Clements says that Nick has a mischievous nature but is irresistible. "One of the things I love about Nick is that he's right on the edge—he's what a good friend of mine calls Very Nearly Naughty," he adds. "But Nick is so smart and funny, and he has such a good heart and such good ideas, that you have to forgive him."

Author website: www.frindle.com

BOOK BITES

Andrew Clements's Hot Cocoa

Andrew Clements craves hot cocoa year-round, and will go to great lengths to create ideal cocoa conditions, even during Massachusetts's warmer months. "I've been known to turn up the air-conditioning in my writing shed in the middle of August un-til hot chocolate feels right," he says. Clements shared his delectable cocoa recipe with us, and now we understand the temptation to drink hot cocoa in the summer!

NOTE: Clements recommends using Dutch-processed cocoa powder, which has a milder flavor than regular unsweetened cocoa powder. He considers Droste's cocoa powder "the best cocoa on the planet," but adds that any good-quality cocoa powder will work in his recipe.

3¼ cups 2% low-fat milk, divided

6 teaspoons unsweetened cocoa powder, preferably Dutch-processed (see note)

3 tablespoons plus 1 teaspoon sugar

½ teaspoon vanilla extract

¼ cup half-and-half or light cream

1. In a 1-quart microwave-safe pitcher, heat ½ cup of milk 1 minute.
2. In a small bowl, whisk together the cocoa powder and sugar. Add to the hot milk, stirring with a long spoon until mixture is smooth and syrupy. If lumps form, whisk to break them up.
3. Add the vanilla and half-and-half or light cream. Fill the rest of the pitcher with milk, stir, and heat in the microwave 2 minutes. Remove and stir, and then heat another minute, or until almost steaming.

YIELD: 4 (8-OUNCE) SERVINGS

PLAY IT!

Word Games

INVENT A WORD

Jen Taggart, who coordinates Books & Bites at the Bloomfield Township Public Library in Bloomfield Hills, Michigan, asked her group to invent words, as Nick did with *Frindle*.

Have several dictionaries on hand when you try this with your group.

Divide members into groups, and ask each group to invent ten words they don't think they will find in a dictionary. (If you know that a suggested word already exists, don't tell!) Have the groups come together to share the words and discuss what each group thinks of the other groups' words—and whether they already exist or not. Then ask the children to look up the words in the dictionary, to find out if they're right.

As a variation, the group leader can present a list of silly-sounding words along with actual words the group might know and ask participants to separate the "real" from the "fake" ones. Discuss their predictions, and then ask the group to look up the words to find out if their predictions were correct. Your group members might be surprised to learn that words they thought were "nonsense" words actually appear in the dictionary.

INVENT YOUR OWN "FRINDLE"

In this game, your group members describe an object using an invented word. Pam Comello, a children's librarian with the Sedona (Arizona) Public Library, had children warm up for their *Frindle* discussion by creating a new word before the meeting. "Everyone was a winner with this game," she says, "and it was a good way to ease the kids into the discussion."

Before the meeting, ask members to bring an object—and an invented name for it—but ask them to keep the object hidden. Ask each member to briefly discuss his or her object, using his or her invented name. The group then guesses what the object might be, and the child reveals the object.

TRY IT!

Visit Webster's Word Central

Webster's Word Central "Build Your Own Dictionary" website (www.wordcentral. com) allows visitors to submit invented words. With adult permission, children can enter their word, its part of speech, definition, history, and a sample sentence including the word—and become part of a unique dictionary. Merriam-Webster editors review the submissions, many of which are posted on the website. Information on how words get into dictionaries can be found in the article "How Does a Word Get into the Dictionary," also on Webster's Word Central.

Topics Discussed

- If Nick acted respectfully toward Mrs. Granger and whether his classroom behavior was appropriate
- Why Mrs. Granger was opposed to the word *frindle*
- If you have ever thought of challenging your teacher
- Fads and trends and how they get started

ASK IT!

What does Mrs. Granger mean when she writes to Nick,
"Every good story needs a bad guy, don't you think?"

This generated a lot of discussion. The kids had a great time discussing fictional villains, whether Mrs. Granger truly was a villain, and whether every good story really needs a villain.

—DEBORAH GRIMMETT, JUNIOR CLIFFHANGER CLUB (GRADES 2 AND 3)
ABINGTON PUBLIC LIBRARY
ABINGTON, MASSACHUSETTS

Maniac Magee

Jerry Spinelli

Little, Brown, 1990
Available in paperback from Little, Brown
184 pages
Fiction

Twelve-year-old orphan Jeffrey Lionel Magee runs away in search of a home, and finds his way to segregated Two Mills, Pennsylvania. The mysterious stranger gains instant celebrity—and the nickname "Maniac"—for his miraculous athletic feats. In his struggle to find a home in a racially divided community, Maniac confronts prejudice and breaks down racial barriers.

AUTHOR SCOOP

- Jerry Spinelli grew up in Norristown, Pennsylvania—a town that became Two Mills in his fiction. He says that like Two Mills, Norristown was racially segregated: African-Americans generally lived on the east side of town and whites on the west side. When Spinelli began playing sports as a young boy he crossed the color line. He recalls

Every day in summer kids from both sides of town met on the Elmwood Park basketball court. Blacks ceased to be blacks and I ceased to be white. Instead, we were teammates or opponents, identified by the color of our uniforms, not of our skin.

You can learn more about Spinelli's childhood in Norristown in his autobiography, *Knots in My Yo-yo String* (Alfred A. Knopf, 1998).

- Spinelli has much to say about all aspects of *Maniac Magee*—its inspiration, writing, and his hope for its legacy. Here are some of his thoughts.

On the writing of *Maniac Magee*:

I write in my office upstairs. I try to write every morning, and sometimes at night. Putting my "game face" on involves reading brief portions of a book or two aloud to myself. The most important tool at my disposal in the writing of Maniac Magee *was my memory, as the book is, in my view, most fundamentally about childhood recollected. It was my sense of the legendary, mythical qualities of that recollection that gave the story its style.*

On the many childhood memories that became part of *Maniac Magee*:

I'll mention two. An old friend of mine who grew up in an orphanage. As a youngster, he ran everywhere he went. This characteristic seemed a good fit for Maniac. I met a sixth-grade girl in New York State who brought her home library to school with her every day in a suitcase. And thus Amanda Beale was born.

On the hope that, if readers could choose one of his books, it would be *Maniac Magee*:

Maniac Magee *is about brotherhood. About different kinds of people getting along. If this story can help promote that ideal in some small way, it will have been well worth the writing. Back in the 1990s the government of South Africa bought and distributed 600 copies as part of their efforts to dispel apartheid.*

• Spinelli shared a little-known fact about how he conceived *Maniac Magee.*

The initial inspiration for Maniac Magee was the 1964 pop song from Martha and the Vandellas "Dancin' in the Streets." It provoked a vision of people of all kinds and colors intermingling in the same community.

Author website: www.jerryspinelli.com
Film adaptation:
Maniac Magee (Nickelodeon, 2003), not rated, 90 minutes
Jerry Spinelli recommends:
The Watsons Go to Birmingham—1963 by Christopher Paul Curtis
(Delacorte, 1993; see p. 180)
Linda Brown, You Are Not Alone: The Brown v. Board of Education Decision,
edited by Joyce Carol Thomas (Jump at the Sun, 2003)

┌ - - - - - - - - - - - - - - - ┐
BOOK BITES
└ - - - - - - - - - - - - - - - ┘

Butterscotch Krimpets

Jerry Spinelli shared his description of Maniac Magee's beloved butterscotch krimpets:

Readers of Maniac Magee *know that butterscotch krimpets are Maniac's favorite food. However, many of those readers don't know what krimpets are. Some think they are candy, some cupcakes. In fact, a krimpet is a small, rectangular (about four inches long), yellow sponge cake with butterscotch icing. The krimpet gets its name from the pan in which it is baked. The pan has fluted, or crimped, sides.*

Tastykake Butterscotch Krimpets, prewrapped frosted cakes created in 1927, are one of the Philadelphia-based Tasty Baking Company's bestselling products. According to a company representative, bakers at that time wanted a sweet butter frosting that they then scorched in copper kettles to give it its distinct flavor. The special baking pan was developed because the crimps in the sides of the cakes makes them easier to hold. For each cake, the bakers had to "crimp it," hence the origin of the word.

Many book clubs have been inspired to sample butterscotch krimpets after reading *Maniac Magee*: On average, the Tasty Baking Company receives approximately ten to fifteen orders per week from parents, teachers, and readers of *Maniac Magee*.

If you live in the mid-Atlantic area of the United States, you might find Tastykake Butterscotch Krimpets at your local grocery or convenience store. You can also order them through the company's website (www.tastykake.com) or by calling 1-800-33-TASTY. Or you might want to try baking some of your own.

While the Tastykake krimpet recipe has never been published, Todd Wilbur re-created it for his book *Top Secret Recipes: Creating Kitchen Clones of America's Favorite Brand-Name Foods* (Plume, 1993). Of course, the cakes will look different without the krimpet pan, but Wilbur claims—and we agree—that these home-baked goods taste similar to the store-bought cakes.

NOTE: Use cake mix only as directed in the recipe below; do not follow the instructions on the package.

If you don't have a 9 x 12-inch baking pan, you can use a 9 x 13-inch pan. Fill the extra inch with aluminum foil, greasing the edge of the foil as if it were the side of the pan.

FOR THE CAKE

4 large egg whites, at room temperature   ⅔ cup water

1 (16-ounce) box golden pound cake
mix (see note)

FOR THE FROSTING

¼ cup butterscotch morsels   1½ cups confectioners' sugar

½ cup (1 stick) unsalted butter, softened

1. To make the cake: Preheat oven to 325° F. Grease a 9 x 12-inch baking pan (see note).

2. In a large bowl, beat the egg whites with an electric mixer on high speed until thick but not stiff. Blend the egg whites with cake mix and water, mixing well.

3. Pour the batter into the prepared baking pan. Bake 30 minutes, or until the top is golden brown and a toothpick inserted in center comes out clean. Remove the pan from oven and cool on a wire rack.

4. To make the frosting: Melt the butterscotch morsels in the top pot of a double boiler over low heat or in a microwave on high 45 seconds.

5. In a bowl, mix butter with melted butterscotch morsels. Add the confectioners' sugar, blending with an electric mixer until smooth.

6. Spread the frosting on top of cooled cake. Cut cake into nine horizontal rows, and then make two lengthwise cuts, dividing the cake into 27 equal pieces.

YIELD: 27 SERVINGS

TRY IT!

Get All Knotted Up

When Maniac arrives in Two Mills, the knot at Cobble's Corner Grocery store has defied attempts at untying for years—until Maniac takes the challenge. The volleyball-sized string knot "had more contortions, ins and outs, twists and turns and dips and doodles than the brain of Albert Einstein himself." Maniac's heroic attempt at unraveling the famous knot draws a crowd—and becomes the talk of the town.

Spinelli told us about the evolution of this scene:

Maniac Magee was a hero to little kids. What makes a hero to little kids? For one thing, the ability to do something they can't do for themselves. Such as untie knots. Logical so far. Then an imaginative leap—hey, let's have him tackle the mother of all knots.

Knots are useful at work and at home, and used in many recreational activities, including sailing, camping, and climbing. Here are two fun ways to test your skills at knot tying—and untying.

MATERIALS

5-to-6-foot plastic or nylon cords or ropes

UNTIE-A-KNOT GAME (FOR PARTNERS)

Distribute one cord to each participant. Have participants create their own knots. Then ask them to trade cords and challenge their partner to unravel the knots.

READY-OR-KNOT RACE (FOR A GROUP)

In this game, adapted from *Family Fun* magazine, team players must untie various knots created by another team. It can be played by four or more players with plastic rope.

1. Sort your players into two teams. You can mix older and younger players and players who are more and less dexterous.
2. Each team receives a five-to-six-foot length of rope. Ask each player to tie one overhand knot OR allow each team one or two minutes to tie as many knots as possible. The teams then trade ropes.
3. To begin the race, ask each player to untie any one knot, and then pass the rope to a teammate. The first team to untie all its knots wins.

Topics Discussed

- What makes Maniac run
- Racial segregation in Two Mills and how Maniac bridges the differences between the two sides of town

- The prejudice, and also the kindness and goodness, that exist on both sides of the track
- If a Maniac character is possible—or if he is too innocent and unbiased for the real world

Maniac Magee's world seems so familiar. Do things happen in the story that do not happen in the real world?

In *Maniac Magee*, things are talked about directly—skin color, cultural difference—that we talk around or simply ignore. Like all good children's books, the story provides vicarious "growing up": strike out on your own with Maniac Magee; watch him choose his own way, assert his independence. The book is an intellectual and possibly spiritual awakening for young readers.

—ANDREW SPENO, CINCINNATI COUNTRY DAY SCHOOL
OPPORTUNITY, APPRECIATION AND KNOWLEDGE (OAK) BOOK CLUB (GRADES 4–5)
CINCINNATI

The Lion, the Witch and the Wardrobe (The Chronicles of Narnia, Book Two)

C. S. Lewis

Geoffrey Bles, 1950

Available in paperback from HarperCollins

208 pages

Fantasy

Series: *Prince Caspian* (Geoffrey Bles, 1951); *The Voyage of the "Dawn Treader"* (Geoffrey Bles, 1952); *The Silver Chair* (Geoffrey Bles, 1953); *The Horse and His Boy* (Geoffrey Bles, 1954); *The Magician's Nephew* (The Bodley Head, 1955); *The Last Battle* (The Bodley Head, 1956)

To escape the London bombings of World War II, Peter, Susan, Edmund, and Lucy Pevensie are evacuated from their city home to the English countryside estate of an eccentric professor. When the children discover a wardrobe in a spare bedroom, and Lucy ventures inside, she finds herself in the land of Narnia, populated by magical creatures, talking animals, and an evil White Witch, whose reign enslaves Narnia in an everlasting winter. All four children eventually find passage to Narnia, where Edmund is lured into treachery by the White Witch. Only the power of the awesome lion, Aslan, can reverse her control and restore spring to the land.

- The idea for *The Lion, the Witch and the Wardrobe* came to C. S. Lewis in 1939, at the start of World War II, when four children who had been evacuated from London came to stay at his home in the English countryside. One of the children asked Lewis what was behind an old wardrobe in a bedroom of the house. To entertain the four, Lewis began writing a story about children who had been evacuated to a big house in the country inhabited by a mysterious professor. Lewis put the story aside until 1948, when he began writing *The Lion, the Witch and the Wardrobe* in earnest.

- According to Lewis, the dreams and "mental pictures" that came to him as a teenager inspired several of the characters that later appeared in *The Lion, the Witch and the Wardrobe*. One image—a faun with an umbrella carrying parcels under his arm in a snowy wood—appears in the book exactly as he first imagined it, as the character Mr. Tumnus. Lewis added the character of Aslan (Turkish for "lion") much later, when he had already written part of the book.

- Lewis was a scholar at Oxford and Cambridge universities in England and a prolific writer of adult fiction, nonfiction, and Christian works before he wrote *The Lion, the Witch and the Wardrobe,* his first children's book. Many readers have recognized a Christian allegory in the book, where the rebirth of Aslan parallels the incarnation of Christ. Lewis claims that he had no intention of writing a Christian allegory but rather intended only to write a good story. In an essay titled "Sometimes Fairy Stories May Say Best What's to Be Said," Lewis wrote: "Everything began with images; a faun carrying an umbrella, a queen on a sledge, a magnificent lion. At first there wasn't even anything Christian about them; that element pushed itself in of its own accord."

- Although written six years after *The Lion, the Witch and the Wardrobe, The Magician's Nephew* depicts the creation of Narnia, long before the Pevensie children entered the wardrobe. Lewis has said that the Chronicles are best read chronologically in Narnian time, in this order: *The Magician's Nephew; The Lion, the Witch and the Wardrobe; The Horse and His Boy;*

Prince Caspian; *The Voyage of the* Dawn Treader; *The Silver Chair*; and *The Last Battle*.

Film adaptations:

The Chronicles of Narnia—The Lion, the Witch and the Wardrobe (Walden Media, 2005), rated PG, 134 minutes

The Lion, the Witch and the Wardrobe (Sesame Workshop, 2005), not rated, 90 minutes

The Chronicles of Narnia—The Lion, the Witch and the Wardrobe (Homevision, 2002), not rated, 169 minutes

The Lion, the Witch and the Wardrobe, Animated (Alpha Omega, 1979), not rated, 95 minutes

BOOK BITES

Turkish Delight

The White Witch entices Edmund to betray his siblings with enchanted Turkish delight. After tasting it, Edmund can hardly think of anything else, and its magical allure keeps him firmly in the Witch's clutches.

Turkish delight has intrigued generations of Narnia readers. Legend has it that Turkish delight was first concocted in the late eighteenth century, in the court of a famous sultan who ordered his confectioner to create a unique sweet to appease his many wives. The confectioner combined sugar syrup, flavorings, nuts, and dried fruits, and bound them together with mastic (gum arabic), and his irresistible treat was thereafter served daily to keep peace in the Ottoman court. Our recipe, from a cookbook written by C. S. Lewis's stepson, has a gelatin base and omits the fruit and nuts, but it retains the delectable sweetness of the original recipe. Turkish delight can be an acquired taste, but we think you'll savor the chance to sample the confection that bewitched Edmund.

The recipe comes from *The Narnia Cookbook: Foods from C. S. Lewis's* The Chronicles of Narnia, by Douglas Gresham (HarperCollins, 1998).

NOTE: This recipe calls for a 6-inch square pan, but a plastic sandwich box works well if you don't have a 6-inch pan. The candy is notoriously difficult to remove from the pan. If you're having trouble, try working the edges of the pan with a knife dipped in boiling water.

The mixture must be chilled overnight in order to set, so plan accordingly.

The texture of this Turkish delight improves after sitting for a day, so feel free to make it at least a day in advance.

3 (.25-ounce) envelopes unflavored gelatin
½ cup cold water
½ cup hot water
2½ cups granulated sugar

¼ teaspoon salt
juice of 1 lemon (about 3 tablespoons)
½ teaspoon lemon extract
About ½ cup confectioners' sugar, sifted

1. Pour the gelatin into the cold water. Set aside.
2. In a medium saucepan, bring the hot water and granulated sugar to a boil, stirring constantly. Reduce heat to low. Add the salt, and stir in the softened gelatin until completely dissolved. Simmer 20 minutes.
3. Remove from the heat and let cool 10 minutes. Stir in the lemon juice and lemon extract.
4. Rinse a 6-inch square pan (see note) with cold water. The pan should be wet but not have standing water. Pour the mixture into the pan. Cover with a lid or plastic wrap and refrigerate overnight.
5. Sift some of the confectioners' sugar onto a plate. Moisten a sharp knife in very hot water and run it around the edges of the pan to loosen the candy. Invert the pan over the plate. It may be necessary to work on the edges to loosen them enough to turn the candy out on top of the sugar (see note). Cut the square into equal-width strips, about 1 inch wide. Coat each strip in confectioners' sugar; then cut into cubes. Coat each cube in additional confectioners' sugar. Store covered at room temperature.

YIELD: 3 DOZEN (1-INCH) CUBES, OR 10 TO 12 SNACK-SIZE SERVINGS

Marmalade Roll

Mr. Beaver, a talking creature, leads the four children to his dam to take refuge from the White Witch, and to tell them the fate of Lucy's friend, Mr. Tumnus. There, they enjoy a meal of fresh fish and buttered potatoes, followed by "a great and gloriously sticky marmalade roll, steaming hot" that Mrs. Beaver pulls from the oven.

In Great Britain, marmalade refers to a jamlike preserve made from the fruit and peel of the bitter, or Seville, orange. Britain leads the world in the production of marmalade, and the city of Oxford, where C. S. Lewis taught, has a reputation for producing some of the finest marmalade around.

Our recipe for marmalade roll—a light, sweet, and lovely-looking jelly-roll cake—is adapted from *The Narnia Cookbook: Foods from C. S. Lewis's* The Chronicles of Narnia, by Douglas Gresham (HarperCollins, 1998).

NOTE: Another type of jam, such as strawberry or apricot, can be substituted for the marmalade in the recipe.

About ¼ cup confectioners' sugar, plus extra for dusting the cake

1 cup sifted cake flour

2 teaspoons baking powder

¼ teaspoon salt

3 large eggs

¼ cup cold water

1 cup granulated sugar

1 teaspoon vanilla extract

½ cup orange marmalade (see note)

1. Preheat oven to 425° F. Line a 10 x 15 x 1-inch jelly-roll pan with buttered parchment paper. Spread out a dish towel and sprinkle it with ¼ cup confectioners' sugar.
2. Sift together the cake flour, baking powder, and salt.
3. In a large bowl, beat the eggs with an electric mixer, until slightly thickened and lemon colored. Continue to beat while adding the water and the granulated sugar.

4. With a spatula, fold the dry ingredients into the egg mixture until thoroughly blended. Stir in the vanilla.

5. Pour the batter into the prepared pan, spreading to the edges. Bake 10–12 minutes, checking for doneness after 10 minutes. The top of the cake should be light golden brown and firm to the touch. Remove from the oven.

6. Invert the cake on the dish towel and carefully remove the paper. Immediately spread all but 2 tablespoons of the marmalade evenly over the surface of the hot cake. Starting with a long edge and using the dish towel to assist you, roll the cake into a log. The cake may crack slightly. Spread the reserved marmalade over the top of the cake and sprinkle with a little confectioners' sugar. Allow the cake to cool before cutting.

YIELD: 1 (15-INCH) JELLY ROLL, 10–12 SERVINGS

MAKE IT!

Snow Globes

During the reign of the White Witch, winter never loosens its grip on Narnia. Andrea Purdy, Youth Services Librarian at East Regional Library in Knightdale, North Carolina, says that making snow globes—an activity she found on the Martha Stewart website—is a great reminder of the chilly setting of *The Lion, the Witch and the Wardrobe*.

NOTE: After the first step of this project, you will need to wait one hour before proceeding, so structure your meeting accordingly.

Purdy suggests browsing discount outlets for figurines. Around the winter holidays, look for figurines that add a seasonal touch, such as carolers.

Glycerin, a skin emollient, may be purchased at most drugstores.

Synthetic evergreen tips are available at floral-supply or craft stores.

Epoxy creates a strong bond through the mixing of two chemical agents, and adult supervision of this product is recommended at all times. You can find epoxy at hardware and craft-supply stores.

MATERIALS

Small glass jars (baby-food or olive jars are good choices, but almost any jar works), one per member

Sandpaper

Clear-drying epoxy (see note)

Small plastic or ceramic figurines (see note)

Tips of synthetic evergreen trees (see note)

Distilled water

Wooden craft stick or plastic spoon

Glycerin (see note)

Glitter

Oil-based enamel paint (optional)

Ribbon (optional)

1. Rub the inside of the jar lid with sandpaper to roughen the surface. Using the epoxy, glue a figurine and/or synthetic trees to the inside of the lid. Be sure to glue the objects toward the middle of the lid, leaving at least ¼ inch of space around the perimeter so the lid can easily be screwed onto the jar. Allow to dry completely, about 1 hour.

2. Fill the jar almost to the top with distilled water. Using a wooden craft stick or plastic spoon, add a few drops of glycerin and stir. (Glycerin keeps the glitter from falling too quickly through the water. Don't add too much glycerin or the glitter will stick to the bottom of the jar.) Add a pinch of glitter.

3. Screw the lid on tightly. If desired, paint jar lid with enamel paint and allow to dry, about 45 minutes. If desired, glue a ribbon around the neck of the jar. Shake the jar up and down, and watch it snow!

Detect the Lie

Edmund's ability to lie—he convinced Peter and Susan that Lucy was lying about the existence of Narnia, even though he knew Lucy was telling the truth—intrigued Lisa Hughes, so she asked the mothers and daughters in her Oregon, Wisconsin, book club if they could lie as well as Edmund. Hughes challenged participants to think up simple true and false statements about themselves, such as "I have a pet hamster named Rufus" or "I know how to play the clarinet." Then, each member took a turn making three truthful statements and one false statement to the group, and the rest of the group guessed which statement was the lie. "In most cases we were able to pick out the lie pretty quickly," says Hughes. Hughes adds that she thinks the girls would have been more convincing if they had been required to write down their statements on paper. "But I told them it's a good thing that they couldn't lie as well as Edmund."

Topics Discussed

- Which scenes in the book might be taken from biblical stories
- How birth order in a family influences siblings' behavior
- How you would describe Edmund's character in the first part of the book, and if, like Edmund, you have ever done anything to a family member that you knew was wrong
- How the White Witch tempted Edmund, and what might tempt you if you were in Edmund's situation

ASK IT!

*What role do you think birth order played in the behavior
of the Pevensie children?*

We discussed how birth order influences everyone's behavior. Edmund is the middle child in his family, and he perceives a lack of attention and respect from his siblings. Many in our group believed that Edmund allied himself with the White Witch because he wanted to be "special" and gain the recognition he felt he was missing. Peter, being the eldest, played the role of the wise sage, and the elder sister was the "caretaker." The youngest fell neatly into the place of the "baby" and was very precocious and cute. The behavior patterns witnessed in the book seemed to ring true in the girls' lives, too, for the most part.

—EDE MARQUISSEE, SUMMIT MIDDLE SCHOOL
GREAT ATTITUDES ABOUT BOOKS (GAB)
FORT WAYNE, INDIANA

The Phantom Tollbooth

Norton Juster

Alfred A. Knopf, 1961

Available in paperback from Random House

256 pages

Fantasy

Milo finds everything—especially learning—dull, until the day a package containing a tollbooth and a map with strange places appears in his room. Driving past the tollbooth in his toy car, Milo arrives at the Lands Beyond, where wordplay and puns rule. When he learns of the feud over whether words or numbers are more important in the Kingdom of Wisdom, Milo embarks on a quest to end the quarrel by rescuing the Kingdom's twin princesses, Rhyme and Reason. In his mission to reunite words and numbers, Milo develops a new appreciation for life and learning.

AUTHOR SCOOP

- According to Norton Juster, inspiration for wordplay in *The Phantom Tollbooth* came from his father and the Marx Brothers.

- An architect who had received a grant to write a children's book about urban aesthetics, Juster was curious about how people experience and use cities. He was bogged down with the book project and began a story to divert himself, which he continually went back to when he sat down to write. That story became *The Phantom Tollbooth*.

- Juster was looking for a device, such as a rabbit hole or a wardrobe, to feature in his story when the idea of the tollbooth came to him. A tollbooth "seemed like a perfect, contemporary way for a kid to go from one world to another one," he says. "It's such a lovely blend of the magical and mundane." Juster thought tollbooths would be familiar to children, but has been surprised to learn in recent years that people on the West Coast of the United States are often no longer familiar with them, as many tollbooths have been removed.

- *The Phantom Tollbooth* wasn't written sequentially, says Juster, but rather in scenes that he pieced together after writing them. One of the first scenes he penned depicted the Mathemagician explaining infinity to Milo. He had a similar conversation with a ten-year-old in a restaurant three weeks earlier. "The child asked me, 'What is the biggest number there is?' and that's where this scene came from," says Juster.

- Juster felt that often he was simply eavesdropping on the characters and recording their words when he wrote the royal banquet scene in Dictionopolis, where characters state their food preferences and the meal they name magically appears. He made sure to include his favorite childhood meal in this scene: hot dogs, corn-on-the-cob, and chocolate pudding.

- Jules Feiffer was a housemate of Juster's in Brooklyn Heights and contributed illustrations as he read *The Phantom Tollbooth* manuscript. Juster thought the drawings were wonderful and brought his book to the publisher with Feiffer's illustrations. His drawings have appeared in the book since the first edition.

Film adaptation:

The Phantom Tollbooth, animated (MGM, 1970), rated G, 90 minutes

Norton Juster's "Subtraction Stew"

Norton Juster contributed his delightful recipe for the dish that Digitopolis's ruler, the Mathemagician, serves to Milo. After nine portions of stew, Milo's stomach is "feeling as empty as he could ever remember," and each bowl makes him "a little hungrier than the one before."

We think this stew will leave you with plenty of thought for food, and hungry for more.

4 lbs. (maybe 6) of less than nothing

5 lbs. mixed nonexistent ingredients

6 cups (maybe 9) of thin air

An iota of celery—chopped fine

3½ teaspoons of inconceivable seasonings

7 large slices of zilch

½ cup of emptiness

A pinch of zero

Less than a trace of not a darned thing

A large bunch of whatever is not there

One small figment of your imagination

Cut less than nothing into chunks and nonexistent ingredients into small pieces. Put them in a big pot. Add thin air and then all the other ingredients that have been either chopped, mashed, or forgotten.

Bring to a boil over high heat; then cover, turn down, and simmer for a long time. Taste it and if it's not ready, simmer some more for even longer, but don't burn it. Serve in deep bowls so you won't spill any.

YIELD: 8 SERVINGS

If you have leftovers, grind them all up and make into a loaf. Bake in a moderate oven.

SERVES 12

If there is still something left, form into small round croquettes and fry.

YIELD: 16 SERVINGS

This dish is particularly good with synonym buns, ragamuffins, and rigamarolls. Careful, if you eat too much you will starve to death.

TASTE IT!

Bites from the Book

Barb Moore brought a package of alphabet cookies to *The Phantom Tollbooth* discussion of the fourth- to sixth-grade Lunch Bunch Book Club at the Wayne County Public Library in Wooster, Ohio, so her group could try "eating their words," as did the characters in Dictionopolis. The children enjoyed the puns and double meanings in the story, and spelling words out and then eating them was a perfect accompaniment to the discussion.

MAKE IT!

Dodecahedrons

Barb Moore also thought members of her book club would enjoy an activity centered on the Dodecahedron, the twelve-sided character named after the mathematical shape in *The Phantom Tollbooth*. The Dodecahedron has twelve faces, each appearing on one surface and each wearing a different expression. After locating paper models of the twelve-sided figures on a website (www.korthalsaltes.com/dodecahedron), Moore enlarged the figures and printed them for each member of her group on two 8½-by-11-inch sheets of card stock. (The final models were roughly the size of softballs.) Each child cut the shape, folded paper on the lines, assembled the figures using glue sticks, and secured the final side with tape. If you find it difficult to secure the sides using glue sticks, you can also use clear tape to assemble the figures.

"Lands Beyond" Map

Barb Moore's Lunch Bunch Book Club enlarged the map of the Lands Beyond from *The Phantom Tollbooth* book jacket to two by three feet and displayed it to show where Milo's journeys had taken him. During the discussion, group members referred to the map to remind them of Milo's adventures and to prompt conversation.

MAKE IT!

Coffee Filter Sunrises

Elisabeth Wright and Kathy Gilmore's fourth- and fifth-grade book club at the Smoky Hill Public Library in Centennial, Colorado, drew symmetrical designs on coffee filters with water-based markers, submerged the tips of the filters in water, and watched the colors fade. The activity was designed to allow participants to experiment with color, says Wright, as Milo did when he attempted to conduct the sunrise, and the sun rose and set seven times, quickly, and the colors went all wrong. The craft was suggested in *A Guide for Using The Phantom Tollbooth in the Classroom* by Kathleen L. Bulloch (Teacher Created Resources, 1998).

Topics Discussed

- Which characters might be your friends
- How the author uses puns and clichés
- What you thought about the argument involving words and numbers
- The characters Milo meets and how they might be similar to people you know

> **ASK IT!**

Who sent the tollbooth to Milo?

I got a kick out of the different points of view of group members when we asked who sent the tollbooth. Many of the children believed that characters from the Lands Beyond, such as the Princesses of Rhyme and Reason, sent the tollbooth. The parents in the group thought Milo's parents or an adult in the "real world" had given him the tollbooth.

—NANCY HINMAN, PARENT-CHILD BOOK GROUP (GRADES 5–7)
SEEKONK, MASSACHUSETTS

Titles for Middle Grade Readers

(GRADES 4–7)

Chasing Vermeer by Blue Balliett

Dave at Night
by Gail Carson Levine

The City of Ember
by Jeanne DuPrau

Esperanza Rising
by Pam Muñoz Ryan

Freaky Friday
by Mary Rodgers

Hatchet by Gary Paulsen

Holes by Louis Sachar

My Louisiana Sky
by Kimberly Willis Holt

No More Dead Dogs
by Gordon Korman

*The Watsons Go to
Birmingham—1963*
by Christopher Paul Curtis

*Harry Potter and the Half-Blood
Prince* by J. K. Rowling

Homeless Bird by Gloria Whelan

Among the Hidden
by Margaret Peterson Haddix

The Breadwinner
by Deborah Ellis

Hoot by Carl Hiaasen

Out of the Dust by Karen Hesse

Skellig by David Almond

Surviving the Applewhites
by Stephanie Tolan

The View from Saturday
by E. L. Konigsburg

Walk Two Moons
by Sharon Creech

The House of the Scorpion
by Nancy Farmer

*Chinese Cinderella: The True Story
of an Unwanted Daughter*
by Adeline Yen Mah

Eragon by Christopher Paolini

Chasing Vermeer

Blue Balliett

Scholastic, 2004
Also available in paperback from Scholastic
272 pages
Mystery

Sequel: *The Wright 3* (Scholastic, 2006)

Sixth-grade classmates Petra and Calder are drawn together by a series of strange events: their teacher's nervous behavior, the discovery of a mysterious book, and letters sent to neighbors about the work of artist Johannes Vermeer. When Vermeer's painting *A Lady Writing* is stolen, the young sleuths combine their creativity, intuition, and research skills to piece together the puzzle.

AUTHOR SCOOP

- Many ideas from *Chasing Vermeer* came from Blue Balliett's own experiences teaching elementary school at the University of Chicago's Laboratory

School, the same school Petra and Calder attend in the story. When her class explored art and visited local museums, Balliett encouraged them to think about art critically. She wanted more fiction that combined adventure and "real" art ideas to read aloud to her class, and decided to try writing it herself. That was the beginning of *Chasing Vermeer,* but because Balliett was teaching full-time, it was five years before she finished the book.

- Growing up in New York City, Balliett visited museums regularly and became familiar with the work of Vermeer, one of her favorite painters. She studied art history in college. She says she has never tired of looking at Vermeer's *A Lady Writing,* the stolen painting in *Chasing Vermeer,* "in part because you're never going to be able to figure out what she's thinking—and yet she seems like the kind of person you would want to get to know."

- The characters in *Chasing Vermeer* are combinations of people in Balliett's life. The children in the story came out of her classroom experience "with a little sprinkling of my own kids added," says Balliett, and the adults in the book all live in Hyde Park and are all based on people she knows.

Author information: www.scholastic.com/titles/chasingvermeer

Blue Balliett recommends:

Charles Fort's *Lo!,* the 1931 book with accounts of inexplicable events that fascinates Petra. "*Lo!* has been reissued and some bookstores now carry it along with *Chasing Vermeer,*" says Balliett. "Depending on the age of the kids, *Lo!* is lots of fun to look at and pass around. It also prompts talk about paranormal goings-on. What does one make of something that can't be explained?"

From the Mixed-up Files of Mrs. Basil E. Frankweiler, by E. L. Konigsburg (Atheneum, 1967), which Balliett read when it first came out, and which she adored. "I still adore it!" she says.

The BFG, by Roald Dahl (Farrar, Straus & Giroux, 1982). Of Roald Dahl, Balliett says, "I've read all of his books, but this is my absolute favorite. It's wild and funny and touching."

Stonewords: A Ghost Story, by Pam Conrad (HarperCollins, 1990), which Balliett says is "very scary, but I love the way real and unreal are all mixed up together in this book."

Blue Balliett's Harper Avenue Rescue Fund Brownies: Finding the Twelve Blue Ones

Petra and Calder share a love of blue M&M's, agreeing that the color blue tastes "strange and mysterious." In *Chasing Vermeer*, the young sleuths eat blue M&M's only at special times—when a break in the case seems likely or has just taken place.

With the addition of twelve blue M&M's, Blue Balliett turns her brownie recipe into a game, suggesting that mysterious events might unfold for your group upon eating them, just as they do for Petra and Calder.

When serving the brownies to your book club, any number of magical things could happen: each person who crunches down on a blue one will know that they either have just made or are just about to make an important discovery of some kind, a discovery that could be an observation, an insight, or a sudden thought. If he or she feels comfortable sharing that discovery with the book club, this could be pretty cool. This is probably what Calder and Petra would recommend.

Or, each person who crunches down on a blue one can come up with a question or idea for the book club to talk about. Such as "If you were to pick a part of Chasing Vermeer *to jump into, what would it be?" or "If you could change the plot or the ending, how would you do it?" or a much wilder question that I haven't even imagined.*

1 box of brownie mix (preferably the kind with the extra package of chocolate syrup)
12 blue M&M's

1. Follow directions on the box for preparing brownie batter.
2. After you have prepared the batter and poured it into the baking pan, hide 12 blue M&M's *inside* the batter (the cooks can then eat the rest of the colors).

3. Bake brownies following package instructions.

4. Cut and serve brownies to the group, and ask participants to find the blue M&M's as they eat the brownies.

YIELD: 16 BROWNIES

Play with Pentominoes

Pentominoes are Calder's favorite mathematical tools. Each set has twelve shapes, and each shape contains five square blocks that share at least one side. Pentominoes can be used to explore mathematical ideas, and to play a variety of puzzles and games. Each piece is named after the letter of the alphabet it resembles.

When she was writing *Chasing Vermeer*, Balliett says, she often played with pentominoes in order to "get her thinking clear." She recommends purchasing a tub or two of plastic pentominoes in advance of your book club meeting, and if possible giving each book club member a set of pentominoes, which they can take home after the meeting. She explains that if each member of the group has their own set, everyone can do what Calder did with his—and possibly receive messages from their pentominoes as Calder does. "Stir the pentominoes around and pick one piece and see what that piece says. I can guarantee some surprises," says Balliett. She adds:

> When I was writing Chasing Vermeer, I felt like the manuscript kept surprising me. Even though the setting is my world and the characters are all based on people I know, it seemed as though the puzzle side of the book kind of jumped in on its own. The idea must have started, for me, with the twelve pentomino pieces, but I don't remember being aware of that. The twelves, for instance, were everywhere once I realized that Calder's and Petra's names were twelves. And then I realized that my own name was a twelve!

Try asking these questions at your book club meeting: Does your mind ever surprise you like that? Do you ever see coincidences in your life, and if so, do they follow any pattern?

You can purchase pentominoes from a math or educational-supply company. An online pentominoes game and printable pentominoes are available on the *Chasing Vermeer* webpage (www.scholastic.com/titles/chasingvermeer).

Find What's Hidden in the Pictures

Artist Brett Helquist has hidden secret messages related to the pentominoes in *Chasing Vermeer*'s illustrations. Look for the messages, composed by Blue Balliett, and see how many your group can decode. For more information, see "About the Artwork: A Challenge to the Reader" in the beginning of *Chasing Vermeer*.

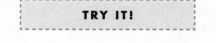

Explore Vermeer's Art

Dorothy Distefano, who facilitates the Families Invited to Read and Share Together (FIRST) Book Club, a school-based parent-child book club in Hilton, New York, organized activities that allowed the fifth- and sixth-graders in the group to play detective with Vermeer's artwork. First, the school's art teacher enlarged photographs of Vermeer paintings to display. Then each child received small details of Vermeer paintings cut from printed copies, and had to match the details with the real paintings. Distefano says the students enjoyed seeing the paintings that were referred to in *Chasing Vermeer*. She also found some works by Vermeer's known art forger, Han van Meegeren, and placed them next to photographs of Vermeer's works so members could guess which ones were forgeries.

Topics Discussed

- The symbology of the number twelve in religion, astronomy, time, math, and science, and the many coincidences involving twelves in the book
- Whether Calder's pentominoes were sending him messages or he was using them to kick-start his own ideas
- How writing letters is different from sending e-mail
- If Ms. Hussey has a similar teaching style to any of your teachers

ASK IT!

Chasing Vermeer begins with a quote taken from Charles Fort's
book Lo!: *"One can't learn much and also be comfortable.*
One can't learn much and let anyone else be comfortable."
What does this quote mean to you?

We discussed how this idea compares with our students' school journey, from the beginning of the year to the end. In order to learn, children need to be willing to step outside of their comfort zone, to open themselves to new ideas. When they allow themselves to reach for these new ideas, they inevitably learn more and also generate more questions. The kids likened this to occasions when they had learned something new in school and couldn't wait to share it with friends, siblings, and parents.

—DOROTHY DISTEFANO, FAMILIES INVITED TO READ AND SHARE TOGETHER (FIRST)
BOOK CLUB (GRADES 5–6)
HILTON, NEW YORK

Dave at Night

Gail Carson Levine

HarperCollins, 1999
Available in paperback from HarperTrophy, 2001
281 pages
Historical Fiction

It's 1926 and Dave, eleven years old and newly orphaned, has just landed in the Hebrew Home for Boys, a drafty, old asylum run by the maniacal Mr. Bloom. By day, Dave commiserates with his "buddies," or fellow orphans. By night, he escapes to the streets of Harlem, where Solly Gruber, a fortune-teller with a Yiddish-speaking parrot, introduces Dave to the vibrant nightlife of the Harlem Renaissance. At one evening gala, Dave befriends Irma Lee, the daughter of a Harlem socialite. Soon he must decide which place—the Hebrew Home or the streets of Harlem—to call home.

AUTHOR SCOOP

- Gail Carson Levine was born and raised in New York City, the setting for *Dave at Night.* To portray life in the city in the 1920s accurately, Levine thoroughly researched the period, making use of the many resources available to her in New York. She recalls:

> *To get into the period of the novel, I read several books about the Harlem Renaissance. I visited the Studio Museum in Harlem. I visited the New York Historical Society and looked at plans of the streets near the orphanage, which showed where buildings and stores were. I looked at old photos, especially of the Lower East Side, at the Forty-second Street branch of the New York Public Library (the main branch). I listened to old jazz. I did more than this, of course, but that's some of it.*

- Levine's father grew up in a Hebrew orphanage in Harlem, and that inspired her to research and write *Dave at Night*. As part of her research, she visited the orphanage where her father had lived. "Because of its connection to my father, *Dave at Night* is my favorite book," says Levine. She adds:

> *My father wouldn't talk about the orphanage, and I don't know why. The brutality may have been the reason. His silence sparked my curiosity. I was told a couple of stories by my uncles, but most of the events are invented.*

- Levine claims that Solly "may be my favorite character in any of my books." Solly was inspired by a line Levine read in a book about the Italian section of Harlem, where an annual church festival took place. She recalls:

> *The book said that an elderly Jewish man with a white parrot always came to the festival and told fortunes using a deck of cards. Although the parrot only spoke Yiddish, it knew enough Italian to tell the fortunes. This was in one sentence of the book, but Solly and the fortune-telling came from it.*

Author information: www.harperchildrens.com
Gail Carson Levine recommends:
Bud, Not Buddy by Christopher Paul Curtis (Delacorte, 1999), which she says "takes place in the 1930s and is about an African-American boy searching for his father."

Double Crossing by Eve Tal (Cinco Puntos, 2005), "about an immigrant experience from Eastern Europe."

Soft Pretzels

When Solly visits Dave at the orphanage, he brings a brown bag filled with goodies: raisins, sucking candy, a banana, and "a big soft pretzel with lots of salt."

Brought to America by European immigrants, pretzels belong to a German group of breads that are moistened before baking to give them a chewy texture. Pretzels take the form of knots, sticks, or rings, and can be hard or soft, but the most popular form in 1920s New York was a soft yeast pretzel covered in salt, commonly sold by street vendors, as they are today.

Some people think that the word *pretzel* derives from the Latin word *pretiola*, or "little reward." For Dave, perpetually hungry and almost always without visitors, Solly's visit—and the soft pretzel in the bag—was a very handsome "little reward."

NOTE: Bread flour has more gluten than all-purpose flour and gives the pretzels their chewiness. It can be purchased at most grocery stores.

These pretzels are best served straight from the oven. To prepare for your book club, follow the recipe through step 4. When the group arrives, complete the recipe, allowing each child to roll and twist his or her own pretzel.

The pretzel dough can be frozen for up to a month. To freeze, place dough in a sealed plastic freezer bag. Thaw the frozen dough for at least four hours in the refrigerator or two hours at room temperature before using.

If you bake the pretzels in advance, before serving, wrap them in aluminum foil and warm gently in a 250° F. oven 20 minutes.

FOR THE DOUGH

2¼ teaspoons (1 packet) active
dry yeast

2 tablespoons light brown sugar

1⅛ teaspoons salt

1½ cups warm water (100° F. to 110° F.)

4 cups bread flour (see note)

FOR THE DIPPING LIQUID

1½ cups warm water (100° F. to 110° F.)

2 tablespoons baking soda

FOR THE TOPPING

2 tablespoons butter, melted

1–2 tablespoons coarse kosher salt or cinnamon-sugar mix

1. In a large bowl, mix the yeast, brown sugar, and salt. Add 1½ cups warm water and stir to dissolve. Add the bread flour and stir to form a soft dough.
2. Place the dough on a floured surface. Knead about 5 minutes, until smooth and elastic.
3. Grease a large bowl with oil. Place the dough in the bowl, then turn the dough upside down to coat the surface. Cover with a damp towel and let rise in a warm place for 1 hour.
4. Lightly grease two baking sheets. Divide the dough into twelve equal pieces.
5. Combine 1½ cups warm water and baking soda in an 8-inch square pan. Roll each piece of dough into an 18-inch rope, ½ inch wide (the ropes should be slightly wider than a pencil). Twist each rope into a pretzel shape (see instructions and diagram below), dip into the baking soda solution, and set on the prepared baking sheets. Let rest 15–20 minutes.
6. Preheat oven to 450° F.
7. Bake 7–9 minutes, or until golden brown. Brush the pretzels with melted butter and sprinkle with the coarse salt or cinnamon-sugar mix. Serve immediately.

YIELD: 12 LARGE PRETZELS

TO FORM PRETZEL SHAPES

1. Lay dough rope in a U shape. Cross the left strand over the right. Each strand should be about 3 inches long above the place where they cross.
2. Bring left strand to lower right side of loop and press firmly into place.
3. Bring right strand to lower left side of loop and press firmly into place.

TASTE IT!

Bites from the Book

The Temple Israel 4th and 5th Grade Girls Book Club in West Bloomfield, Michigan, enjoyed butter cookies, the treat Dave's aunt brought him at the orphanage, for their *Dave at Night* discussion. They also served fruit and bite-size veggies as a reminder of the apple and little carrots Dave stuffed in his pockets to bring back to his hungry buddies at the Hebrew Home for Boys.

TRY IT!

Become a Fortune-teller

Dave and Solly, along with Solly's Yiddish-speaking parrot, Bandit, predict the fortunes of fashionable partygoers with nothing but a deck of cards.

Book clubs can re-create this miraculous feat, thanks to Cynthia Richey, coordinator of the Just for Guys Book Club, a father-son book club at the Mt. Lebanon Public Library in Pittsburgh. "We thought fortune-telling with cards would be a great activity after reading *Dave at Night*," says Richey. "The fathers told their sons' fortunes, and then they switched. They had a lot of fun!"

You might want to start each round with the words of Solly and Bandit: "Tell for you your fortune?"

MATERIALS

1 deck of cards for each pair of participants

Divide the participants into pairs. One partner tells the other's fortune by turning over cards and interpreting their meaning. Think about events past, present, and future, and offer your opinion about what things—good and bad—are in store for this person. For example, "A jack of hearts means you're headed for disaster!" or "If the next card is a club, the crisis will be averted." Be creative! Partners then switch roles.

TRY IT!

Book Link: An Idea from Gail Carson Levine

DISCOVER NEW YORK CITY MUSEUMS

If you live near or plan to visit New York City, and want to immerse yourself more fully in the era depicted in *Dave at Night*, Gail Carson Levine highly recommends visiting two of the museums she explored while researching the book.

The Studio Museum in Harlem displays historical and contemporary art by African-American artists. The museum's collection includes photographs chronicling the Harlem Renaissance by African-American photographer James Van Der Zee, and portraits of many Harlem Renaissance figures—including Countee Cullen, W. E. B. Du Bois, and Langston Hughes, who appear in *Dave at Night*—by writer and photographer Carl Van Vechten. The museum rotates its exhibits, so call ahead or check the website to find out when these pieces will be on display.

The Studio Museum in Harlem
144 West 125th Street
New York, New York 10027
www.studiomuseum.org

At the Lower East Side Tenement Museum, visitors are offered guided tours of restored tenement buildings and apartments on Manhattan's Lower East Side that reflect the lives of immigrants at various times in history. Several of the apartments date to the late 1800s and early 1900s and give insight into the lives of Jewish immigrants, like the character Solly, during the period when *Dave at Night* was set. If you can't visit in person, Levine suggests browsing the Lower East Side Tenement Museum's website, whose address is given below.

Lower East Side Tenement Museum
108 Orchard Street
New York, New York 10002
www.tenement.org
(To schedule a tour, call well in advance, as tour-group sizes are limited.)

If a trip to New York City is not in your plans, look for local museums devoted to African-American, Jewish, or immigrant history, or art museums featuring artwork or photographs from the Harlem Renaissance period.

Topics Discussed

- The importance of friendship to Dave, and who his true friends are
- How Dave and Irma Lee have common needs but dissimilar lifestyles
- The perception of Jews and African-Americans, and their relationships to each other, during this time period
- The character of Solly, and whether the fact that he is a *gonif* (Yiddish for a dishonest or shady person) makes him bad

Solly refers to his own children as "alrightniks," or people who take other people for granted. Is it worse to be a thief like Solly or an alrightnik?

The group agreed that labels are not always accurate, and that some people who are looked upon as good people are not always so good. At one point, Dave realizes that Mr. Bloom, who seems respectable to the outside world, is actually an alrightnik. And Solly, although he cheats people with fortune-telling, is a good friend to Dave. This led to a discussion of labeling at school, and how labels can discourage kids from really getting to know one another.

—STACEY WEINBERG, CHARLES E. SMITH JEWISH DAY SCHOOL
PARENT-CHILD BOOK CLUB (GRADES 5–6)
ROCKVILLE, MARYLAND

Grades 4–7

The City of Ember

Jeanne DuPrau

Random House, 2003
Available in paperback from Random House
288 pages
Science Fiction

Series: *The People of Sparks* (Random House, 2004); *The Prophet of Yonwood* (Random House, 2006)

Twelve-year-old Lina Mayfleet longs for a world of lightness and color, a world re-moved from the dark, forlorn city of Ember, where the only source of light—an enor-mous generator—is failing. Everyone tells Lina no such place exists, but her friend Doon is convinced an escape route from Ember can be found. When Lina discovers and begins to decode a cryptic letter, she suspects Doon may be right.

AUTHOR SCOOP

- The widespread fear of nuclear war in the 1950s and 1960s, when Jeanne DuPrau grew up, partly inspired the story of Ember. In writing about a city built to protect people from a catastrophe, DuPrau also became intrigued with the idea of a city cut off from the sun, and lit only by electricity. She explains:

What would it be like to live in such darkness, and to know that light and food and supplies were all running out? And not to know about weather or trees or animals, except for a few rats and insects, or any other places? All this grabbed my imagination. And once I'd written The City of Ember, *I hoped it would make people think about our world—about the sun and the moon, the forests and the ocean, the wind and the rain—and how precious it all is.*

- Readers may find it surprising that DuPrau intended the name of the main character—Lina—to be pronounced with a long *i*. "My editor warned me that people would call her 'Leena,' so I put in a clue about the right pronunciation—I had her baby sister call her Wyna," DuPrau explains. "My clue didn't work very well, though. It would have been better if I'd had Lina's friends call her 'Lima Bean.' Oh, well."
- DuPrau says she is reflected in both Lina and Doon. "Lina likes running and drawing and watching things grow; Doon likes collecting bugs, figuring out word puzzles, and exploring. These are all things I like, too," she says.
- DuPrau first wrote *The City of Ember* about twenty years ago, but says she put it aside because "it just didn't sound right." Twenty years later, upon reading J. K. Rowling's *Harry Potter and the Sorcerer's Stone,* she identified the problem with her first draft, and found a way to improve it. Unlike Rowling's fantasy, DuPrau felt her story "moved too slowly, and the characters weren't active enough," she explains. "I rewrote it so that each chapter left readers wanting to know what would happen next, and the characters were always engaged in doing things, figuring things out, and getting in danger and finding a way out of it."
- DuPrau claims the work of Charles Dickens, whom she has long admired, indirectly influenced the writing of *The City of Ember*. "I love the names of characters in Dickens's books, and I think my characters' names might

have been influenced by them," she says. "I also love the complicated plots and odd people in Dickens's novels, and maybe mine bear some faint resemblance to those."

Author website: www.jeanneduprau.com
Jeanne DuPrau recommends:
Airborn by Kenneth Oppel (Eos, 2004)
The Fire-Us Trilogy by Jennifer Armstrong and Nancy Butcher
    (HarperCollins, 2002)
The Giver by Lois Lowry (Houghton Mifflin, 1993; see p. 340)
Gregor the Overlander by Suzanne Collins (Scholastic, 2003)

BOOK BITES

Jeanne DuPrau's Apple-Pineapple Salad

The people of Ember prepare unusual—sometimes unappetizing—dishes from their limited food supplies, and Jeanne DuPrau enjoyed contemplating their menus: "I love food and cooking, so I felt very sorry for the people of Ember, with their dreary diet. It was fun, though, thinking about the things they would eat, like beet tea, mushroom gravy, and turnip stew."

We hoped DuPrau would come up with an appealing recipe to pair with *The City of Ember,* and she obliged with this tasty salad featuring canned pineapple—"the fruit Lina's grandmother remembered with such longing." DuPrau adds:

The people of Ember couldn't have made this recipe—they didn't have apples, or nuts, or really any of the ingredients except the pineapple, before it all ran out. In this way—actually, in lots of ways!—you're much luckier than the people of Ember.

Serve this salad on its own, as a luncheon side dish, or as part of a buffet.

NOTE: Low-fat mayonnaise and/or low-fat yogurt can be used. DuPrau says she favors low-fat yogurt with a little mayonnaise stirred in.

2 apples, cored and chopped

1 (20-ounce) can pineapple chunks, drained, with 1–2 tablespoons juice reserved

½ cup chopped walnuts

½ cup raisins or chopped dates

¼ cup mayonnaise, or a mixture of mayonnaise and plain yogurt (see note)

1. In a medium bowl, combine the apples, pineapple, walnuts, and raisins or dates.
2. In a small bowl, mix the mayonnaise or mayonnaise-yogurt combination with the pineapple juice.
3. Pour the dressing over the fruit. Chill until ready to serve.

YIELD: 4 TO 6 SERVINGS

TRY IT!

Book Links: Ideas from Jeanne DuPrau

DECODE A MISSING-LETTER PUZZLE

Jeanne DuPrau suggests challenging your group with a missing-letter puzzle similar to the one Lina and Doon struggle to decode in *The City of Ember*.

Compose a short message to your book club on the computer. Try to include both short, familiar words (like "and" and "you") and longer, less common words. As you compose, leave blank spaces in place of some of the letters. For the shorter words, leave out one letter, and for longer words, leave out one or two letters. The length of the message and the number of blank spaces will vary depending on the ages of the participants. (If you add an underscore mark in each blank space, decoding the message will be easier.)

Give out copies of the puzzle. Let members work in pairs, and see who cracks the code first!

RAISE CATERPILLARS TO BUTTERFLIES

To experience the awe Doon feels when he finds that his green worm has become a moth, Jeanne DuPrau suggests raising caterpillars and watching them metamorphose into butterflies.

Butterfly kits, complete with butterfly larvae, food, and an observation house, are available online. The kits include instructions for caring for adult butterflies without releasing them, which is advisable during the winter months.

If you'd prefer to collect and raise your own caterpillars, you can find instructions in books and many online sites (see www.rearing-butterflies.com).

PLANT A BEAN SEED

Lina and her friend Clary wonder at the miracle of a bean seed. "Something in this seed knows how to make a bean plant. How does it know that?" Clary muses.

Jeanne DuPrau suggests planting bean seeds during your *City of Ember* meeting. Then, she says, "Take your seed pot home, put it in a warm window, water it, and see how mysterious and exciting it is to watch the stem come up and the leaves unfold." (For materials and instructions for planting seeds, see *My Louisiana Sky*, p. 167.)

TRY IT!

Pick a Profession

At the age of twelve, the children of Ember choose their life's work by picking slips of paper randomly from a bag. This practice inspired Cynthia Rider, a librarian at the Foster City (California) Library, to ask her middle school book club members to pick professions from a hat, then investigate the salary and qualifications for their chosen jobs. "I wanted to expose the group to a variety of jobs, and also encourage them to use reference books to gather information," says Rider.

Write the name of a different profession (e.g., veterinarian, janitor, actor) on an index card for each member of your group. Place the cards facedown on a table and ask each book club member to randomly choose one. Then ask them to research the salary and qualifications of their jobs, using career reference books, and report their findings. Finally, you might allow them to trade careers.

Topics Discussed

- What sorts of environmental or social problems could have led to the building of the city of Ember
- How Lina's and Doon's personalities complement each other and how their friendship helps each of them
- The importance of color and light in the novel
- How the people of Ember react to danger

ASK IT!

What would it be like to live in Ember?

We imagined what it would be like to live that way, not knowing what the taste of peaches or pineapple is. This is what we take for granted. None of the people in the city of Ember had ever tasted these things, and we imagined how hard that would be, or how hard it *wouldn't* be. If you don't know it, do you miss it?

—FAITH HOCHHALTER, TWEEN BOOK CLUB (GRADES 4–6)
CHANGING HANDS BOOKSTORE
TEMPE, ARIZONA

Esperanza Rising

Pam Muñoz Ryan

Scholastic, 2000
Available in paperback from Scholastic
262 pages
Historical Fiction

Fourteen-year-old Esperanza and her mother are forced to flee their privileged lives in Aguascalientes, Mexico, and adjust to harsh conditions in a California migrant labor camp in 1930. Esperanza confronts numerous challenges in her new community: acceptance by fellow Mexicans, caring for younger children, hard labor picking fruits and vegetables in the fields, and nursing her ailing mother. As she faces the difficult circumstances of her new life, Esperanza's hope and courage guide her.

AUTHOR SCOOP

- Pam Muñoz Ryan considers herself truly American: She is half Mexican and, culturally, half Oklahoman. Her grandparents on her mother's side came to the United States from Aguascalientes, Mexico, in the 1930s, and worked in a Mexican farm labor camp, where Ryan's mother was born. Her father came to California from Checotah, Oklahoma, during the dust bowl and years later, coincidentally, worked for the same company farm.

- *Esperanza Rising* is a fictional story, which parallels Ryan's grandmother's immigration experience. Ryan stresses that the character of Esperanza is not her grandmother, but rather "a character based on what I imagined that my grandmother could have been at that age." When Ryan was a young girl, her grandmother related stories of her life in the farm camp, but it was not until much later that Ryan learned about her grandmother's past. She explains:

> *I was an adult before I knew anything about my grandmother's Mexican life in Aguascalientes, and what it was like for her to grow up there. It was a revelation to discover that she was actually wealthy and that she had servants, because I always thought that her beginnings were in the farm labor camp. In my mind, there wasn't anything before that. And so it was very much an epiphany to discover that she had this other princess life in Mexico.*

Author website: www.pammunozryan.com
Pam Muñoz Ryan recommends:
Adaline Falling Star by Mary Pope Osborne (Scholastic, 2000)
A Corner of the Universe by Ann M. Martin (Scholastic, 2002)
Homeless Bird by Gloria Whelan (HarperCollins, 2000; see p. 197)

(see p. 197)

-------------------------------- BOOK BITES --------------------------------

Pam Muñoz Ryan's Rice and Bean Burritos

The characters in *Esperanza Rising* frequently eat burritos—flour tortillas often filled with rice, beans, and other ingredients. Ryan grew up with extended family nearby and recalls the burritos she ate as a child: "When I was a girl, my grandmother almost always had a pot of beans and pan of rice on the stove," says Ryan. "I made burritos with a variety of ingredients: beans, rice, cheese, avocados, salsa, and sour cream."

NOTE: If you prefer a spicier filling, you might want to add additional black pepper or your favorite diced chiles to the beans or rice.

You can serve the burritos with Salsa (see p. 263).

FOR THE BEANS

1 (16-ounce) bag dried pinto beans

1 large onion, chopped

4 cloves garlic, minced

2 (14-½ ounce) cans chicken or vegetable broth

2 (14½-ounce) soup cans of water

½ teaspoon salt

¼ teaspoon ground black pepper (see note)

FOR THE RICE

2 tablespoons vegetable oil

⅓ cup minced onion

⅓ cup minced bell pepper

1½ cups uncooked long-grain white rice

1 (14½-ounce) can chicken or vegetable broth

¼ cup tomato sauce stirred into 1½ cups water

FOR THE BURRITOS

8 large (at least 10-inch) flour tortillas

2 cups shredded Monterey Jack or cheddar cheese (optional)

FOR THE GARNISHES

Sour cream, salsa (see p. 263), avocado (optional)

1. To make the beans: Follow directions on back of bag for cleaning and soaking the beans. Drain water.
2. In a large saucepan, combine the beans, onion, garlic, broth, and water. Season with salt and pepper. Bring to a boil. Reduce heat to low and simmer 2½–3 hours, until beans are plump and soft, stirring often. Add salt and pepper to taste.

3. To make the rice: Pour the oil into a large skillet. Add onion, bell pepper, and rice and sauté over medium heat until rice is lightly toasted.

4. Add the broth and tomato sauce water. Bring to a boil and cover. Reduce heat to low. Simmer 20–25 minutes, or until liquid has been absorbed. Do not stir while simmering or rice will be mushy.

5. Remove from heat and let stand 5 minutes. Carefully fluff with a fork.

6. Heat tortillas according to package directions.

7. To make the burritos: Place tortilla on a flat surface. Mound ¼ cup rice, ¾ cup bean mixture, and ¼ cup shredded cheese (if desired) on one side of tortilla, leaving enough tortilla to cover the filling when you fold it over. Fold once over filling, tucking edge under filling. Alternate folding in each side of the tortilla as you roll, and tightly roll into a bundle. Repeat process for remaining tortillas.

8. If desired, serve with sour cream, salsa, and avocado.

YIELD: 8 BURRITOS

TASTE IT!

Book Links: Tasty Ideas from Pam Muñoz Ryan

TEA

Pam Muñoz Ryan suggests trying Celestial Seasonings Red Zinger tea, made from hibiscus flowers and rose hips. These flowers are prominent in *Esperanza Rising,* and the tea is reminiscent of *agua de Jamaica,* the hibiscus flower water drink served at the plentiful fiestas held by the migrant laborers. Ryan adds that the herbal tea can be made as a pitcher of cold tea or served hot.

FRUIT

Each *Esperanza Rising* chapter title takes its name from fruits and vegetables harvested in Mexico and then in California's San Joaquin Valley. Ryan explains the importance of the produce in her novel.

As I read through my story, I began to feel a parallel between the harvest and what was happening in Esperanza's life. The fruits or vegetables began to take on the feel of metaphors. For example, the smashed figs for her smashed life and the resentment she felt. Their [the characters'] lives were dictated by the rhythm of the harvest seasons, so the story lent itself to this organization.

Sample the fruits named in the chapter headings—including grapes, papaya, cantaloupe, plums, and peaches—with your book club. Simply cut up fruit or mix to serve as fruit salad.

Book Link: An Idea from Pam Muñoz Ryan

YARN DOLLS

Pam Muñoz Ryan told us how yarn dolls became part of Esperanza's story.

When I was a young girl, about ten years old, I received a pillow octopus craft kit as a gift. The instructions were similar to the yarn doll, except for the lower half of the body. For the octopus, after the head is tied off, you simply divide the rest of the yarn into eight legs and braid it. It came with a Styrofoam ball that fit under the yarn for the head, cute googly eyes, and colored ribbons to tie on each leg. Much more yarn was used as well, so it was considerably larger than the yarn dolls. With the leftover yarn, I made a few yarn dolls. Memories like these often work their way into books.

Yarn Dolls

Sharon Coppola, a librarian with the St. Petersburg (Florida) Public Library, says making yarn dolls, as Esperanza's mother made in the book, was a favorite activity at the mother-daughter book club she facilitates. "The girls loved the scene on the train where the girl is given a yarn doll to play with, and discussed what it would be like to be so poor that this was their only toy," says Coppola. "It made a real impact. Some girls made their one doll to give as a gift."

MATERIALS (FOR ONE YARN DOLL)

Ball of yarn

Ruler

Scissors

Book, at least 5 ¼ x 7 ½ inches, for wrapping yarn

1. Cut 7 (12-inch) pieces of yarn. Set aside.
2. Holding ball of yarn in one hand and book in the other, wrap yarn around book approximately 50 times (or until you are tired!). This will determine how plump the yarn doll will be.
3. Slip a small piece of yarn between the book and the yarn, and tie a knot. Slip the yarn off the book.
4. Tie another piece of yarn about 1½–2 inches below the first knot. This will be the head.
5. Cut the bottom loops and separate the strands into three sections: two for the arms and one for the torso. (The torso section should be slightly thicker than the two arm sections.) Tie another piece of yarn around the middle section, about 2½ inches below the doll's head, to form the torso.
6. Braid the arms, using string to tie each section. Leave an inch or so of loose yarn at ends for the hands and feet.

7. If you want a dress, leave the remaining yarn hanging free. If you want legs, separate yarn below the torso and braid each section. For an extra touch, braid or twist a yarn of a different color to make a belt.

THINK ABOUT IT!

Explore Immigrant Stories

In Orlando, Florida, teens and their parents—all from immigrant families, and many with poor English-speaking skills—gathered at the Orange County Library's Southeast Branch in the spring of 2005 to explore their experiences as they related to the immigrant story in *Esperanza Rising*. The Parent-Teen Get Together Placticamos program gave teens the opportunity to meet peers, and allowed parents time to converse.

Esperanza Rising was a perfect choice for this group, says coordinator Lisa Stewart, because its simple language is accessible to those struggling with English, but also because of its mature themes. "Esperanza faces situations in which fellow Mexicans living in the United States view her as snooty and arrogant because she was a member of the Mexican upper class," explains Stewart. "This is a situation that many of our attendees have faced. They have also felt embarrassed about family members even though they love them, and experienced ridicule due to lack of English competence, and the pressures of living within another culture." Stewart posed the following questions to the group:

- What is your fondest memory from your native country, and what is the hardest thing about adapting to life in the United States?
- What is your favorite holiday memory?
- What is your favorite food, and which childhood memories do you associate with this food?

The questions successfully drew the members into the conversation, eliciting many touching and funny responses, and making members more comfortable speaking to the group, says Stewart.

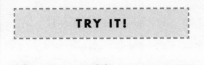
Visit a Vineyard

When the Summer Young Readers Program at the Chautauqua Institution, a center for the arts, religion, education, and recreation in Chautauqua, New York, discussed *Esperanza Rising*, the group visited a local vineyard to learn firsthand about grape harvesting. Most group members had never been on a farm and were fascinated by the behind-the-scenes look at grape growing and harvesting. They were able to discern the differences between grape picking in Esperanza's day and modern grape harvesting, says program director Jack Voelker, and realized that even in today's mechanized grape farms, a great deal of hand labor is required. "They learned how much is required to plant, grow, and harvest the grapes," says Voelker, "so they had a sense that there is more to it than walking down the grocery aisle."

Topics Discussed

- Entering another country and culture and leaving family and friends behind
- The transition from being very rich to being very poor and being unaccustomed to doing simple things for yourself
- Esperanza's quick maturation, where she had to care for both herself and her mother
- The lives of migrant children, who have to move around with the different growing seasons and crops

Have you ever moved? What was it like to be the new kid?

Asking if children had ever relocated helped them relate to Esperanza's disloca-tion when she moved to California. It was an excellent way to begin the discussion.

—KAREN SPANO, BOCA PARENT-CHILD BOOK CLUB (GRADES 3–5)
SOUTHWEST COUNTY REGIONAL LIBRARY
BOCA RATON, FLORIDA

Freaky Friday

Mary Rodgers

HarperCollins, 1972
Available in paperback from HarperCollins
176 pages
Fiction

Series: *A Billion for Boris* (HarperCollins, 1974); *Summer Switch* (HarperCollins, 1982)

Thirteen-year-old Annabel awakens one Friday morning to discover she's in her mother's body. Annabel is at first thrilled with her new independence, and eager to experience life with all the privileges her mother enjoys. After an eye-opening day of mishaps and revelations—while running the household and attending a parent-teacher conference—Annabel discovers that being her mother is not as easy as it seems.

AUTHOR SCOOP

- Apart from writing fiction, Mary Rodgers is an accomplished screenwriter and composer. She created and wrote lyrics for several Broadway musicals, including *Once Upon a Mattress, Hot Spot, Working, The Mad Show,* and *The Griffin and the Minor Canon.* She also compiled the collection of songs *Free to Be... You and Me.* She is the daughter of composer Richard Rodgers.

- Rodgers was a mother of five when she wrote *Freaky Friday*—her first published book. In an interview about writing the book, Rodgers commented—with tongue in cheek—about her free time to write the story:

> *Since I had nothing to do but take care of five children, a nine-room apartment, an eleven-room house in the country and show up once a month at the Professional Children's School Board of Trustees meeting, once a month at the Dramatist Guild Council meeting, and eight times at the A&P, I thought I'd be delighted to write a children's book because I had all this extra time on my hands. (Between the hours of two and five a.m., I just loll around the house wondering how to amuse myself.)*

Film adaptations:
Freaky Friday (Walt Disney, 2003), rated PG, 93 minutes
Freaky Friday (Walt Disney, 1995), rated G, 98 minutes
Freaky Friday (Walt Disney, 1976), rated G, 95 minutes

BOOK BITES

"Beetloaf" (Hot Milk) Cake

In choosing a dessert for her suburban Boston mother-daughter book group's *Freaky Friday* meeting, Jill Oetheimer turned the beetloaf Boris volunteers to make for Annabel's dinner company into a beetloaf cake. She enjoyed the scene where Boris tells Annabel he's preparing "beetloaf" but Annabel assumes he means meat loaf because his adenoid problem causes him to pronounce *m* like *b.* "The story at this point gets very chaotic," says Oetheimer. "The cake seemed like a fun way to go along with that theme of 'Nothing is what it appears to be.'"

Oetheimer added red food coloring to her grandmother's recipe for hot milk cake to give it a pink tinge, baked the cake in a loaf pan, and voilà!—beetloaf. She tops the cake with chocolate sauce.

NOTE: Oetheimer says to add food coloring until batter is "beet juice" pink.

FOR THE CAKE

2 large eggs, at room temperature

1 cup sugar

1 cup all-purpose flour

1 teaspoon baking powder

⅛ teaspoon salt

½ cup whole milk

1 tablespoon unsalted butter

4–5 drops red food coloring (see note)

FOR THE CHOCOLATE SAUCE

¼ cup semisweet chocolate morsels

1–2 tablespoons unsalted butter

1. To make the cake: Preheat oven to 375° F. Grease a 9 x 5 x 3-inch loaf pan.
2. In a large bowl, beat the eggs and sugar with an electric mixer on high speed until well blended.
3. Add the flour, baking powder, and salt, mixing well.
4. In a saucepan, heat the milk and butter until butter is melted and milk is hot but not scalded. Add the milk mixture to batter and mix thoroughly (batter will be thin). Add food coloring (see note). Pour batter into prepared pan.
5. Bake 20–30 minutes, until cake is golden brown or toothpick inserted in the center comes out clean. Cool completely, then turn out onto a wire rack.
6. To make the chocolate sauce: Place the chocolate morsels and butter in a saucepan over low heat until chocolate is completely melted and mixture is smooth. Or heat the morsels and butter in a microwave, stirring at 30-second intervals. Spread the sauce over top of cake.

YIELD: 1 LOAF CAKE, 6 SERVINGS

"Freaky" Bookmarks

Since it was "freaky" that Annabel and her mother traded places, says Jill Dean, she asked her Junior Book Club fourth-, fifth-, and sixth-graders at the Wardsboro (Vermont) Public Library to create a freaky bookmark when they discussed *Freaky Friday*.

On one side of a bookmark cut from neon-colored card stock, the girls used their imaginations to create what is freaky to them, or as Dean described, "anything that they felt was strange or unusual, or uncomfortable for them to do." On the other side, they glued a one-inch mirror (purchased from a craft store), so that all the children could see their own face, just as Annabel did before the switch with her mother.

Switch Places with Your Mother or Your Daughter

When the fourth-grade girls and their moms arrived at Jill Oetheimer's house for their *Freaky Friday* book club meeting, they had already traded roles in keeping with the theme of the book: The mothers had dressed like the daughters and the daughters like the mothers.

"They loved it," recalls Oetheimer. The girls arrived in long earrings and scarves and the mothers in sweatpants and pigtails. A few girls felt uncomfortable in "grown-up" clothes, recalls Oetheimer, but one pair shared similar tastes and didn't look all that different.

The mothers and daughters then divided into two groups. Each group took five minutes to imagine what the other's day might be like, followed by a sharing session.

Oetheimer recalls that things got pretty silly. "The girls imagined the mothers had interesting days full of manicures and shopping sprees, and the moms thought the girls had way too much homework and fights with their brothers," she recalls. "This exercise really got the book discussion going."

TRY IT!

Take a Mother-Daughter Trust Walk

At the Needham, Massachusetts, Youth Commission's Books and Bridges Mother-Daughter Book Club, Katy Colthart, the group's facilitator, planned a trust walk as a *Freaky Friday* icebreaker. She gave each mother-daughter pair a blindfold and had each take turns leading the other around the room for several minutes without touching and only using words, steering clear of obstacles. As a group, they discussed whether it is hard to trust your mother or daughter to keep you from bumping into walls, chairs, and obstacles, and the different ways in which their partners made them feel safe. Colthart says the icebreaker was important for reminding the moms and daughters that relying on each other is not always easy, but through trust you can avoid some of the obstacles you might face.

Topics Discussed

- How you would react if you were in Annabel's situation that morning
- What Annabel learned from her family and what her family learned from her
- What the characters (Annabel, her mother, Ape Face, Boris) could have done differently
- What you thought of how Annabel handled the parent-teacher conference

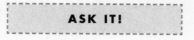

What did you think of the similarity between the beginning and the end of the book?

We had an excellent discussion about the book's ending. The last paragraph repeats the opening lines from the beginning: "You are not going to believe me . . . but it's true, it really is." We talked about whether the book was a fantasy story, or whether it was Annabel's English essay—the product of a very wild imagination.

—JILL OETHEIMER, MOTHER-DAUGHTER BOOK CLUB (GRADE 4)
NEEDHAM, MASSACHUSETTS

Hatchet

Gary Paulsen

Macmillan, 1987
Also available in paperback from Aladdin
208 pages
Fiction

Sequels: *The River* (Delacorte, 1991); *Brian's Winter* (Delacorte, 1996); *Brian's Return* (Delacorte, 1999); *Brian's Hunt* (Wendy Lamb, 2003)
Companion book: *Guts: The True Stories Behind* Hatchet *and the Brian Books* (Laurel-Leaf, 2001)

Thirteen-year-old Brian Robeson is the sole passenger on a small plane that crashes in the Canadian wilderness. Armed only with his wits, a windbreaker, and a hatchet, a gift from his mother before he left on the trip to visit his father, Brian must learn to survive in an unforgiving environment, where food is scarce and wild animals threaten. Brian's fear and self-pity gradually harden into a determination to understand his new home and how to survive within it.

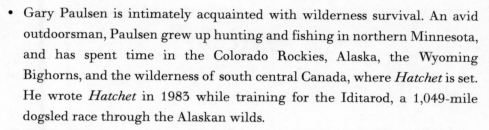

AUTHOR SCOOP

- Gary Paulsen is intimately acquainted with wilderness survival. An avid outdoorsman, Paulsen grew up hunting and fishing in northern Minnesota, and has spent time in the Colorado Rockies, Alaska, the Wyoming Bighorns, and the wilderness of south central Canada, where *Hatchet* is set. He wrote *Hatchet* in 1983 while training for the Iditarod, a 1,049-mile dogsled race through the Alaskan wilds.

- Readers have consistently asked Paulsen to explain how personal life events inspired the action in *Hatchet*. Paulsen responded with *Guts: The True Stories Behind* Hatchet *and the Brian Books,* in which he describes the many events in his life that parallel the events in *Hatchet*, including:

WATCHING A MAN DIE OF A HEART ATTACK

Before becoming a well-known writer and while living in a prairie town, Paulsen served as a volunteer ambulance driver. He sometimes arrived too late to save heart-attack victims, and one experience in particular, when he watched a man die before his eyes, inspired the scene of the pilot's death in *Hatchet*.

BEING ATTACKED BY A MOOSE

While training for his first Iditarod in Alaska, Paulsen was viciously attacked by a cow moose. Although he knew she was just an animal, the brutality of the attack shook him. "She made it personal, as the moose that went after Brian made it personal," he writes in *Guts*.

TASTING RAW TURTLE EGGS

During his Iditarod training in 1983, Paulsen's favorite dog, Cookie, discovered buried turtle eggs. Imagining that the character he was writing about, Brian, would likely come across buried turtle eggs, Paulsen tried to eat some—unsuccessfully. Paulsen decided to include the scene in *Hatchet* because he imagined Brian would be hungry enough to eat the raw eggs.

Spoiler Warning: Plot and/or ending details follow.

- Paulsen wrote one of the sequels to *Hatchet*, *Brian's Winter*, in response to comments from readers who felt Brian's rescue before the winter months left his story unfinished. Paulsen, who by then had twice run the Iditarod, became interested in what strategies Brian would employ to survive a winter in the north woods. At the start of *Brian's Winter*, Paulsen asks readers to imagine that two key events in *Hatchet*, including Brian's rescue, never happened.

Author website: www.garypaulsen.com
Film adaptation:
A Cry in the Wild (MGM, 1994), rated PG, 81 minutes

BOOK BITES

Trail Mix

Trail mix—a nutritious, high-energy combination of nuts, seeds, dried fruit and berries, and candy—is traditional survival food. Also known as GORP (good old raisins and peanuts; or granola, oats, raisins, and peanuts), this lightweight, portable food has been carried on the trail by travelers throughout history—from Native Americans to pioneers to current-day scouts and hikers.

Pam Grover, facilitator of the Middle School Book Club at the Smoky Hill Public Library in Centennial, Colorado, has paired trail mix with several books with survival themes, including *Brian's Winter*, a sequel to *Hatchet*. Grover set out ingredients, including Cheerios, peanuts, banana chips, raisins, M&M's, dried fruit, sunflower seeds, and Chex cereal, and let group members compose their own trail mix in small plastic bags. For additional ingredients, she recommends granola, chocolate chips, and other nuts, such as almonds.

Test Your Memory

Cynthia Richey put the observation and memory skills of her Just for Guys Book Club to the test at the Mt. Lebanon Public Library in Pittsburgh when the group discussed *Hatchet*. "Brian survived by being observant," explains Richey. "It's important to observe carefully, and to see things you might not recognize, and to remember what you've seen."

Richey placed about twenty-five objects of varying sizes on a large tray, including a pen, a paperweight, a plastic action figure, and a clay pot. She placed the tray in the center of a table and asked participants to observe the tray for one minute and try to remember what they saw. She then removed the tray, handed out paper, and asked participants to write down what was on the tray. "Everything came from the library, and one dad's strategy for remembering was to think about what objects one would find in a library," says Richey. "The boys did a little better than the dads, which tells you something about the aging memory!"

Outdoor Survival Packs

Pam Grover of the Smoky Hill Public Library in Centennial, Colorado, created survival packs with her Middle School Book Club when they read *Brian's Winter* but says the activity is also appropriate for its predecessor, *Hatchet*, because survival is its central theme. "We included a discussion on how to survive a winter storm and the basic contents of a survival kit," Grover says.

Before the group met, Grover's supervisor, Donna Geesaman, sewed small fabric drawstring bags. At the meeting, Grover asked participants to begin by creating a first-aid kit in a reclosable plastic sandwich bag with items such as safety pins, Band-Aids, gauze pads, and alcohol swabs. Next, Grover asked participants to place the first-aid kit in their drawstring bags, along with other items for survival, such as matches, a candle, a water bottle, and a whistle.

Topics Discussed

- How you would survive if you found yourself in Brian's shoes, and what strengths and weaknesses you would bring to the situation
- How the story compares to other survival stories, such as the television show *Lost*, the books *My Side of the Mountain* by Jean Craighead George and *The Sign of the Beaver* by Elizabeth George Speare, and the film adaptation of *Hatchet*, *A Cry in the Wild*
- What you would bring if you suspected you might need to survive on an island or in a cold climate
- The meaning of the secret involving Brian's mother

If you were missing, to what lengths do you think your parents
or the government would go to find you?

We compared Brian's situation with that of Natalee Holloway [the eighteen-year-old from Alabama who disappeared on the island of Aruba in May 2005], and discussed all the efforts being made to find her. One member brought up John F. Kennedy, Jr., and the lengths the government went to to retrieve his body after his plane crashed. We talked about how much of the search efforts relate to money and influence, and we wondered who would rally around us to find us—or our remains.

—DIANNE HAPP, TALK ABOUT GOOD! (GRADES 4–8)
PEORIA PUBLIC LIBRARY, LAKEVIEW BRANCH
PEORIA, ILLINOIS

Grades 4–7

Holes

Louis Sachar

Farrar, Straus & Giroux, 1998
Available in paperback from Yearling
240 pages
Fiction

Sequel: *Small Steps* (Delacorte, 2005)
Companion book: *Stanley Yelnats' Survival Guide to Camp Green Lake* (Yearling, 2003)

In keeping with the Yelnats family's history of misfortune, supposedly due to an ancestral curse, young Stanley Yelnats is falsely accused of stealing a famous athlete's sneakers and sentenced to eighteen months at the Camp Green Lake juvenile detention facility. At the camp, set on a dry lakebed infested with poisonous reptiles, inmates must dig holes under the scalding Texas sun. Stanley is suspicious of the prison warden's obsession with digging holes. When Stanley discovers strange parallels between events in his family's past and the camp's history, he attempts to resolve the mystery of the holes—and to reverse his family's curse.

- Louis Sachar says the initial idea for *Holes* and Camp Green Lake came from the oppressive summer heat he experienced after returning to his Texas home from a refreshing summer in Maine. "Anybody who has ever tried to do yard work in Texas in July can easily imagine Hell to be a place where you are required to dig a hole five feet deep and five feet across day after day under the brutal Texas sun," explains Sachar.

- Of the many children's books he's written, *Holes* is Sachar's favorite. Sachar says *Holes* was challenging to write, with its adventure-filled plot, characters that span four generations, and many settings including Latvia, the Old West, and contemporary Texas.

- Creating the multilayered story of *Holes*—telling the stories of schoolteacher-turned-outlaw Kate Barlow, and the story of Elya Yelnats, Stanley's great-great-grandfather, alongside Stanley's story—also challenged Sachar. For example, in the scene in which Stanley digs his first hole, Sachar wanted to relate the misery of Stanley's experience without too much repetition. To avoid monotony in his writing, Sachar chose to interweave the story of Elya Yelnats's story with the story of Stanley's digging.

- It took Sachar a year and a half and five drafts to complete *Holes*—much longer than for other books he's written. The time period, he notes, is the same amount of time for which Stanley was sentenced to Camp Green Lake. "I arbitrarily chose the length of his sentence early on," writes Sachar. "Maybe on some unconscious level, I knew how long it would take [to write the book]."

- Sachar says children connect with the character of Stanley Yelnats because he isn't a typical hero. Sachar explains:

  [Stanley is] a kind of pathetic kid who feels like he has no friends, feels like his life is cursed. And I think everyone can identify with that in one way or another. And then there's the fact that here he is, a kid who isn't a hero, but he lifts himself up and becomes one. I think readers can imagine themselves rising with Stanley.

Author website: www.louissachar.com

Film adaptation:

Holes (Walt Disney, 2003), rated PG, 117 minutes

Dirt Treasure Pudding Cups

In San Carlos, California, Libby McCord and her daughter served treasure-filled dirt—a mixture of pudding and chocolate sandwich cookie crumbs with gold chocolate coins hidden inside—for their book club's *Holes* discussion. "The dessert represented the treasures and dirt dug up by the 'campers,'" says McCord, "and we added yellow spotted gummy lizards to represent those nasty lizards in the story."

McCord left the chocolate coins wrapped when she buried them in the pudding, and explained to the girls that they needed to dig holes and look for treasures as Stanley had done.

Our recipe is adapted from the Kraft Foods/Jell-O Pudding recipe for Oreo Sand and Dirt Cups.

1 (3.9-ounce) package vanilla flavor instant pudding & pie filling

1 (3.9-ounce) package chocolate flavor instant pudding & pie filling

4 cups cold milk, divided

1 cup nondairy whipped topping, such as Cool Whip, thawed, or whipped cream, divided

20 chocolate sandwich cookies, such as Oreos, finely crushed

8 foil-wrapped chocolate coins (optional)

16 gummy lizards (or worms)

1. In medium bowls, prepare vanilla and chocolate pudding mixes separately with milk as directed on the packages (preparing each with 2 cups of cold milk). Let stand 5 minutes. Gently stir ½ cup of the whipped topping or whipped cream into each bowl of pudding.

2. Sprinkle 1 tablespoon cookie crumbs into the bottom of each of 8 (6-ounce) dessert cups. Top cookies with layers of ¼ cup vanilla pudding, followed by 1 tablespoon cookie crumbs, and then ¼ cup chocolate pudding. Sprinkle evenly with the remaining cookie crumbs. If desired, insert one gold coin into each cup.

3. Refrigerate at least 1 hour, or until ready to serve. Top each dessert with two gummy candies just before serving.

YIELD: 8 SERVINGS

TASTE IT!

Bites from the Book

At the Woodmont Library in Des Moines, Washington, Lisa Barkhurst's book discussion group thought it was hilarious when she served Peach Snapple, a peach juice drink, during their *Holes* discussion, representing the "Sploosh" peach nectar from stored peaches that Zero and Stanley drank to survive.

TRY IT!

"Surviving Camp Green Lake" Treasure Hunt

At the Enoch Pratt Free Library in Baltimore, librarian Lily Rozaklis coordinated a "*Holes* Survivor" theme meeting for children who had read *Holes* as part of a citywide community reading program. Children could test their survival skills at Camp Green Lake with a treasure hunt that Rozaklis devised involving art, science, movement, critical thinking—and even snacks. You might want to try one or all of these *Holes*-related exercises with your group.

To begin, all members created their own nicknames (because *Holes* characters Zero and X-Ray have nicknames), and wrote them on name tags. Rozaklis read aloud the chapter of *Holes* describing Stanley's arrival at Camp Green Lake to introduce the camp idea for those who weren't able to read *Holes* prior to the meeting. She then explained the rules of the hunt: Each attendee should complete, or at least attempt to complete, each station to make it to the final destination.

All "survival" stations—tables where activities take place—were labeled with Camp Green Lake–themed signs, such as "Tent A," "Tent B," "Rec Hall," or "Dining Room," and a "Welcome to Camp Green Lake" sign was posted outside the door to the meeting room. Volunteer "camp counselors" were on hand to help facilitate and lead campers through activities.

THE CAMP STATIONS

Art Station: (1) Make a yellow spotted lizard bookmark. (2) Make Model Magic (or clay) scorpions and tarantulas.

Fitness Station: Participate in a relay race in which members of each team will need to empty a bucket of dirt into another bucket using a small shovel.

Critical Thinking Station: (1) Learn the definition of a palindrome, and identify words that are palindromes from a list. (2) Play a concentration/memory/matching game where you match images of camp life and yellow spotted lizards.

Science Station: Learn about venomous reptiles and deserts from science books in the library.

Snack Station (the final destination): Sample *Holes*-related foods: peach cobbler, Funyuns (onion-flavored snack rings), Life Savers, root beer, and chocolate milk (representing muddy water).

Invent Palindromes

As "Stanley Yelnats" is a palindrome—a word or phrase that reads the same backward or forward—many book clubs have enjoyed experimenting with palindromes for their *Holes* discussions. Lisa Barkhurst of the Woodmont Library in Des Moines, Washington, asked book club members to turn their names into palindromes on stand-up name tags (hers read "LISASIL"). Dorothy Distefano's Families Invited to Read and Share Together (FIRST) Parent-Child Book Club in Hilton, New York, distributed a list of palindrome phrases such as "Never odd or even" and "Was it a hat I saw?" She says the children found that coming up with their own palindromes was much harder than they had initially thought.

MAKE IT!

Chain-of-Events Questions

Lisa Barkhurst made a chain of questions to go with the chain of events in the *Holes* plot for her book club. Barkhurst wrote discussion questions on strips of paper and stapled them into a paper chain to represent the fact that many of the book's events are linked. To get the discussion going, she asked each member to tear off a piece of the chain and ask a question.

Topics Discussed

- What Stanley might have sacrificed by trying to fit in with the campers
- Whether it was a curse or a coincidence that Stanley was accused of stealing the sneakers

- Whether you have ever misjudged someone at first, as Stanley misjudged Zero
- If you were Stanley, whether you would rather go to Camp Green Lake or prison

ASK IT!

Why did the song that Stanley recalls his father singing to him change by the end of the book?

One of our best discussion points involved comparing the song at the beginning of *Holes* to the song at the end of the book. I found the question particularly interesting because when reading the book, I hadn't noticed that the song had changed. We didn't reach a conclusion about the meaning of the song, but it was an interesting discussion because everyone had different interpretations of the changes.

—LIBBY McCORD, MOTHER-DAUGHTER BOOK CLUB (GRADE 4)
SAN CARLOS, CALIFORNIA

My Louisiana Sky

Kimberly Willis Holt

Henry Holt, 1998
Available in paperback from Yearling
176 pages
Fiction

In Saitter, a small Louisiana town in 1957, twelve-year-old Tiger Ann Parker copes with feelings of shame for her mentally slow parents, ambivalence toward her neighbor, Jesse Wade, and the desire to be accepted into the "secret world" shared by the girls in her class. When Tiger's granny, who takes care of her, dies, Tiger is forced to decide whether she will stay with her parents in Saitter or move to the "big city" of Baton Rouge with sophisticated Aunt Dorie Kay.

AUTHOR SCOOP

- When she was a child, the idea of "home" eluded Kimberly Willis Holt, who moved frequently. When her family settled in Forest Hill, Louisiana, for several months, Holt quickly adopted the town as her own. She recalls:

I grew up in a military family and that meant, every two years or so, we moved. My younger sister seemed content with saying she was from nowhere, but I wanted to be from somewhere. Home quickly became Forest Hill, the small town nestled in the piney woods of central Louisiana. My parents grew up there and two of my grandparents live there today. Our roots run deep in that soil because seven generations of our family called that area home.

As a child, I dreamed of living in Forest Hill and at thirteen, my dream came true. My mom, sisters, and I moved there for seven months during my dad's assignment in Washington, D.C. For a while I got to live a life a million miles away from a military childhood. Cousins became best friends. I caught the bus in front of my grandmother's house, just as my dad had years before. I attended worship services in a little church where my ancestors had been founding members.

- In *My Louisiana Sky*, Tiger Ann's fictional hometown of Saitter closely resembles Forest Hill. Holt told us:

The town in My Louisiana Sky *is called Saitter, but my heart knows every inch of it is Forest Hill. Holloway's plant nursery that my dad had worked at became Thompson's nursery where Tiger's dad worked. Tiger's Saitter Creek is my beloved Hurricane Creek that crosses Butter's Cemetery Road. Most importantly, I gave Tiger my grandmother's white framed house with a tin roof.*

- A childhood memory inspired Holt to create mentally retarded characters. She recalls:

When I was nine years old, my mother and I passed a woman walking on the side of the road. My mother told me that the woman was mentally retarded and that her husband was too. She said they had a lot of children. I always wondered what happened to those children. And I never forgot the woman on the road.

- The original draft of *My Louisiana Sky* was set in 1958 and didn't include a hurricane. Holt was struggling to add action to the story. After learning that Hurricane Audrey struck in 1957, and that farmers used to predict the weather from unusual signs of nature, Holt had a breakthrough.

I was excited because I knew what was going to happen in the rest of my story. Lonnie was going to be sensitive to nature and predict the hurricane. That meant I had to do more research because the year would change to 1957. But at that point, I knew it was the right thing to do. The ironic thing is, I was born in a hurricane. So maybe I was destined to write about one.

Author website: www.kimberlywillisholt.com
Film adaptation:
My Louisiana Sky (Showtime, 2001), rated PG, 90 minutes
Kimberly Willis Holt recommends:
Where the Lilies Bloom by Vera and Bill Cleaver (HarperCollins, 1969)

BOOK BITES

Kimberly Willis Holt's Buttermilk Pie

Granny bakes a buttermilk pie for the monthly church picnic in Saitter, where Tiger Ann eats so much, her side "felt like it could split open."

Buttermilk pie, a sweet, custardlike pie made from buttermilk, eggs, sugar, and vanilla, has long been associated with the South. In Texas, where Kimberly Willis Holt now makes her home, buttermilk pie is a favorite dessert—and has been for more than a century. Two recipes for buttermilk pie appeared in *The First Texas Cookbook*, published in 1883.

Holt first tasted buttermilk pie at a church dinner in Forest Hill, Louisiana, in 1974. After years of experimenting with the ingredients, Holt created this delicious recipe for the pie, and she thinks back to her hometown whenever she bakes it.

[This is] my version of the pie I first experienced at the Elwood Southern Baptist Church's Fifth Sunday Dinner in Forest Hill, Louisiana. There were plenty of pies to choose from that Sunday in July 1974, but I decided on a slice of one of the four buttermilk pies. They had each been made by different women, and after trying that first slice, I thought it only fair to try each of the other three. I'm certain my recipe doesn't do those ladies' pies justice. I hope they will forgive me for that. Because every time I bake it, it's a tribute to them and the place I have always called "home."

Holt recommends serving the pie warm, straight from the oven.

NOTE: The surface of the pie can easily overcook. Be sure to check the pie after the first 10 minutes in the oven. If the surface has browned, immediately reduce heat and continue cooking as instructed.

You can use either whole or low-fat buttermilk.

If using frozen piecrust, defrost the crust before baking.

4 large eggs, at room temperature

1½ cups sugar

3 tablespoons all-purpose flour

½ cup (1 stick) butter, melted and cooled

1 tablespoon fresh lemon juice

1½ teaspoons vanilla extract

1 cup buttermilk (see note)

1 unbaked 9-inch deep dish pie shell (see note)

1. Preheat oven to 425° F.
2. In a bowl, beat the eggs with an electric mixer on medium-high speed until lemon-colored and frothy. Gradually add the sugar, beating until thick.
3. Add the flour, melted butter, lemon juice, and vanilla, beating well after each addition.
4. Gradually add the buttermilk, beating on low speed until thoroughly combined.
5. Pour the filling into the pie shell. (You may have extra filling, which you can pour into individual custard cups and bake until set, if desired.) Bake 10–15 minutes, or until golden brown, then lower the oven temperature to 350° F. Bake an additional

35–40 minutes, or until a toothpick inserted between the center and edge of the pie comes out clean.

6. Let the pie cool on a wire rack 10–15 minutes. Serve warm.

YIELD: 1 (9-INCH) PIE, 6 TO 8 SERVINGS

Guess Your Parent's or Your Child's Favorite Dessert

Autumn Gonzalez, facilitator of the Mother-Daughter Book Club at the Carmel Clay Public Library in Carmel, Indiana, asked participants to guess each other's favorite desserts to break the ice for their discussion of *My Louisiana Sky*. "When I saw the buttermilk pie mentioned in the book, I decided to see if the moms and daughters could guess each other's favorite desserts," Gonzalez says. "No one could!"

Decorate Flowerpots and Plant Seeds

Tiger's father, Lonnie, cares for Mr. Thompson's beloved Louisiana Lady camellias, tenderly transplanting the tiny cuttings and shielding them from harm as a storm approaches.

The Fifth Grade Mother-Daughter Book Club at Solomon Schechter Day School of Greater Boston suggested decorating flowerpots and planting seeds as an activity to complement a discussion of *My Louisiana Sky*. Shira Goodman, a mother in the group, says this activity highlights the importance of the flower featured in the book, a plant "clearly so important to Tiger's family, and evocative of the book's southern setting."

Camellias—both shrubs and trees with a variety of colorful flowers—originated in China and Japan, and thrive on the moist air and well-drained soil of the Gulf States. Although Holt says she invented the Louisiana Lady hybrid depicted in her book, thousands of camellia hybrids exist, many that have adapted to cooler climates. New camellia plants are generally grown from cuttings, as depicted in *My Louisiana Sky*, although with the right conditions and patience, plants will emerge from seeds. For specific instructions on planting camellia seeds, ask a gardening store or look on the Internet. Other flower seeds, such as marigolds, nasturtiums, or dwarf sunflowers, germinate easily and are excellent alternatives to camellias.

NOTE: You can purchase clay flowerpots at a gardening or art-supply store. Be sure to buy markers designed for use on clay, available at art-supply stores.

MATERIALS (FOR ONE FLOWERPOT)

*Clay flowerpot and under plate
(see note)*

*Markers for decorating clay pot
(see note)*

4–6 small pebbles

About 2 cups of potting soil

*Flower seeds (e.g., marigolds,
nasturtiums, dwarf sunflowers)*

1. Decorate clay flowerpots using markers.
2. If pots have drainage holes, fill with small pebbles to prevent potting soil from leaking out.
3. Fill pots with soil to about 1½ inches from the top. Place 2 or 3 seeds in soil and sink to the depth indicated on the seed package. Pat soil firmly. Water.
4. Follow care instructions on the package, and watch your flowers grow!

Topics Discussed

- The effects of guilt on Tiger Ann's family
- Why Granny kept it a secret that Corrina had been born "normal"
- How Tiger Ann coped with being ashamed of her parents
- Granny's role in holding the family together

How does Dorie Kay change throughout the story?

We talked a lot about Dorie Kay's motivations. Growing up with a slow sister made her feel like an outcast. She also resented all of the extra responsibilities she had taking care of her sister. We discussed how Dorie Kay's feelings of guilt may have influenced her desire to leave Saitter. At the end of the discussion, we talked about Dorie Kay's transition into a person who wants to be connected to her family and who is now able to reach out and make personal connections of her own.

—CONNIE MATHEWS, GIRLS NIGHT OUT BOOK CLUB (GRADES 4–8)
MT. LEBANON PUBLIC LIBRARY, PITTSBURGH

No More Dead Dogs

Gordon Korman

Hyperion, 2000
Available in paperback from Hyperion
192 pages
Fiction

Eighth-grade football star Wallace Wallace prides himself on his honesty. When Wallace expresses his low opinion of the book *Old Shep, My Pal* in a school essay, his teacher, Mr. Fogelman, who considers the book a personal favorite, takes offense. Wallace's refusal to rewrite his essay results in his suspension from the football team and detention, where he must attend rehearsals for the school play Mr. Fogelman is directing, the stage version of *Old Shep, My Pal.* Wallace's honest opinions for improving the play are warmly embraced by the drama students, and Mr. Fogelman has to decide whether to incorporate Wallace's changes or risk losing his cast.

- Gordon Korman wrote his first novel in seventh grade, when a new English teacher, a track and field coach who hadn't taught language arts before, took over the class. The teacher instructed students to work on whatever they liked for the remainder of the year, and the novel that Korman produced during this time—*This Can't Be Happening at Macdonald Hall*—was published when he was fourteen and in ninth grade. Korman later wrote the book *The 6th Grade Nickname Game*, featuring a character, Mr. Huge, a football coach who is unexpectedly sent to take over a sixth-grade class, inspired by his experience in seventh grade.

- Korman was intrigued by the idea that in classic novels about dogs, the dog always dies. Korman says:

> *Growing up, it always used to drive me nuts that every time we read a book about a dog, the dog always died at the end. Not that the books were bad, but as the canine body count mounted up, it was just depressing. And because so many of those books are considered classics, it seemed as if we were studying one or two of them every year. I felt like I was being buried in dead dogs. So* No More Dead Dogs *was my not-so-subtle shot back.*

- Korman explains the origins of Wallace's character—and how he felt about Wallace while writing *No More Dead Dogs*.

> *The character Wallace is an eighth-grade version of my dad—an immensely admirable stand-up guy and the straightest shooter I've ever met. But sometimes he can be so pathologically honest that he offends people.*
>
> *Wallace is a very admirable character because his value system is set in stone. But there were several times during the writing of* No More Dead Dogs *that I just felt like hitting him over the head and saying, "Come on! You're making a mountain out of a molehill, and the person suffering the most for it*

is you!" And if I, Wallace's creator, was losing patience with him, I can only imagine how exasperating his stubbornness must be to some readers.

- At the age of two, Korman wanted to be a dog when he grew up. "I don't actually remember this, but my parents tell me that I used to eat dinner under the table in preparation for this career," Korman says.
- Korman balances his humorous writing with a number of adventure series, including Island, On the Run, and Kidnapped. "Strangely, the structure is similar in humor and adventure. In both, the goal is to keep the audience turning pages. In a funny book, the laughs perform that function, while in adventure, the key is suspense and heart-pounding action," he explains.

Author website: http://gordonkorman.com

Gordon Korman recommends:

The Dog Who Wouldn't Be (1957) by Farley Mowat, which Korman calls "my favorite dead-dog book. It's very old and probably next to impossible to find."

Flipped by Wendelin Van Draanen (Alfred A. Knopf, 2001; see p. 294), which Korman likes "since the narrator keeps changing."

see p. 294

BOOK BITES

No More Dead Dogs Puppy Chow

Gordon Korman liked the idea of munching on "human" puppy chow—an easy to prepare mixture of cereal, chocolate, peanut butter, sugar, and butter during a *No More Dead Dogs* discussion. He has sampled many versions of the mix while visiting schools to talk about *No More Dead Dogs,* and pronounces them all "great." He adds that the puppy chow "is a lot more appetizing than what I got when I went on tour to promote *Nose Pickers from Outer Space.*"

Both Kate Van Auken of the Rawson Memorial District Library in Cass City, Michigan, and Vickey Long of the Basehor (Kansas) Community Library made puppy chow fit for human consumption when their book clubs discussed *No More Dead Dogs*. Both librarians confirm that the kids were intrigued by the nuggets, and quickly gobbled them up. Long suggests asking members if they have or know a dog and, if so, to share some details about the dog while munching on the chow.

NOTE: This chow is intended for human consumption only. It should not be fed to dogs, for whom chocolate can be harmful.

½ cup (1 stick) unsalted butter

⅓ cup peanut butter

2 cups semisweet chocolate morsels

9 cups crispy corn or rice cereal squares, such as Corn or Rice Chex

4 cups confectioners' sugar (more as needed)

1. In a medium saucepan, stir the butter, peanut butter, and chocolate morsels over low heat until all the ingredients are melted and well mixed. Cool slightly.
2. Place the cereal in a large bowl. Pour the warm mixture over cereal and gently fold until the cereal is completely covered by the mixture.
3. Pour the confectioners' sugar into a large paper bag. Place the coated cereal in bag with the sugar and shake until completely covered with sugar. Add more sugar as needed.
4. Spread the mixture in a single layer on a sheet of wax paper and allow to cool completely. Store in an airtight container in the refrigerator.

YIELD: 9 TO 10 (1-CUP) SERVINGS

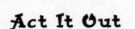
Act It Out

In *No More Dead Dogs,* a middle school theater group is rehearsing for the school play—an idea that prompted Pam Grover of the Smoky Hill Public Library in Centennial, Colorado, to incorporate the school performance theme into her middle school book club meeting. Grover asked the children to try their hand at acting in front of a camera and then watch their own performances.

Grover says her students enjoy any opportunity to act and get in front of a camera, and she gave them some time to practice before performing. Using scripts from Aaron Shepard's Readers Theatre Page (www.aaronshep.com/rt/), a website that provides free original and adapted scripts of children's novels, each performer read from a script with his or her part highlighted. Grover chose funny scripts to complement the humor in *No More Dead Dogs,* and encouraged the actors to use facial expressions and their voice to convey their part.

Gordon Korman offers some advice about acting—and writing:

Don't feel too much pressure to be hilarious. The truth is, nothing is more painful than watching someone trying too hard to be funny. Just act naturally, and let the humor in the script work its power. This is also true when I'm writing. If I'm obsessed with creating a laugh-a-minute riot, the jokes become too forced or over-the-top. The funniest parts of my novels always come when I allow the characters to be themselves, and let their personalities guide the story.

Topics Discussed

- If you recall books in which a dog has died
- If you have had experiences with cliques such as the jocks and thespians described in the story, and what some of the stereotypes about groups in your school might be

- Whether it is all right to tell a lie if telling the truth would hurt someone's feelings
- How Mr. Fogelman changes by the end of the story

If you were Wallace, would you have rewritten the essay
as Mr. Fogelman wanted it written?

Every one of the teens said that they would have tried to stick to their guns like Wallace did. But they also said they have had teachers for whom it would be difficult to refuse to rewrite the essay.

—KATE VAN AUKEN, YOUNG ADULT BOOK CLUB (GRADES 5–9)
RAWSON MEMORIAL DISTRICT LIBRARY
CASS CITY, MICHIGAN

The Watsons Go to Birmingham—1963

Christopher Paul Curtis

Delacorte, 1993
Available in paperback from Delacorte
224 pages
Historical Fiction

Ten-year-old Kenny narrates the antics of his family, dubbed the "Weird Watsons" by neighbors, in Flint, Michigan, in 1963. When Kenny's older brother, Byron, gets into trouble, the Watsons pile in the "Brown Bomber" for a road trip to Birmingham, Alabama, to visit the notoriously strict Grandma Sands. Their trip is timed with a horrific moment in American history: Birmingham's 16th Street Baptist Church bombing.

AUTHOR SCOOP

- Christopher Paul Curtis was raised in Flint, Michigan, where he worked for thirteen years after high school hanging car doors on Buicks on the assembly line at the Fisher Body plant. Unhappy with his job and seeking an escape from the noise of the factory, Curtis began keeping a journal during his breaks at work. His wife, Kaysandra, suggested he take a year off to write. During that year, Curtis wrote *The Watsons Go to Birmingham—1963* in the children's room of his local public library.

- While working at the auto factory, Curtis enjoyed listening to stories of African-Americans who had come from the South to Michigan for jobs. Through these stories, Curtis became intrigued by the idea of visiting the South. Eventually he drove from Michigan to Florida with his wife and children, and the trip inspired him to write *The Watsons Go to Birmingham—1963*, which he originally titled *The Watsons Go to Florida*. The book's story line changed when his son, Steven, brought home a poem from school about the bombing of the 16th Street Baptist Church in Birmingham, Dudley Randall's "The Ballad of Birmingham." Curtis knew the Watsons' destination would be Birmingham, instead of Florida.

- Curtis hopes young readers will gain a better understanding of and curiosity about the historical events depicted in *The Watsons Go to Birmingham—1963*, and says the story has generated many questions from children about the civil rights movement. In particular, he is often asked if the men who planted the bomb in the church were caught. Curtis believes children want the answer to feel reassured and because "they often have a strong sense of justice."

- Curtis explains that the "Wool Pooh" scene in the book fascinates and provokes many questions from readers. "They understand that it represents death, and they find that both frightening and interesting," he explains. "I wrote the character in a style that is called magic realism, and I think that causes some confusion. It's simply a method of describing a magical event in a realistic way."

Author website: www.nobodybutcurtis.com

Christopher Paul Curtis recommends:

The Power of One: Daisy Bates and the Little Rock Nine by Judith Bloom
    Fradin and Dennis Brindell Fradin (Clarion, 2004)

Kaysandra Curtis's Swedish Creme Cookies

When Byron learns that his family can buy food on credit at the Mitchell's store, he purchases a bag of Swedish Creme Cookies and gorges on the large cookies with pink frosting. We asked Christopher Paul Curtis's wife, Kaysandra, if she had a recipe for Swedish Cremes, and she created this delicious sandwich cookie version of the treat that Byron craves. She began by adapting a recipe for Swedish Spritz Cookies from *The Better Homes and Gardens Cookbook* (Better Homes and Gardens, 1962). For the filling, she adapted a recipe for Seven-Minute Frosting from *The Best of Gourmet: A Year of Celebrations* (Random House, 2005), replacing water with cream soda for a boost of "cream" flavor and adding red food coloring to make the frosting pink, true to the Swedish Cremes in the story. She created a winning sandwich cookie, one that lives up to Kenny's exclamation: "Man! Swedish Cremes have got to be the best cookies in the world."

NOTE: Kaysandra Curtis says you can make larger single-layer cookies and spread each with frosting and sprinkles, instead of making sandwich cookies.

FOR THE COOKIES

1½ cups (3 sticks) unsalted butter, softened

1 cup sugar

1 large egg

½ teaspoon vanilla extract

½ teaspoon almond extract

4 cups all-purpose flour, sifted

1 teaspooon baking powder

FOR THE FILLING

1 large egg white

½ cup sugar

2 tablespoons cream soda

Several drops red food coloring

1 teaspoon light corn syrup

½ teaspoon vanilla extract

½ teaspoon fresh lemon juice

1. To make the cookies: Preheat oven to 400° F.
2. In a bowl, beat butter and sugar with an electric mixer on high speed until fluffy. Add the egg, vanilla, and almond extract, beating well.
3. Sift the flour and baking powder and add to the creamed mixture, 1 cup at a time, until thoroughly combined.
4. Remove the dough to a lightly floured work surface and roll to ¼-inch thickness. Using a cookie cutter or plastic bottle cap, cut out 1½-inch circles. You can also use a cookie press to make the circles.
5. Place the cutouts on an ungreased baking sheet and bake 8–10 minutes, or until golden brown around the edges.
6. Cool the cookies on the sheet for several minutes, then remove to a wire rack to cool completely.
7. To make the filling: Fill a medium saucepan three-quarters full with water and heat on burner set to high.
8. In a large metal bowl, beat the egg white, sugar, cream soda, food coloring (enough to turn frosting desired pink color), and corn syrup with a handheld electric mixer until well combined.
9. When the saucepan of water comes to a boil, reduce the heat to low. Set the metal bowl over the simmering water and beat with an electric mixer on high speed 5–7 minutes, until stiff, glossy peaks form. (Humid weather may necessitate additional beating time.) Remove the bowl from heat.
10. Add the vanilla and lemon juice and continue beating 6–10 minutes, until frosting is cooled and very thick. Frosting can be made 4 hours ahead and chilled, covered.
11. To assemble the cookies: Spoon 1 teaspoon of the filling on a cookie, cover with another cookie and press down to make a sandwich. Repeat with the remaining cookies and filling.

YIELD: APPROXIMATELY 4 DOZEN SANDWICH COOKIES

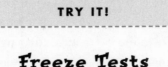

Freeze Tests

The Watsons lived in Michigan, where Kenny describes winters as "a zillion degrees below zero." On one such "super-duper-cold" day, while practicing his kissing techniques, Byron manages to freeze his lips to the side-view mirror of the family car.

To find out what could have caused Byron's lips to stick to the mirror and how water reacts to freezing temperatures, you can conduct the following activities with your group.

These activities are adapted from *The Watsons Go to Birmingham—1963: Random House Teachers Guide* (Random House, 2004).

THE STICKING ICE TRAY

MATERIALS

A tray of ice just out of the freezer

Pass the tray around and ask the group for their observations. They should note that the tray will stick to their fingers.

Explain: If the tray and ice cubes are below the freezing point of water, the warmth of the hand will melt a thin layer of frost. Then, as the hand is cooled, the layer of water will freeze again. It is possible that the finger can freeze so tightly to the tray that a little skin is torn as it is pulled loose.

FREEZE WITH FINGERS

MATERIALS

Two ice cubes

Ask the group to press the cubes together, one flat surface tightly against the other. The cubes will freeze together.

Explain: The increase in pressure lowers the melting point and some of the ice melts where the cubes are in contact; then the water freezes again as the pressure is reduced.

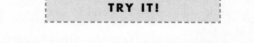

TRY IT!

Investigate Local History

Shannon Peterson, a librarian with the Islands Branch Library in Savannah, Georgia, selected *The Watsons Go to Birmingham—1963* for her fifth- and sixth-grade Page Pals Book Group's black history month meeting. Peterson wanted to connect local civil rights history to her book discussion. After the group snacked on peanut butter and jelly sandwiches, the Watson kids' fare during their car trip, Peterson asked the members to devise questions about race relations in their community in 1963, and then sent them around the library to interview staff and patrons who had lived in Savannah during that time. When the group reconvened, many of the children reported that they had learned how segregated Savannah had been, and that residents told them that they hadn't grown up seeing white and black children together.

TRY IT!

Watch *Voices of Civil Rights*

Shannon Peterson watched this film with her Savannah, Georgia–based Page Pals Book Group, from the Voices of Civil Rights Project sponsored by the AARP, the Leadership Conference on Civil Rights (LCCR), and the Library of Congress, through the website of the same name (www.voicesofcivilrights.org). The website features thousands of personal stories and oral histories of the civil rights movement. "The interviews and the film made the kids realize that events in *The Watsons Go to Birmingham—1963* were a solid piece of history," says Peterson.

TRY IT!

Map the Watsons' Route

Jenne Laytham asked her middle school book group at the Basehor (Kansas) Community Library to locate United States maps in the library stacks. When the group returned with maps, they plotted the route the Watsons took from Flint, Michigan, to Birmingham Alabama. Together the group traced the route on the largest map. "I wanted them to see the scope of the Watsons' trip," says Laytham. "It was valuable to see where the Watsons lived and to plot the places the children had read about on the map. And it was a good way for them to learn about all of the resources in our library."

TRY IT!

Listen to "Yakety Yak"

Cynthia Richey played Kenny's favorite song—the Coasters' 1958 hit "Yakety Yak"—for the fathers and sons in the Just for Guys Book Club she facilitates at the Mt. Lebanon Public Library in Pittsburgh. "The group thought music was such an important part of the story," says Richey. "They were interested in how music brought the Watson family together. They understand that families can bond in a variety of ways, and music is one of them."

Topics Discussed

- How the author skillfully turned a funny story into a tragedy
- The meaning of the "Wool Pooh" experience
- Connections between the bullying and prejudice toward Rufus in the first part of the book and the church bombing in the second part
- If you were surprised by the change in Byron in Birmingham

ASK IT!

Have you encountered situations where there was prejudice?

Most of the boys in our group were unaware of racism and had no idea what it was like in the United States during the time before the Civil Rights Act. Adults who grew up in the United States during the 1960s can talk about the things they remember from their childhood, and as a group, they can compare these recollections to their impressions of race relations today.

—CYNTHIA RICHEY, JUST FOR GUYS BOOK CLUB (GRADES 5–8)
MT. LEBANON PUBLIC LIBRARY, PITTSBURGH

Grades 4 and up

Harry Potter and the Half-Blood Prince

J. K. Rowling

Scholastic, 2005
Available in paperback from Scholastic
652 pages
Fantasy

Series: *Harry Potter and the Sorcerer's Stone* (Scholastic, 1997), also published as *Harry Potter and the Philosopher's Stone* (Bloomsbury, 1996); *Harry Potter and the Chamber of Secrets* (Scholastic, 1999); *Harry Potter and the Prisoner of Azkaban* (Scholastic, 1999); *Harry Potter and the Goblet of Fire* (Scholastic, 2000); *Harry Potter and the Order of the Phoenix* (Scholastic, 2003); *Harry Potter and the Deathly Hallows* (Scholastic, 2007)

As Harry Potter enters his sixth year at the Hogwarts School of Witchcraft and Wizardry, nonwizards and wizards alike are threatened by attacks from Death Eaters, followers of the evil Lord Voldemort. When a returning Potions professor, Horace Slughorn, gives Harry a textbook formerly owned by the mysterious Half-Blood Prince, Harry consults the handwritten notes in the book—and suddenly begins to excel in the class. Headmaster Albus Dumbledore uses a memory device, the Pensieve, to show Harry flashbacks of Lord Voldemort's past. As Harry and Dumbledore explore

Voldemort's life, they are drawn further into their quest to understand his immortality and ultimately to defeat him.

- *Harry Potter and the Half-Blood Prince* is one of J. K. Rowling's favorite books in the series: "Book Six does what I wanted it to do and even if nobody else likes it (and some won't) I know it will remain one of my favourites of the series. Ultimately you have to please yourself before you please anyone else," Rowling writes.
- Rowling says she had considered using a chapter much like "The Other Minister," the opening chapter of *Harry Potter and the Half-Blood Prince*, in several other Harry Potter books. When you read the first chapter of *Harry Potter and the Half-Blood Prince*, says Rowling, you should know that "it's been about thirteen years in the brewing."
- The Pensieve, or memory storage device Dumbledore uses in *Harry Potter and the Half-Blood Prince*, reflects reality and does not give the memory owner's interpretation of an event. Rather, explains Rowling, the Pensieve re-creates a moment, as if you could delve into your own memory and relive things you hadn't noticed.
- One of Rowling's favorite childhood books was Elizabeth Goudge's *A Little White Horse*, originally published in 1946. The fact that "the feasts at Hogwarts are fulsomely described" and that Rowling knows what her characters eat, she says, is due to Goudge's influence.
- Rowling says Harry's maturity has been gradual, but she's not sorry to see Harry and his friends grow up. "I have always found it slightly sinister when you read children's books in which the children are not allowed any romantic feelings and are not allowed to get angry," she explains.

Author website: www.jkrowling.com

Chocolate Cauldrons

Romilda Vane, Harry's classmate, has a crush on him, and gives Harry a box of firewhiskey-filled Chocolate Cauldrons. When Harry's friend Ron Weasley mistakenly eats the Cauldrons, believing them to be one of his own birthday gifts, he begins to profess his love for Romilda. It becomes clear to Harry that Romilda has concealed love potion within the chocolates, intended for Harry, and he brings Ron to Professor Slughorn to reverse the spell.

Nur Kilic, owner of Serenade Chocolatier in Brookline, Massachusetts, makes handmade chocolates in the Viennese tradition and created a delicious Chocolate Cauldrons recipe for us to share with Harry Potter fans. These cauldrons can be filled with your favorite candies (instead of firewhiskey), and they are certain to cast a spell on the lucky eater!

NOTE: In order to make a cauldron from chocolate, you need some form of a mold. You can use the plastic cauldrons that party stores sell during Halloween and cut each in half along the seam, from the top edge to the bottom, or you can purchase a plastic cauldron mold online (www.onestopcandle.com). We also created cauldron shapes by pouring the liquid chocolate into plastic containers for cupcakes commonly sold in grocery stores.

In candy making, chocolate should be tempered in order for it to release easily from the molds; the process also gives the chocolate a glossy sheen, keeps it from becoming streaked with cocoa butter crystals that might form, and gives it a smooth flavor. In tempering, a portion of the chocolate is melted, cooled slightly, and then the remainder of the chocolate is added and reheated. Temperatures are very critical in the tempering process so a candy thermometer is necessary.

1 pound milk or dark chocolate　　　　　*Cocoa powder for dusting*

1. Chop the chocolate on a cutting board with a large knife. Heat water in the bottom portion of a double boiler. The water should be hot, but not boiling. Place half

of the chopped chocolate in the top pot of the double boiler. Stir until the chocolate is melted.

2. Remove the chocolate from the heat. Add the remaining chopped chocolate to melted chocolate, stirring until chocolate reaches 88–90° F. Pour the chocolate into a mold until mold is full. Place the mold in the refrigerator 5 minutes, or until the chocolate begins to set along the perimeter of the mold. The center should still be liquid.

3. Remove the liquid chocolate by inverting the mold over the pot. (You can reuse this chocolate for another mold, as long as it is maintained at 88° to 90° F., and stirred.) Scrape the top of the mold with a spatula. Place the mold with the remaining chocolate in the refrigerator for 15 minutes, or until the chocolate is firm. When the chocolate is set, it will release from the mold easily.

4. Remove the chocolate from the mold. Dust with cocoa powder to give it a rustic look.

5. Fill with your favorite candies or sweet drink!

YIELD: 4–12 CAULDRONS, DEPENDING ON THE SIZE OF THE MOLD

BOOK BITES

Iced Butterbeer

Amber Lowery includes a recipe for iced butterbeer, one of her first *Harry Potter* recipe creations in *Magical Munchies for Muggles to Make*, a cookbook she compiled for her library book clubs at the Peoria (Illinois) Public Library. "Harry and his friends drink butterbeer as a special treat when they go into Hogsmeade, or when Fred and George sneak out for after-Quidditch celebrations," says Lowery. "The students at Hogwarts seem to really enjoy the supersweet frothy drink at a bargain price of two silver sickles each."

Lowery says butterbeer is a fun recipe that can be prepared for big groups. "Those not adventurous enough to try butterbeer can still have a tasty root beer float," she adds. Lowery prefers to use Muggle—or nonwizard—root beer.

1–1½ cups root beer   *Butterscotch syrup*

1 scoop (½ cup) vanilla ice cream

Fill a glass two-thirds full with root beer. Add 1 scoop of ice cream. Top with butterscotch syrup.

YIELD: 1 DRINK

> **MAKE IT!**

Harry Potter Celebration

At the Peoria (Illinois) Public Library's Lakeview Branch, Amber Lowery leads Lakeview's Leaky Cauldron Book Club, an intergenerational group with fifty members, including children, teens, and adults devoted to reading Harry Potter books. Leaky Cauldron Book Club members celebrated the release of *Harry Potter and the Half-Blood Prince* with a party, and Lowery shared some of the group's favorite activities, including sorting hats, and parchment and potion making.

> **MAKE IT!**

Sorting Hats

Amber Lowery turned ice-cream cones into sorting hats—the hats used to tell new students which house they are destined for at Hogwarts. Having your members sort themselves into houses is a fun way to begin the event, says Lowery, who chose four colors of candies, each representing a Hogwarts house—red for Gryffindor, green for Slytherin, blue for Ravenclaw, and yellow for Hufflepuff—based on book and film references to Hogwarts' house colors. After filling each cone with one color of candy and covering the opening with a cookie, Lowery asked members to choose a cone. The candies that spilled out when they removed the cone from the cookie dictated their house.

NOTE: The cookies should be slightly bigger than the opening of the cone. Use the pointy sugar ice-cream cones.

Frosting

Sugar ice-cream cones, one for each member (see note)

Chocolate-coated candies, such as M&M's, in red, green, blue, and yellow, sorted by color (approximately 30–40 candies will fill one 13-gram cone)

Sugar or chocolate-chip cookies (see note)

1. Place the frosting in a small plastic bag, and cut off one of the bottom corners of the bag. Pipe an even layer of frosting around the rim of a cone.
2. Fill the cone with one color of the candies. Center the flat side of the cookie over the opening of the cone and press it on. Carefully turn over. Repeat with each cone and arrange the cone hats on a tray.

MAKE IT!

Parchment

Harry Potter writes letters on parchment rather than Muggle writing paper, so Lowery made homemade parchment with her group, and then sent notes to her book club members on their parchment. Using the materials mentioned in the book evokes the spirit of *Harry Potter* for their get-togethers, says Lowery.

NOTE: A hair dryer will speed up the drying process and make the paper appear more distressed.

The parchment can be used to write secret messages that can be revealed with

"Aparecium," the spell to make invisible ink visible. Dip a cotton swab in lemon juice and write a message on the parchment. Let the paper dry completely. To read the message, remove a lampshade and carefully place the paper near the hot lightbulb. The acids in the lemon juice will darken when heated, and the writing will become visible.

CAUTION: Be careful not to let the paper get too close to the lightbulb.

MATERIALS

White paper with torn edges, a few sheets per member

Tray or bowl

Dark tea or cold leftover coffee (about ½ cup per sheet of paper)

Paper towels

Handheld hair dryer (optional; see note)

Plate

1. Tear the edges of a sheet of paper to make the parchment appear older, and crumple paper into a tight ball. Carefully unfold the sheet. Repeat until paper looks severely distressed.
2. Soak paper in a bath of dark tea or coffee for approximately 5 minutes, or until thoroughly wet. (The longer you soak it, the darker the paper becomes.)
3. Remove paper, unfold, and lay flat to dry. Brush as much water off as possible, then pat dry with a paper towel. Drying will take approximately 1 hour. If you are using a hair dryer, place the paper on a plate and dry for approximately 5 minutes.

MAKE IT!

Potions

Harry Potter and the Half-Blood Prince focuses more on Potions—the class where students learn to brew magical potions—than the previous books in the series, says Amber Lowery. "Harry is helped by a mysterious guide, the Half-Blood Prince, and never before has he done so well in Potions," she adds. "Making your own potions, such as

Felix Felicis, a potion that provides its drinker with liquid luck, is a great opportunity to mix a bit of science with your love of reading."

Potion bottles are an easy project for any group, and make a colorful decoration for a desk, shelf, or mantel, says Lowery, who recommends creating a few potion bottles before the event for decorations.

NOTE: You cannot drink these potions!

It's fine if some glue oozes out when you place the cork stopper in the bottle. For extra staying power, put additional glue around the outside of the cork at the top of the glass. The potions bottles can be turned over when they are dry, but over time the cork will absorb the oil and it may become slightly stained. The bottles are available at art- and craft-supply stores. Mineral oil is available at most drugstores.

To make a gold-colored potion reminiscent of Felix Felicis, mix six drops of yellow food color with one small drop of purple or green color.

MATERIALS

Food coloring	Water
4- to 6-ounce glass bottles with corks (in various shapes and sizes), one per member	Glitter, and glitter stars and sparkles in a variety of colors
	Towels
Mineral oil	Glue

1. Place 3–6 drops food coloring into an empty bottle.
2. Fill one-third to one-half of the bottle with mineral oil.
3. Slowly fill with water to the neck of the bottle (do not overfill). Add a few sparkles, glitter, and/or stars. Wipe the edges and inside of the bottle's neck clean.
4. Coat the bottom half of the cork with glue and place the stopper in the bottle. Allow to dry. The two liquids will remain separated and the water will be colorful, with the glitter and stars remaining suspended between the oil and the water.

Topics Discussed

- Why Dumbledore wants Harry to learn about Lord Voldemort's past
- What your favorite bit of magic in the book is
- Why Draco Malfoy hesitates at the end of the book
- Where the horcruxes are hidden and if there is one at Hogwarts

Is Severus Snape evil?

We had a brilliant conversation about Snape's character. So many of the kids thought Snape was definitely evil, but many adults thought he was acting on Dumbledore's orders. We considered the conversation between Snape and Narcissa Malfoy as well as Snape's interactions with Dumbledore. We discussed Dumbledore's plea to Snape at the end of the book, Snape and Harry's duel, as well as the two facts that Snape stopped another Death Eater's Cruciatus Curse on Harry, and managed to get Draco away from the battle without injury.

—AMBER LOWERY, LAKEVIEW'S LEAKY CAULDRON BOOK CLUB
PEORIA PUBLIC LIBRARY, LAKEVIEW BRANCH
PEORIA, ILLINOIS

Homeless Bird

Gloria Whelan

HarperCollins, 2000
Available in paperback from HarperTrophy
240 pages
Fiction

In India, thirteen-year-old Koly faces an arranged marriage to a boy she has never met, and leaves the security of her family and small village to start a new life. Dire circumstances soon force Koly to find her way alone in a society that has no place for her, and she must summon her courage and creativity to survive.

AUTHOR SCOOP

- In 1998, Gloria Whelan read a *New York Times* article about the thousands of white-saried widows in the Indian city of Vrindavan; this sparked the idea for *Homeless Bird*. She recalls:

One of the widows mentioned in the article had been widowed at thirteen and she stayed in my mind. A few weeks later, I happened to see an exhibition at Asia House in New York City of quilts embroidered by Indian women. I don't know how it is for other writers, but for me two things have to come together for a story to make me want to write it. It's as if you couldn't trust just one thing, but you needed the second thing; as if someone were looking over your shoulder and saying, "Now will you believe me." When I saw the exhibition of quilts I began to write Homeless Bird.

- While she has never visited India, Whelan "traveled" there in her head, a feat made possible by the severe winters in northern Michigan, where she wrote *Homeless Bird*.

Our cabin was on a small lake, the nearest house a mile away. It's a magical place in the summer, but the northern Michigan winters are long. It's not unusual to be snowed in. As the winter grows, I begin to have the feeling that the snow will creep through the windows and doors and bury me. So each year I decide where I want to spend the winter months, figuratively—that is, in my head. The great thing about being a writer is that you can live in the world you choose, or—as so often happens—somewhere in the world that chooses you.

- To research her novel, Whelan spent time at two libraries near her home in Michigan, where she stumbled upon many "treasures" to enhance her story. She says:

When I research books there are specific things I am looking for, but the greatest fun is coming upon surprises that either fit into my book or suggest new aspects of my story. I knew that Koly's first job would be threading marigolds for weddings and funerals, so I was delighted to find a description of how the fibers of the banana plant were used in the process. I discovered that bats hang out (literally) in the temples and when the monsoon rains come, snakes appear everywhere. The bats and snakes went right into my book.

Author website: www.gloriawhelan.com

Gloria Whelan recommends:

Shabanu: Daughter of the Wind by Suzanne Fisher Staples (Alfred A. Knopf, 1989)

Shiva's Fire by Suzanne Fisher Staples (Farrar, Straus & Giroux, 2000)

Kira-Kira by Cynthia Kadohata (see p. 310)

BOOK BITES

Gloria Whelan's Favorite Kachumber (Tomato and Cucumber Salad)

While researching *Homeless Bird*, Gloria Whelan came upon this recipe for kachumber, a tangy Indian relish, and it has since become one of her favorites. Whelan enjoys kachumber as a cooling accompaniment to spicy curry dishes, but it also makes a delicious salad on its own.

NOTE: Adjust the amount of chile to the taste of the group.

Wear plastic or rubber gloves while handling the chiles to protect skin from the oil in them. Avoid direct contact with eyes, and wash hands thoroughly after handling.

2 tomatoes, diced

1 medium cucumber, peeled, seeded, and diced

3 scallions, chopped

1 fresh jalapeño chile, cored, seeded, and diced (see note)

2 tablespoons fresh lemon juice

2 teaspoons sugar

Cilantro leaves, chopped

Salt

In a medium bowl, combine all the ingredients, adding the cilantro leaves and salt to taste. Keep refrigerated until ready to serve.

YIELD: 4 SERVINGS AS A SALAD, 6 TO 8 SERVINGS AS A RELISH

TRY IT!

Embroider Your Name

Koly's embroidery gives expression to her memories and helps her survive. The girls of the Fifth Grade Mother-Daughter Book Club of Solomon Schechter Day School of Greater Boston tried their hands at embroidery while they discussed *Homeless Bird*. "The girls loved embroidering while they talked about the book," says coordinator Stephanie Maroun. "Because embroidery was so central to Koly's life, trying it made them feel more connected to the book. And they seemed to speak more freely when their hands were occupied!"

NOTE: Supplies for this project may be purchased at a local sewing- or crafts-supply store. If no one in the group knows how to embroider, you may want to purchase a book that demonstrates simple embroidery stitches, or ask a crafts store employee for guidance.

MATERIALS

8½-inch squares of smooth cotton fabric, in solid colors, one per member

Embroidery hoops, about 7 inches in diameter, one per member

Embroidery needles, one per member

Embroidery thread in various colors

Pencils

Place a fabric square in an embroidery hoop to pull it taut. Thread an embroidery needle with up to three strands of embroidery thread, knotting the end. Using a pencil, draw your name or a simple design of your choice on the fabric. Embroider over the pencil lines.

Book Links: Ideas from Gloria Whelan

WRAP A SARI

Gloria Whelan has found that girls enjoy winding saris, the traditional wraps worn by Indian women. "Though it looks like it would be simple to wind a sari around your waist, it is a challenge, and hard to learn without a lot of slippage and laughter," she says.

If you know someone who owns a sari and who can instruct group members in how to wrap it, invite her to your meeting.

HELPING BIRDS FIND A HOME

The central metaphor of *Homeless Bird* is rooted in Gloria Whelan's long-standing love of birds. She told us:

> *I have always been a bird-watcher and when I write a book, it's the first thing about the new country I research. For years we had a phoebe who attached its nest to our floodlight. We had to tape the switch to "off" so there would be no scrambled eggs. Our greatest thrill has been the return of the eagles to Michigan and though we were seeing them almost every day, at every sighting we would call out, "Eagle," drop whatever we were doing, and rush to the window.*

Each spring, at her home in Michigan, Whelan unravels fibers from hemp rope and scatters them over bushes and tree limbs. "Orioles use the fibers for their nests, and once they find them, they return each year," says Whelan. She suggests that book clubs might enjoy this simple activity at a spring meeting.

Bagel Bird Feeders

The symbolism of birds seeking a home inspired Jan Seerveld to create bagel bird feeders with her San Carlos, California, mother-daughter book group when they discussed *Homeless Bird*. Seerveld used a combination of peanut butter and shortening to make it easier for the birds to swallow.

MATERIALS

Approximately ½ cup peanut butter

Approximately ¼ cup vegetable shortening

3 bagels, sliced in half

2 cups birdseed

6 ribbons, about 10 inches long

Jelly-roll pan (optional)

Plastic bags (optional)

1. Combine the peanut butter and shortening.
2. Spread each bagel half with the peanut butter mixture.
3. Sprinkle a layer of birdseed in the bottom of a jelly-roll pan, and place the bagel halves facedown in the seed to coat them. Or place the birdseed in a plastic bag, add the bagels, and shake.
4. Tie a ribbon through each bagel hole.
5. Hang the bird feeders on a tree or trees, and enjoy watching the birds!

MAKES 6 BAGEL BIRD FEEDERS

Topics Discussed

- How your life would be different if you were expected to marry in your early teens

- How embroidery can tell a story, and what other skills are passed down in families
- Differences between American and Indian cultures, especially in how decisions are made for young girls, including arranged marriages
- How the rest of Koly's life is affected when she learns to read

How would you have reacted if you found yourself in Koly's situation?

It was interesting for the girls to imagine a life—marriage, leaving parents—so different from their own at a similar age. They saw Koly as more resourceful and independent than they imagined they would be at her age. One of the girls remembered the part of the story where Koly went to the city with Mala and let herself be led into bad behavior, like stealing. She felt that Koly was more agreeable and passive than she would have been in the same circumstances.

—JAN SEERVELD, MOTHER-DAUGHTER BOOK CLUB (GRADE 5)
SAN CARLOS, CALIFORNIA

Among the Hidden

Margaret Peterson Haddix

Simon & Schuster, 1998
Available in paperback from Aladdin
160 pages
Science Fiction

Sequels: *Among the Impostors* (Simon & Schuster, 2001); *Among the Betrayed* (Simon & Schuster, 2002); *Among the Barons* (Simon & Schuster, 2003); *Among the Brave* (Simon & Schuster, 2004); *Among the Enemy* (Simon & Schuster, 2005); *Among the Free* (Simon & Schuster, 2006)

In a society that has banned third children, twelve-year-old Luke spends his days at home with the shades drawn, fearful that the Population Police might somehow learn of his existence. Bored and lonely, Luke often watches the activity in his neighborhood, including the building of a new housing development next to his family's farm, from a hidden attic window. One day, Luke spies movement in the upper window of a neighboring house, and his sheltered life changes forever.

- Margaret Haddix told us she conceived the idea for *Among the Hidden* when she was contemplating expanding her family. She recalls:

  I first started thinking about Among the Hidden *when my husband and I were trying to decide whether to have a third child, or whether to stop with two. All the reasons we could come up with for having, or not having, another baby seemed entirely subjective, more emotional than rational—except the possibility that the world was overpopulated, and it might be irresponsible to have more than two kids. I remember thinking in frustration one night, "Well, how bad a problem can overpopulation be, anyway? If the situation were that dire, there'd be a law against third children." My next thought was, "What if there was a law against third children?" I knew instantly that I had a good idea for a book, regardless of what my husband and I decided.*

- Haddix invented the "two-child" rule depicted in *Among the Hidden*, but says the idea is "not entirely far-fetched."

  For many years, China has had a more stringent law: Families are limited to one child there. But the circumstances and enforcement methods in China aren't exactly the same as in my book. (You could probably tell that Among the Hidden *wasn't set in China.) When I was researching my book, I read a lot about China's efforts at population control—and efforts in other countries—but there's certainly a lot more fiction than fact in the book. I feel very bad for people in countries that have serious overpopulation problems. It really bothered me that none of the books and articles that I read seemed to have what I would consider a good solution.*

Author information: www.simonsayskids.com

Margaret Haddix recommends:

The Giver by Lois Lowry (Houghton Mifflin, 1993; see p. 340). "Several people have compared *Among the Hidden* to *The Giver*, mainly, I think, because they're both about societies whose extreme efforts to control people have backfired," Haddix says. She suggests reading age-appropriate books about Anne Frank, another child in hiding. "There are certainly plenty of powerful and incredible books about children hiding during World War II, and several interesting ones about the challenges they faced coming out of hiding after the war ended."

BOOK BITES

Margaret Haddix's Favorite Chocolate-Chip Cookies

To feed a growing population, the government in *Among the Hidden* forced factories making "junk food"—potato chips, soda, cookies—to produce healthy food instead. Junk food became illegal. "I included the notion of banning junk food mostly to show how controlling the government was," says Margaret Haddix. "I don't think that would be a particularly helpful public policy, if there truly were a food shortage."

Banning junk food resonates strongly with the readers of *Among the Hidden*, according to Haddix. "One school I visited offered kids extra credit if they were able to go without junk food for an entire weekend—the kids reported that it was very, very difficult, and many did not succeed."

Haddix herself might have trouble succeeding: "I'm not much of a junk-food junkie except that I have a pretty strong sweet tooth. I could easily live without potato chips, but I'd really, really miss brownies and chocolate-chip cookies. . . ."

This cookie recipe, an adaptation of the original Nestlé Toll House Cookies recipe, is one that Haddix's mother made often when Haddix was a child, and now Haddix's children consider them favorites, too.

NOTE: To make bars instead of drop cookies, spread dough in a greased 9 x 13-inch pan and bake for 20 to 25 minutes.

*1 cup (2 sticks) butter or
margarine, softened*

¼ cup firmly packed brown sugar

¼ cup granulated sugar

2 large eggs

1 teaspoon vanilla extract

1 teaspoon water

1 teaspoon baking soda

2½ cups all-purpose flour

1 teaspoon salt

2 cups semisweet chocolate morsels

1 cup chopped nuts (optional)

1. Preheat oven to 375° F.
2. In a large bowl, beat the butter, brown sugar, and granulated sugar with an electric mixer on high speed until fluffy. Add eggs and vanilla, mixing well.
3. In a small dish, mix the water and the baking soda. Add to the butter mixture, blending well.
4. Sift the flour and salt together, then add to the batter. Mix 15 to 20 seconds, until just combined. Stir in the chocolate morsels and, if desired, nuts.
5. Drop the batter by rounded teaspoonfuls onto an ungreased cookie sheet, about two inches apart. Bake 8–10 minutes, or until cookies are light golden brown and outer edges begin to crisp. Cool cookies on sheets 1–2 minutes before removing to wire racks to cool completely.

YIELD: ABOUT 4½ DOZEN COOKIES

PLAY IT!

Up, Baby!

Because *Among the Hidden* focuses on hidden children, Jane Ahern played a hiding game with her after-school book club for fourth- and fifth-graders at the Jefferson

County Library in Madras, Oregon. Ahern devised a twist on the classic British coin-hiding game called Up, Jenkins! "Instead of using a coin we used a token with a picture of a baby on it, so we called it Up, Baby!" Ahern explains. She says that if you don't have time to make a token with a picture of a baby, you can simply use a quarter. Ahern calls the game "addictive" and says that keeping score is optional. "Some of the kids were really good at tricking each other," she adds.

Players: 8 or more

Equipment: A long table, chairs or benches, and a coin or token with the image of a baby or child on it

Object: To win points for your team by discovering where the "baby" is hidden

1. Divide players into two teams with equal numbers of players, and have the teams sit on opposite sides of the table. Choose a captain for each team.
2. To start the game, the players on one team begin passing the token back and forth among themselves, underneath the table. The object of the game is to pass the token so carefully that the opposing team cannot guess which player has it.
3. At any time, the captain of the opposing team may call out, "Up, Baby!" At this signal, the players on the team with the token raise their clenched fists above their heads. The captain then calls out, "Down, Baby!" and the players slap their hands with palms flat on the table, keeping the token hidden under one of the palms. The players on the opposing team should listen carefully for any clinking sound to determine which player is concealing the token.
4. The first two players on the opposing team then guess which player has the token. One of them calls the name of the player he or she thinks has the token. This player must lift up both hands to show if the token is on the table. If it isn't, the second player gets to guess.
5. If one of the guesses is right, the opposing team gets a point, and wins a chance to hide the token. If the guesses both are wrong, the first team receives a point and the token stays with that team. In the next round the third and fourth players on the opposing team get to guess, and so on. Set a time limit for play, about twenty minutes or so. The team with the most points wins.

Topics Discussed

- What it might be like to be a child in hiding, or to have a sibling in hiding
- Whether you would choose to stay in hiding or try to get a fake identification, as Luke did
- The relationship between Luke and his parents, and how he was treated as a "hidden child"
- Whether governments have the right to restrict the size of families, and how different governments and countries differ

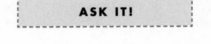

ASK IT!

What is your birth order in your family, and what might it be like to hide a sibling?

The discussion naturally came around to the kids' families and how many siblings they have, and they discussed the pros and cons of big versus small families. Many of the kids commented on how they were third children themselves. They were interested in imagining how it would be in their families if they had to hide one of the kids.

—JANE AHERN, AFTER-SCHOOL BOOK CLUB (GRADES 4–5)
JEFFERSON COUNTY LIBRARY
MADRAS, OREGON

The Breadwinner

Deborah Ellis

Groundwood, 2001
Available in paperback from Groundwood
170 pages
Fiction

Sequels: *Parvana's Journey* (Groundwood, 2002); *Mud City* (Groundwood, 2003)

In Taliban-controlled Afghanistan, eleven-year-old Parvana is forbidden to attend school and risks beatings by soldiers if she ventures outside her home. When her father disappears, Parvana dons her brother's old clothing and steps out as a boy, determined to find a way to save her family from starvation.

AUTHOR SCOOP

- Deborah Ellis is a mental health counselor in Toronto, Canada, and has been an antiwar activist and feminist since the age of seventeen.
- The idea for *The Breadwinner* came out of Ellis's visits in 1999 to Afghan

refugee camps in Pakistan, where she was interviewing women for an adult nonfiction book titled *Women of the Afghan War* (Praeger, 2000). During one of these conversations, she met a woman whose daughter was masquerading as a boy to earn a living for her family, and this is what she recalls:

> *The woman who told me this had been smuggled out of Afghanistan to attend an International Women's Day rally in Pakistan, and had to return shortly to Kabul. She said her daughter was incredibly brave for doing this, for risking terrible consequences in order to keep the family from starving. She told me her daughter preferred being out in the streets, working, to being walled up in their house, and worried what would happen when the girl grew and could no longer get away with the disguise. She thought it would be terribly difficult to be stuck inside after being somewhat free.*

- Many of the women living in the refugee camps told Ellis of the hardships they endured, stories that became a part of *The Breadwinner*. She told us:

> *The burqa is a restrictive garment and the women I met hated being forced to wear it. Many said, though, that the burqa was the least of their worries. Much worse was the lack of education, not being able to feed their children, being beaten in the street, lack of health care, and feeling abandoned by the rest of the world.*
>
> *It was a real honor for me to be able to hear these women's stories of survival and courage, and to share a bit of that courage with others through Parvana's story.*

- Although several scenes in *The Breadwinner* may be disturbing to young readers, Ellis believes that depicting violence is sometimes necessary to illuminate the lives of children in other parts of the world. She explains:

> *We—all of us—have created a world where children are starved, poisoned, enslaved, and cut off from the riches of their own minds. Children everywhere have to deal with these struggles, even in wealthy countries, and those struggles should be reflected in literature, in addition to all the wonderful*

fantasy and lighter books. I think we all aspire to be courageous, and learning about others who have found their courage makes it seem possible for us to face our own challenges with dignity and generosity.

- After the American invasion of Afghanistan in 2001, Ellis noticed a heightened interest in *The Breadwinner* among the American public. "People wanted a way to understand what was happening in this very faraway place," she says.

Author information: www.groundwoodbooks.com
Deborah Ellis recommends:
Kiss the Dust by Elizabeth Laird (Heinemann, 1992)
From Anna by Jean Little (HarperCollins, 1972)

BOOK BITES

Nan (Afghan Bread)

A flattish bread with a crisp crust, *nan* is a staple of the Afghan diet and appears throughout *The Breadwinner*—for breakfast, as a snack, and as an accompaniment to afternoon tea. When Parvana ventures into the marketplace to buy supplies for her family, her first stop is the baker's stall, where she buys ten loaves of *nan*. With the warm bread clutched to her chest, the smell of the *nan* is so tempting, Parvana feels "she could have swallowed a whole loaf in one gulp."

Traditionally, *nan* is made from Middle Eastern whole-wheat flour and a sourdough starter and cooked in a tandoor—a clay oven built into the ground, capable of reaching temperatures approaching 900 degrees Fahrenheit. A round of dough is slapped onto the side of the hot oven, and in less than sixty seconds, the bread browns, puffs slightly, and is ready to be removed. The clay and the smoke from the tandoor combine during the cooking process to give *nan* its distinctive, lightly smoky flavor.

Even without a tandoor, you can prepare tasty and attractive loaves of *nan* at home to serve with your discussion of *The Breadwinner*. Though it is traditionally served without butter, our testers liked *nan* with butter and jam. The bread is best eaten warm, straight from the oven, and Deborah Ellis recommends drizzling it with honey.

NOTE: This recipe, from Helen Saberi's *Afghan Food & Cookery: Noshe Djan* (Hippocrene Books, 2000), calls for *chapati* or *ata* flour, available at Indian groceries, but Saberi says bread flour (a high-gluten flour available in most grocery stores) may be substituted.

The bread dough must be quite soft, and the amount of water you use will depend on the type of flour and the humidity in the air. Adjust the quantity of water suggested in the recipe as necessary.

To "freshen up" *nan* after it has gone cold or been removed from the freezer, sprinkle it with a little water on both sides and quickly warm it up under a hot broiler.

Sia donna, or nigella seeds, have a nutty, peppery flavor, and are used in India and the Middle East to flavor vegetables, legumes, and bread. You can find them at Indian groceries.

5¼ cups chapati *or* ata *flour (see note)*

1½ teaspoons salt

2¼ teaspoons (1 packet) quick-rising yeast

4–5 teaspoons vegetable oil

2 cups warm water (see note)

Sia donna *(nigella seeds), poppy seeds, sesame seeds (optional; see note)*

1. Sift the flour and salt into a medium bowl. Add the yeast, and mix to combine the dry ingredients. Mix in the oil, and rub in with the hands. Gradually add the warm water to flour mixture and mix with the hands until a smooth, round, soft dough is formed. Knead for another 7–10 minutes, until the dough is elastic and smooth, essentially the same as ordinary bread dough. Form into a ball, cover with a damp cloth, and let rest in a moderately warm place for about 1 hour, or until the dough has doubled in bulk.

2. Preheat oven to 500° F. Line a baking sheet with aluminum foil and place in the oven to get hot.

3. When dough has risen, punch down and divide into four equal-size balls. Shape or roll out the dough on a lightly floured surface into oval shapes of about ½-inch thickness. After shaping the dough, wet your hand and use your finger or thumb

to form deep grooves down the center of each loaf. Sprinkle with the *sia donna* (or poppy or sesame seeds), if desired. Press the seeds lightly into dough.

4. Remove the hot baking tray from the oven and place dough on it, leaving a couple of inches between the dough pieces. Bake 8–10 minutes, until golden brown. The bread should be fairly crisp and hard on the outside. Repeat the process with the remaining balls of dough.

5. When removed from the oven, the *nan* should be wrapped in a clean tea towel or aluminum foil to prevent drying.

YIELD: 4 (6 X 10-INCH) LOAVES

┌─────────────────┐
│ **TASTE IT!** │
└─────────────────┘

Book Links: Tasty Ideas from Deborah Ellis

TEA

As in other Middle Eastern countries, the ritual of drinking tea is an important part of Afghan culture, and book clubs reading *The Breadwinner* enjoy serving tea to accompany their discussions. Deborah Ellis recalls sharing tea—and conversation—with Afghanis:

> *A big part of Afghan culture is being hospitable to strangers. I have so many wonderful memories of sitting with Afghan families in their mud hovels or rag tents, lantern-light casting shadows around us, drinking tea and talking.*

For your book club meeting, Ellis suggests serving tea flavored with cardamom or mint tea, along with a small dish of candied almonds, dried mulberries or apricots, or other sweets.

QABILI PILAU

Ellis discovered *qabili pilau*, often described as Afghanistan's national dish, during her time in that country. In *qabili pilau*, long-grained rice is cooked with onions, slivered carrots, raisins, and chicken or lamb; this popular dish can be served alone or with vegetables. A recipe can be found in *Afghan Food & Cookery: Noshe Djan* by Helen Saberi (Hippocrene, 2000).

MAKE IT!

Book Links: Ideas from Deborah Ellis

TOYS FROM RECYCLED MATERIALS

Ellis says children living in refugee camps turn everyday items—things we might discard—into toys. For example, they might find a plastic shopping bag in a garbage dump and create a makeshift kite by tying a string to the bag, and running with it fluttering behind them.

For this activity, gather assorted household "junk" such as plastic shopping bags, toilet-paper rolls, bits of string or yarn, or Styrofoam packaging. Place all the items on a table, and ask children to come up with ideas for toys made out of the materials. They may want to try making and "flying" the kite described above.

MOSAIC DESIGNS

According to Ellis, some of the world's great mosaic artwork resides in Afghanistan's huge buildings decorated in tiny colored tiles. She suggests giving the children in your book club the opportunity to create their own mosaics.

To inspire the artists in the group, show them photographs of Afghan buildings adorned with mosaics, from books or the Internet. Cut small squares of colored paper (about 75 to 100 per artist), and allow children to design and glue mosaic patterns onto sheets of paper.

Topics Discussed

- Similarities and differences between Parvana's life and the daily lives of children in America
- Parvana's changing relationship with her older sister, and the way her role in the family shifts after her father's disappearance
- The various ways characters in the story choose to fight against the Taliban
- Who is behind the blackened window in the marketplace, and why they choose to drop things onto Parvana's blanket

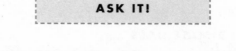

How could such a terrible situation have been allowed to develop in Afghanistan?

This book was an eye-opener for the kids. They know they have fairly cushy lives, but they had no idea that some children have it so bad. We talked about how adults could have let this situation develop, and we decided that not enough good people had stood up and said no. Maybe they were afraid. Then we talked about how many times in our own history people were too afraid to stand up and say no. This was a lesson the moms really wanted the girls to internalize.

—JANICE BUCHANAN, MOTHER-DAUGHTER BOOK CLUB (GRADES 5–7)
MOUNT VERNON CITY LIBRARY
MOUNT VERNON, WASHINGTON

Grades 5–9

Hoot

Carl Hiaasen

Alfred A. Knopf, 2002
Available in paperback from Alfred A. Knopf
304 pages
Fiction

Roy Eberhardt has just moved to Coconut Grove, Florida, and is contending with the challenges of being a newcomer at Trace Middle School: making new friends and warding off bullies like big Dana Matherson, who tries to strangle him each day on the school bus. One day, Roy spies a barefoot boy running by the bus. His determination to uncover the identity of this stranger thrusts Roy into an adventure involving owls, snakes, alligators, and a pancake house—and forces him to confront powerful forces threatening his environment.

AUTHOR SCOOP

- Carl Hiaasen has been a lifelong resident of South Florida. Born and raised in Fort Lauderdale, near Coconut Grove—the setting for *Hoot*—he now lives in the Florida Keys. As a child, Hiaasen loved exploring the woods and swamps near the Everglades, and he says his adventures gave him "a passion for wild places, and something that I knew was worth fighting for."

- The tiny burrowing owls featured in the novel actually inhabit South Florida. During Hiaasen's childhood, the owls were abundant, but in recent years their habitats have been all but wiped out by real estate development, leading Hiaasen to depict their plight in *Hoot*.

- *Hoot* is Hiaasen's first children's book. Hiaasen says his adult novels contain language inappropriate for children, and he wrote *Hoot* to give his stepson, nieces, and nephew, all between the ages of ten and fourteen, something to read "without worrying about the salty language or adult situations."

- A year younger—and smaller—than his classmates in grade school, Hiaasen was the target of frequent beatings. He claims he developed a sharp wit so he could defend himself with words. His experiences of being intimidated as an adolescent inspired him to explore themes of bullying in several of his books, including *Hoot*. After reading *Hoot*, many young readers have written to Hiaasen with accounts of their own problems with bullies.

Author website: www.carlhiaasen.com
Film adaptation:
Hoot (New Line Cinema, 2006), rated PG, 90 minutes

BOOK BITES

Buttermilk Pancakes

Pancakes are a natural choice to pair with *Hoot*, because the book's central conflict concerns the building of a pancake house and its effects on the environment. Dorothy Distefano, facilitator of Families Invited to Read and Share Together (FIRST) Book Club in Hilton, New York, says *Hoot* prompted terrific discussion among the fifth- and sixth-graders and their parents in her group. She shared her family recipe for buttermilk pancakes with us.

NOTE: Distefano recommends dropping the batter by tablespoons to make silver-dollar pancakes that kids can pick up with their hands and dip in syrup.

Ideally, these pancakes should be served straight from the pan, so if possible, prepare the batter in advance and cook the pancakes when the group has gathered. If necessary, the pancakes may be kept warm on a wire rack in a 200° F. oven for up to five minutes.

2 large eggs

2 cups buttermilk

¼ cup canola oil

2 cups all-purpose flour

2 tablespoons sugar

2 teaspoons baking powder

1 teaspoon baking soda

1 teaspoon salt

Oil or cooking spray

1. In a large bowl, beat the eggs with a fork or whisk. Stir in the buttermilk and oil. Add the remaining ingredients and stir just until large lumps disappear. The batter should be thick.
2. Heat a large skillet over medium-high heat. Lightly grease the griddle with oil or cooking spray.
3. When droplets of water sizzle when sprinkled in the pan, drop batter by the tablespoon into pan. Fry until bubbles form on top and edges dry and brown slightly. Flip to cook other side. Serve immediately.

YIELD: APPROXIMATELY 35 SILVER-DOLLAR PANCAKES

MAKE IT!

Duster Owls

Participants in Natick Reads, a monthlong program of events and activities centered recently around *Hoot*, made owls out of recycled materials. Kristen Arnold, director of children's services at Bacon Free Library in Natick, Massachusetts, conceived the idea for the project when she spotted a Swiffer Duster—a white, fluffy casing that attaches to a handle and is used for dusting. "When I saw one, it looked just like the shape, size, and color of an owl," she says. She made the Swiffer Duster look like an owl by inserting a coat hanger wire inside, and then gluing on various objects. "One of the themes of the book is environmental awareness, so I wanted to bring in the idea of using materials that are just lying around and can be recycled," says Arnold. She placed the owls on branches she had collected, so they appear to be perched on top.

The results were impressive. "The owls look more alive because they don't stand up straight," says Arnold. "Each owl has its own personality—some are funky, with purple feathers attached, and others are more sedate and authentic." Arnold has created duster owls with children of all ages, as well as adults and seniors, and these have always been well received.

NOTE: It can be challenging to attach facial features and other decorations to the owl's body, as sometimes the glue fails to cling to the fuzz, according to Arnold. She recommends a hot-glue gun to secure the decorations, although she says white glue will also work.

If wire cutters do not cut the hangers, simply work the wire back and forth with your hand until it snaps.

Swiffer Dusters can be purchased in grocery or cleaning-supply stores. Arnold bought less expensive, off-brand dusters in bulk at a discount club.

MATERIALS

Coat hangers

Swiffer Dusters, or other brand dusters (see note), one per member

Wire cutters

Tree branches, about 2–3 inches in diameter, gathered from outside

Recycled materials (feathers, rubber washers, pieces of yarn, wire, coffee cans, fabric scraps, etc.)

Hot-glue gun or white glue (see note)

1. Put a stiff object such as a coat hanger inside the Swiffer Duster to form the owl's body, leaving enough wire at the bottom to wrap around the branch.

2. Wrap the excess coat wire around the branch.

3. Decorate the owl with recycled materials, attaching with glue or glue gun.

Dissect Owl Pellets

Owls swallow their prey whole, absorbing the nutrients into their systems and regurgitating the bones, skin, and hair in a soft pellet. Asking children to dissect the soft, furry masses of undigested material is a hands-on way for them to investigate the lives of these birds of prey, and many book clubs throughout the country have tried this activity when discussing *Hoot*. Many sources for purchasing owl pellets can be found on the Internet. Give each child a pellet, tweezers, rubber gloves, a paper plate to collect their findings, and a diagram of bones and other objects that the children can expect to find (often this comes with the pellets). Participants might extract rat skeletons and the feathers of various birds, and can then use their artifacts to make inferences about the daily lives of owls.

Live Owls

Karen Perkins, coordinator of special programming for the Morse Institute, a library in Natick, Massachusetts, invited two licensed raptor rehabilitators to bring live owls to the library for their monthlong celebration of *Hoot*. Jim Parks of Wingmasters, a group dedicated to increasing public understanding and appreciation of North American birds of prey, brought five live owls to the library, four of them species found in Natick. In addition, Parks had read *Hoot* and explained the differences between the burrowing owls in the book and the owls he had brought.

Topics Discussed

- If the company had the right to build a pancake house where endangered animals were living
- Different ways Roy could have dealt with Dana's bullying
- If you have had personal experience with bullies, and how to deal with them
- How frequent moves impacted Roy and his ability to make and develop friendships

Is it okay to break the rules for a good reason?

We discussed the unconventional things Mullet Fingers did to try to stop the pancake house from being built. Many of the things he did, and what Roy did, for that matter, were not necessarily considered "right." We talked about whether it is okay to break the rules for a good reason. The group generally agreed that if breaking a rule was the only way they could think of to fix a problem, and it was really important, then it was justified.

—DOROTHY DISTEFANO, FAMILIES INVITED TO READ AND SHARE TOGETHER
(FIRST) BOOK CLUB (GRADES 5–6)
HILTON, NEW YORK

Grades 5–8

Out of the Dust

Karen Hesse

Scholastic, 1997
Available in paperback from Scholastic
240 pages
Historical Fiction

Writing in free-verse poetry, fourteen-year-old Billie Jo Kelby tells of her family's struggle to survive in the Depression-era Oklahoma dust bowl, a region plagued by dust storms and their aftermath. After Billie Jo's mother dies from a tragic accident that also leaves Billie Jo's hands scarred, she summons the courage to withstand personal hardship as her family—and the community—persist in farming, against the elements.

AUTHOR SCOOP

- Karen Hesse was working on another book when she began *Out of the Dust*, "a picture book in which a young urban girl longs for rain during a particularly hot, dry summer," she explains. "My writing group asked why she wanted rain so much. My mind shot back to the Dirty Thirties, when rain came so infrequently. Before I knew it, I was knee deep in Oklahoma dust. The result—*Out of the Dust*. I also completed the picture book. It's called *Come On, Rain!*"

- The Walker Evans photograph of Lucille Burroughs featured on the cover of *Out of the Dust* was Hesse's inspiration for the novel and the character of Billie Jo Kelby. The daughter of an Alabama cotton sharecropper in the 1930s, Burroughs struggled along with her family during the Depression. The photograph was included in James Agee and Walker Evans's *Let Us Now Praise Famous Men: Three Tenant Families* (Houghton Mifflin, 1941). According to Hesse:

  Let Us Now Praise Famous Men is one of many volumes in our personal family library. When I begin a new book, before I visit our local library, I comb our home shelves, pulling down books relevant to my intended period or subject. Agee's book joined the stack of resources in those earliest stages of research for Out of the Dust. *The images of Lucille Burroughs and her family drew me in, they spoke to me. Fortunately, I had the good sense to listen.*

- Hesse read numerous period news articles from the *Boise City News*, a daily paper published in the Oklahoma panhandle. She also listened to music to gain an understanding of the Oklahoma dust bowl during the Depression era. "I listened to Woody Guthrie's *Dust Bowl Ballads* over and over to get the cadence right," adds Hesse. "You can only go so far with paper research alone. Without an Oklahoma background, I had my work cut out for me in re-creating an authentic representation of that time and place."

- Hesse, who began her writing career as a poet, says she "never attempted to write this book in any other way than in free verse." In her Newbery Medal acceptance speech for *Out of the Dust*, Hesse said, "The frugality of the life, the hypnotically hard work of farming, the grimness of conditions during the dust bowl, demanded an economy of words." The novel's poetic form has received "remarkably positive" response from readers. "An uncluttered page invites readers to take more time with each word, each metaphor, each small journey," Hesse told us. "This kind of compression of language provides the reader a vivid, direct reading experience. Happily, from the start, readers were receptive to a nonconventional novel form."

Karen Hesse recommends:

Children of the Dust Bowl: The True Story of the School at Weedpatch Camp
by Jerry Stanley (Crown, 1992)

Children of the Dust Days by Karen Mueller Coombs (Carolrhoda, 2001)

Driven from the Land: The Story of the Dust Bowl by Milton Meltzer
(Benchmark, 1999)

BOOK BITES

Apple Pandowdy

Sugar was scarce during the Great Depression. In *Out of the Dust,* when Sheriff Robertson seizes a half ton of sugar from bootleggers and delivers it to the school, Billie Jo rejoices that she can now bake, among other treats, apple pandowdy.

Karen Hesse says she makes note of details when researching her books—including what people are eating. "When you find food listed in one of my books, you can feel fairly comfortable that it was eaten during that period," she told us. Her frequent references to apples in *Out of the Dust* also have roots in her childhood: "I spent much of my childhood reading in the crotch of an apple tree in my Baltimore city backyard," says Hesse. "Is it any wonder both I and my characters have a fondness for apples?"

Hesse thought apple pandowdy would be the perfect dish to sample when discussing *Out of the Dust.* Apple pandowdy was one of the first desserts she baked for her family, after discovering a Bisquick recipe years ago. She prefers a biscuit topping rather than a thinner crust to cover the pandowdy, and suggests topping the dessert with ice cream. "There's nothing like eating apple pandowdy fresh and warm from the oven with a scoop of vanilla ice cream melting over and into it," she adds.

In apple pandowdy, apples, sugar or molasses, and spices are combined and topped with a biscuit topping or piecrust. The deep-dish dessert is thought to get its name from its plain or dowdy appearance. Traditional apple pandowdy was baked until the topping became crisp, and then removed from the oven so the crust could be "dowdied," or broken up. The topping was then pushed into the fruit and baked longer. And while pandowdy is traditionally made with molasses, there are many variations calling for sugar or combinations of sugar and molasses. We created an apple pandowdy recipe using the topping from Mark Bittman's recipe in *How to Cook Everything* (Wiley, 1998).

You might want to take a moment to discuss the symbolism of apples in *Out of the Dust*, while sampling the apple pandowdy.

NOTE: This pandowdy recipe calls for sugar, but you may substitute ⅔ cup molasses for the sugar in the filling if you prefer. You can use your favorite baking apples for the filling. We like a combination of McIntosh and Granny Smith.

For an easy "dowdy" crust, simply cut the pie dough into 2-inch squares and arrange in a patchwork pattern over the apples.

FOR THE DOUGH

1⅛ cups all-purpose flour, plus extra for dusting the work surface

½ teaspoon salt

2 tablespoons sugar

½ cup (1 stick) cold unsalted butter, cut into about 8 pieces

1 egg yolk

About 3 tablespoons of ice water, plus more if necessary

FOR THE FILLING

6 cups peeled, cored, and thinly sliced apples (about 6 medium apples; see note)

½ cup firmly packed brown sugar (see note)

1 tablespoon fresh lemon juice

¼ teaspoon ground cinnamon

⅛ teaspoon ground nutmeg

FOR THE TOPPING

1 tablespoon milk

2 tablespoons granulated sugar

½ teaspoon ground cinnamon

1. Preheat oven to 375° F. Lightly grease an 8-inch square or 9-inch round baking pan.

2. To make the dough: In the bowl of a food processor, combine flour, salt, and sugar and pulse once or twice. Add butter and process about 10 seconds, until the butter and flour are blended and the mixture has the texture of cornmeal. To mix by hand: Cut the stick of butter into bits and rub the butter and flour very quickly between your fingers, or cut butter into flour with a pastry blender.

3. Place the mixture in a bowl and add egg yolk and ice water. Use a wooden spoon or rubber spatula to gradually gather the mixture into a ball; if the mixture seems dry, add another ½ tablespoon of ice water. Form the dough into a ball with your hands. Wrap dough in plastic, flatten into a small disc, and freeze 10 minutes (or refrigerate 30 minutes) to ease rolling.

4. While dough is chilling, prepare the filling: In a large mixing bowl, stir the apples with the brown sugar, lemon juice, cinnamon, and nutmeg. Spread the mixture in the prepared pan.

5. To roll the dough: Unwrap the dough and place on a floured work surface, and sprinkle top with flour. (If the dough is hard, let it rest a few minutes. It should give a little when you press your fingers into it.) Roll with light pressure from the center out. Add flour to the dough if it sticks. Roll, adding flour, rotating dough and turning over once or twice. When dough is about 10 inches in diameter and less than ¼ inch thick, place over fruit, tucking the edges of the dough under the sides of the fruit. You may also cut the dough in small squares (see note).

6. For the topping: Brush the top of the dough with the milk. Combine the sugar and cinnamon, and sprinkle on top.

7. Bake 30–40 minutes, or until the crust is golden. Serve warm with vanilla ice cream.

YIELD: 6 TO 8 SERVINGS

Book Link: An Idea from Karen Hesse

LISTEN TO *DUST BOWL BALLADS*

Karen Hesse suggests listening to Woody Guthrie's *Dust Bowl Ballads* with your book group.

Folksinger and songwriter Woody Guthrie grew up in Oklahoma during the Dust Bowl era and chronicled the catastrophic effects of dust storms in songs such as "The Great Dust Storm" and "Dust Bowl Blues." In his original liner notes for the album, Guthrie writes: "They are 'Oakie' songs, 'Dust Bowl' songs, 'Migration' songs about my folks and my relatives, about a jillion of 'em that got hit by the drouth [*sic*], the dust, the wind, the banker, and the landlord, and the police all at the same time."

Dust Bowl Ballads (Buddha, 2000) is available at many local libraries.

See the Dust Bowl

Lisa Hughes's mother-daughter book club in Oregon, Wisconsin, watched footage of dust storms in Pare Lorentz's 1936 documentary film *The Plow That Broke the Plains,* which they rented from an online movie rental service. The group didn't watch the entire movie, much of which deals with politics and farming practices, says Hughes. "But when the girls saw the dust storm images, it really brought home the fact that characters in the book did experience these dust storms." Hughes says the girls were amazed that all the dust in the film was real, and that there could really be so much dust.

Topics Discussed

- How sorrowful Billie Jo's life was and yet how hopeful the reader feels
- If you would return the pennies for overpayment for cake ingredients and how valuable the change of just a few pennies was to Billie Jo
- The dust bowl and its effects on Billie Jo's family and her community
- The theme of forgiveness and whether it is realistic that one would always forgive family

ASK IT!

How would you keep going under the weight of all the misery Billie Jo experienced? Would you have run away?

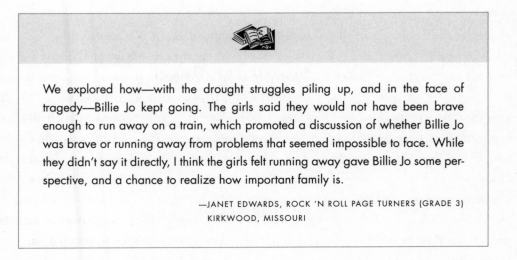

We explored how—with the drought struggles piling up, and in the face of tragedy—Billie Jo kept going. The girls said they would not have been brave enough to run away on a train, which promoted a discussion of whether Billie Jo was brave or running away from problems that seemed impossible to face. While they didn't say it directly, I think the girls felt running away gave Billie Jo some perspective, and a chance to realize how important family is.

—JANET EDWARDS, ROCK 'N ROLL PAGE TURNERS (GRADE 3)
KIRKWOOD, MISSOURI

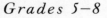

Skellig

David Almond

Random House, 1998
Available in paperback from Random House
192 pages
Fiction

Michael's family has just moved to a new neighborhood of Newcastle, England, and his baby sister is hospitalized with a serious heart condition—leaving Michael feeling isolated and fearful for her well-being. While his parents are preoccupied with his sister, Michael discovers Skellig, a mysterious birdlike creature in the shadows of the garage. With the help of Mina, a new friend from the neighborhood, Michael finds comfort in nurturing Skellig and exploring the mysteries of love and friendship.

AUTHOR SCOOP

- David Almond describes how the idea for *Skellig*, his first children's novel, came "out of the blue"—and almost seemed to write itself. He completed *Skellig* in six months. He explains:

[The story] started telling itself in my head as I was walking along the street one day. Yes, it does have many connections to my own life, but it had an energy and life of its own. When I began to write it down, it often seemed to be writing itself. As I wrote, I had to read [the works of William] Blake again, and to keep referring to bird books, in order to keep up with Mina. This was the first time I had written for a young readership, and that fact gave my work a new excitement and energy.

- Almond is often asked, "Who is Skellig?" He explains that he is happy to have Skellig remain a mystery: "Lots of life, to me, seems pretty mysterious, and to evade straightforward definitions and explanations," says Almond. "I think it would have cheapened the story if I had come in at the end and tried to define exactly what Skellig is."

- Almond drew on life experiences to write *Skellig*. "The story is set in a house in which I used to live, in Newcastle-upon-Tyne," he explains. "When we moved into the house, it had a toilet in the dining room, just like in *Skellig*. And an old man had died in the house. My mother had terrible arthritis. I had a poorly baby sister when I was a boy."

- Mina is Almond's favorite character. "Without her, the story could have been rather weak and sentimental," says Almond. "As I wrote the book, it felt as if she had a guiding hand."

Author website: www.davidalmond.com

BOOK BITES

Ruby Foo's Spring Rolls (#27) with Sesame Soy Dipping Sauce

Skellig begs Michael for "27 and 53," numbered dishes from the local Chinese takeaway. "According to Skellig, 27 and 53 are the food of the gods!" says Almond, who claims the numbers have no particular significance. "They just sounded good when spoken together." As for why Chinese food was Skellig's favorite: "The book is set in a house in which I used to live. There was a very good Chinese takeaway just down the street from us, so it fit well," says Almond.

Number 53 (pork char sui, or barbecued spareribs) was part of Almond's first-ever takeaway Chinese meal and number 27 (spring rolls) was also a longtime favorite. Almond suggested asking Ruby Foo's, a favorite Pan-Asian restaurant in New York City, for its spring rolls recipe. Executive chefs Shawn Edelman and Scott Drewno obliged. We think their recipe will add up to a delicious treat for your club—one that Skellig would have savored.

NOTE: Do not form the spring rolls more than thirty minutes before cooking, or the filling may seep through the wrapper dough.

The Ruby Foo's chefs use the crispy spring-roll wrappers found in Asian or specialty food stores, but they say it's fine to use the soft egg roll wrappers found in most grocery stores in place of the spring roll wrappers.

You will need enough oil to fill half of a wok or fryer; the amount of oil will vary depending on size of pan. The chefs at Ruby Foo's use soybean oil, but they suggest you can substitute corn oil, safflower oil, or peanut oil to fry the rolls.

While the spring rolls on Ruby Foo's menu are filled with a combination of lobster and shrimp, we've adapted the recipe to include shrimp or tofu, or a combination of the two. If you use both the shrimp and tofu, simply include half of each of the amount called for in the recipe.

FOR THE FILLING

4 ounces bean thread noodles (also called cellophane or sai fun noodles)

¼–½ cup soybean, corn, safflower, or peanut oil, plus 3–4 cups for frying rolls (see note)

½ small head green cabbage, thinly sliced (approximately 1½–2 cups)

1 (12-ounce) can thinly sliced bamboo shoots

2 carrots, peeled and julienned

½ cup thinly sliced shiitake mushrooms

1 (14-ounce) package firm tofu, drained and crumbled, or 1 pound uncooked shrimp, peeled, deveined, and cut into thirds, or a combination (see note)

¼ cup cilantro, finely chopped

2 tablespoons sugar

2 tablespoons sesame oil

½ cup fish sauce

1 teaspoon salt

½ teaspoon white pepper

FOR THE SESAME SOY DIPPING SAUCE

½ cup soy sauce

2 tablespoons rice vinegar

1 tablespoon sesame oil

⅛ cup sugar

1 tablespoon minced ginger

1½ teaspoons minced scallion

FOR THE SPRING ROLLS

1 egg, lightly beaten

1 package spring-roll wrappers (see note)

1. To make the filling: Soak the bean thread noodles in hot water to soften, according to package directions.

2. Heat ¼–½ cup vegetable oil in a wok over medium-high to high heat. Sauté the cabbage, bamboo shoots, carrots, and mushrooms 5–7 minutes, or until tender. Remove from the heat.

3. Drain the noodles, chop coarsely (approximately 3 inches in length), and add with the tofu, if using, to the vegetables. Add the cilantro, sugar, sesame oil, and fish sauce, and season with salt and pepper. Stir to combine.

4. Place the filling in a strainer or colander set over a bowl. Place in the refrigerator approximately 15 minutes, until the filling is completely cooled and all liquid is drained. You may have to press down on the mixture to extract the excess moisture.

5. To make the dipping sauce: Place sauce ingredients in bowl and stir. Set aside.

6. Remove the filling from the refrigerator. Add the shrimp, if using, and stir to combine.

7. To assemble the spring rolls: Place the beaten egg in a bowl and have a pastry brush handy. Place a spring-roll wrapper on a work surface, with one point facing you. Spoon ¼ cup of the filling near the bottom corner in an oblong shape. Fold the bottom corner of the wrapper up to the center and then fold in the sides and pull tightly together. Brush the point farthest from you with a small amount of

beaten egg to allow the wrapper to adhere to itself once it is rolled. Roll like a carpet and press gently to seal. Repeat with the remaining filling and wrappers.

8. Pour at least 3 inches of vegetable oil into a pot for deep-frying and heat to 350° F. Add the spring rolls in small batches and fry 2–3 minutes, until crisp and light brown. Drain well on brown paper or paper towels and serve immediately with the dipping sauce or keep warm in oven.

YIELD: 15 TO 20 SPRING ROLLS

TASTE IT!

Bites from the Book

Dorothy Distefano brought Chinese fortune cookies to her Families Invited to Read and Share Together (FIRST) Book Club in Hilton, New York, for the club's *Skellig* discussion. "While I would have loved to bring pork char sui and spring rolls for the kids to try, fortune cookies were an easier choice," says Distefano. The group was delighted when Distefano read her fortune: "You will have a stimulating discussion with a great group of friends."

Just as Mina introduced pomegranates to Michael, the FIRST book group sampled pomegranates at their meeting, using pinwheel toothpicks for skewering seeds. While everyone nibbled the fruit, Distefano related the story of Persephone eating pomegranates in the Underworld, the myth Mina mentions to Michael. "Michael wants to name the baby Persephone because she stands for rebirth and hope, and the group was fascinated with the symbolism of Persephone's name," adds Distefano.

Create a Sound Map

Almond thinks nature journaling is a "brilliant" idea for a book club outing, "and something very close to Mina's heart," he adds.

Mark Baldwin, director of education at the Roger Tory Peterson Institute in Jamestown, New York, led a nature journaling exercise with the Chautauqua Institution, a center for the arts, religion, education, and recreation in Chautauqua, New York, as part of the Summer Young Readers Program's *Skellig* discussion.

Baldwin began by noting that the barn owl (*Tyto alba*) that Mina and Michael discover in *Skellig* is one of the most widely distributed birds in the world—and one of the most interesting. "Owls generally are well adapted to hunting prey in low-light conditions, but the barn owl is actually able to locate and capture prey in complete darkness, using its incredibly sensitive hearing alone," says Baldwin.

Baldwin asked the group to make a sound map—a way to focus attention on what you're hearing and record what you hear in a journal—to hone their sense of hearing. He has found that the activity has also prompted exploration of other topics. "All sorts of discussions about the natural world, noise in the environment, the importance of cultivating keen senses and having firsthand experiences in order to write, come out of it," he adds.

NOTE: After distributing index cards and pencils to the group, go outdoors, preferably to a natural environment, to begin this activity.

MATERIALS
Lined 4 x 6-inch index card and a pencil, one of each per member

1. Draw a circle on the blank side of the card. The circle represents the limit of what you can hear all around you. Outside the circle, record the date, time of day, where you are, and a note about the weather.
2. Place an X in the center of the circle to indicate your position, and then start to listen carefully.

3. Each time you become aware of a sound, note its direction, loudness, and apparent distance away, and represent it graphically in some way in the circle. For example, represent a bird singing with a small sketch of a bird and a musical note. Or, the hum of traffic on a distant highway with a sketch of cars and the letters *hmmmm.* You decide how to represent sounds; the important thing is to record them in some way that will help you remember.

    While doing this activity you may want to think of the way a cat or a rabbit rotates its outer ears in response to a sound. Enhance your own ears' ability to catch sound waves by cupping your hands behind them, and bending your outer ears forward with thumb and forefinger. Listen for a while like this, and note how your perception of sound changes.

4. After listening and recording for about ten minutes, review what you have heard. Ask yourself the following questions, and record your response on the back of the card (the side with lines):

- What sounds were man-made?
- What sounds were "natural"?
- What sounds were annoying to hear?
- What sounds were pleasant?
- What sounds were mysterious?

5. Summarize your sound-scape by writing about it for five minutes.

Book Links: Ideas from David Almond

DRAW SKELLIG

"Drawing makes you look at the world more closely. It helps you to see what you're looking at more clearly," says Mina in *Skellig*. Just as Mina sketches Skellig, Almond thought drawing Skellig would be a good exercise for a book club. He emphasizes to artists: "Everyone sees Skellig in different ways. For every reader, there is a different Skellig." You might want to read Almond's description of Skellig to your group before you begin.

EXPLORE *SKELLIG* THROUGH HISTORY, GEOGRAPHY, AND POETRY

- Find out about the history and geography of the Skellig Islands. The name Skellig comes from the Skellig Islands off the southwest coast of Ireland, which have a fascinating history, says Almond.
- Read William Blake's *Songs of Innocence* and *Songs of Experience*.
  Mina introduces Michael to the poet and painter William Blake. His complementary books of poetry *Songs of Innocence* (1789) and *Songs of Experience* (1794) have contrasting themes.
- Write a poem of your own. Maybe it could contain a blackbird, a cat, some owls, a garage, or a baby's laughter, suggests Almond.

Topics Discussed

- Who (or what) Skellig was
- If you would have kept the secret of finding Skellig
- How the author felt about public education versus homeschooling
- If you ever had a paranormal experience

What is the meaning of the following passage?
"'What does it mean,' I said, 'if Skellig eats living things
and makes pellets like the owls?' She shrugged.
'We can't know,' she said. 'What is he?' I said. 'We can't know.
Sometimes we just have to accept there are things we can't know.'"

Mina's response to Michael's question led to a discussion of how difficult it is for us to accept and how frustrating it can be that there are things we may never understand, especially in a time when we believe information should be right at our fingertips. Faith, belief in the absence of proof or evidence, comes so much easier to some. It was tough for some of the kids to accept that we never really find out exactly who or what Skellig is.

—DOROTHY DISTEFANO, FAMILIES INVITED TO READ AND SHARE TOGETHER
(FIRST) BOOK CLUB (GRADES 5–6)
HILTON, NEW YORK

Surviving the Applewhites

Stephanie Tolan

HarperCollins, 2002
Available in paperback from HarperTrophy
224 pages
Fiction

After being kicked out of every school in Rhode Island, Jake Semple has been sent to live in North Carolina with his grandfather, who enrolls him in the Creative Academy, a homeschool run by the eccentric Applewhite family on their sixteen-acre compound. In spite of his rebelliousness, the artsy Applewhites embrace Jake—with the exception of E.D., the only family member who relishes schedules and resents Jake's intrusion. At first, Jake assumes he'll breeze through this unstructured homeschool. But the Applewhites bring out qualities in Jake that he never knew existed, and his attitude—and self-image—begin to change.

AUTHOR SCOOP

- The Applewhite family was born of Stephanie Tolan's desire to write a comic novel after having published an intensely serious one. Tolan says:

After writing Flight of the Raven *[HarperCollins, 2001], a young adult novel that takes place in a terrorist compound, I wanted to write something funny, so immediately thought of inventing a highly creative family— since such a family would provide nearly infinite comic possibilities. I know many homeschooling families, so I decided this family would be home- schooling their children. As for Jake, I saw a short blurb in our newspaper about a boy who got kicked out of the whole public education system in his state, and I decided to bring such a boy into the Applewhites' world.*

• According to Tolan, several members of the Applewhite family share qual- ities with members of her own family:

My husband and our youngest son are both theater directors, our oldest is an organized, take-charge doctor, I am a writer, and we share our lives with a number of animals. People sometimes ask whether the Applewhites are modeled after my own family. I take the Fifth!

• Tolan made butterflies a part of the school program in *Surviving the Apple- whites* for practical reasons, and only later realized their symbolic function. She explains:

The butterflies got into the book not as conscious symbols of transformation, as many kids who've been learning about symbolism in school believe, but because as I was writing the book, black swallowtail butterflies were devour- ing the parsley in my garden. This happens every year. I always pick the caterpillars off, give them store-bought parsley to eat, raise them in an aquarium till they go into the chrysalis stage, then give them to neighbor children to take to school so their classmates can watch them emerge as but- terflies. It was only after I incorporated our caterpillar/butterflies into the story that I noticed the symbolic dimension they added. Some authors may work at putting symbols into their work, but I suspect a good many useful symbols come about this way as a part of the "magical" creative process.

- Tolan did not homeschool her children, although, she says, she considered it briefly:

> *I seriously considered [homeschooling] for our youngest, who was so bright it was hard to find academic challenge for him, even though he was grade-skipped a couple of times—he went from first grade directly to fourth. When we proposed homeschooling as an option, he objected strenuously. He was (and still is) a strong extrovert who needs to be with people. He was horrified at the idea of being at home with only his mother for companionship. Actually, since I'm as much of an introvert as he is an extrovert and treasured my solitary writing time, I was relieved at his response.*

Author website: www.stephanietolan.com

Stephanie Tolan recommends:

The Bagthorpe Saga by Helen Cresswell, a series Tolan says "would probably appeal to kids who enjoyed the Applewhites. The Bagthorpes, who are very British, are a similarly eccentric family, all of whom believe themselves to be 'geniuses'—except for Ordinary Jack, who is the title character of the first book in the series [Faber, 1977]." Tolan says the books can be found in many libraries.

BOOK BITES

Govindaswami's "Fried Chicken"

Govindaswami, Aunt Lucille's spiritual leader, instructs the Applewhites in meditation, and doubles as the family cook. When Stephanie Tolan came across this recipe for "fried chicken" on the Internet, posted to an Indian cooking website by Raj Nair, who got it from his grandmother, she knew it would work perfectly for the important dinner party Govindaswami prepares in the story.

The guests of honor at the dinner party, being from the American South, expect something very different when told the meal is to be fried chicken. The spicy mixture of chicken and potatoes combined with onions, dried red chiles, and curry leaves cause one dinner guest to mop her reddening face, and her young daughter to shriek pitifully and gulp down Kool-Aid. To cut the spiciness of the dish, serve the chicken with rice, bread, or yogurt on the side. Tolan adds that a sweet food—such as the Kool-Aid mentioned in the book—works well to reduce the heat of a spicy dish.

NOTE: Curry leaves, an essential ingredient in Indian cooking, are thin, shiny, and dark green. Although similar in appearance to bay leaves, curry leaves exude a unique aroma and flavor. There are no substitutes for curry leaves (curry powder, for example, should not be used). You can find fresh curry leaves at Indian grocers. They have a short shelf life but freeze nicely.

This version of the dish is only moderately hot. (Govindaswami would have used many more chiles!) You may wish to adjust the number of chiles you use to fit the group's taste.

2 pounds boneless chicken breasts, cut into ¼-inch cubes

3 onions, peeled and chopped into ½- to ¼-inch pieces

10 whole dried red chiles (see note)

1 tablespoon ground cinnamon

1 tablespoon ground cloves

2½ teaspoons salt, divided

1 cup water

5 medium potatoes

½ cup vegetable oil

½ cup (1 stick) lightly salted butter

½ teaspoon mustard seed

1 bunch curry leaves (see note)

1. In a large, nonstick skillet, mix the chicken, onions, chiles, cinnamon, cloves, 1½ teaspoons of salt, and water. Cover with a tight-fitting lid and cook about 1 hour over medium-low heat.
2. While the chicken is cooking, place the potatoes in a large saucepan and cover with water. Bring the water to a boil and cook potatoes 15–20 minutes, until their skins are soft and can be removed by hand. Let the potatoes cool slightly. Using rubber

gloves if the potatoes are too hot to handle, peel the potatoes either by hand or with a peeler. Thinly slice the potatoes.

3. In another large, nonstick skillet, heat the oil and butter until butter melts. Add a single layer of potatoes to the oil (you may need to fry half or a third at a time). Fry the potatoes in the oil and butter mixture until they turn medium brown, sprinkling 1 teaspoon of salt on the slices while frying. Remove to paper towels to drain. Place the mustard seed in the same pan, and simmer until broken in the oil remaining in the pan, then add the curry leaves.

4. Once the chicken is cooked, remove the chicken pieces to a bowl. Discard the chiles or, if desired, leave them in the pan to add color to the dish. Make a coarse paste out of the cooked onions by mashing them in the pan with a large spoon.

5. Add the cooked chicken to the mustard seed and curry leaves and fry 2–3 minutes. After the curry leaves darken, add the onion paste, mix thoroughly, and cook 5 minutes more. Add the fried potatoes and lower the heat. Cook an additional 5 minutes. Serve immediately.

YIELD: 6 SERVINGS

TRY IT!

Book Link: An Idea from Stephanie Tolan

AUNT LUCILLE'S BREATHING MEDITATION

When bad news visits the Applewhites, they clench their fists, rant, and stomp off. All, that is, except Aunt Lucille, who copes with stress through meditation. Below, Tolan guides us through a breathing meditation Aunt Lucille might have employed to take her mind off the troubles at home.

According to Lucille, breathing meditation calms your mind and body and can be useful in many situations:

- *When everyone around you is driving you crazy*
- *When you have to do something that makes you really nervous, like making an important phone call or taking an important test*
- *When you need to sleep but you can't stop thinking about how wonderful/awful today was or how wonderful/awful tomorrow will be*
- *At the beginning of a group activity, to get everyone in the group on the same wavelength and avoid conflict, and again at the end of a group activity, to defuse any conflict that may have happened anyway*

If you're doing breathing meditation with a group, someone can read the instructions while the others follow them.

If you're doing it alone, it's a good idea first to find yourself a quiet place where you won't be interrupted. (If you have a particularly difficult younger sibling, like Destiny, you may have to choose a closet, or lock yourself in the bathroom.)

Sit comfortably on the floor with your legs crossed, or in a chair with your back straight and both feet on the floor, your hands resting, palms up, on your knees. Closing your eyes may be a good idea. Take three long, deep breaths, breathing in through your nose and blowing the air out strongly through your mouth. (This should make a noise!)

Raise your shoulders toward your ears and let them drop once or twice, and let your body feel relaxed.

Take a long, very slow breath in, and when it feels as if you have taken in as much air as you can, try to take in just a little more. Then, let the air slowly out through your nostrils, and when you think it's all out, try to let out just a little more.

Then let yourself breathe normally, but focus your attention on each in-breath and each out-breath, feeling the air as it moves through your nostrils, being fully aware of how your body feels as you breathe in and out. Don't try to control your breaths; just be aware of them. Keep your full concentration only on your breath and the feeling of breathing in and breathing out. If you start to think of something else, like what you need to do next, or what the dog is barking at, or whether you're being able to do this, let that thought go, and refocus your attention on your breath. To help you do this, you might think breathing in as you breathe in, breathing out as you breathe out. Or you might count each breath in and each breath out, till you get to six, and then begin the count over. When other thoughts come, let them go.

At first, try to do this for three minutes or five minutes. Set a timer so that you don't have to try to keep track of the time. With practice, you may be able to do it for much longer.

But Lucille wants you to know that you don't always have to do the whole meditation. Even a few focused, slow, even breaths can help any stressful situation. Breathe while the test is being handed out and before you read the first question. Breathe while you're dialing—or answering—the phone. Breathe when someone is yelling at you—or when you're tempted to yell at someone else.

We have to breathe, Lucille reminds us, but focusing on our breaths may help us all feel more like the "radiant light beings" we really are.

TRY IT!

Act It Out

The Applewhites prepare a grand production of Rodgers and Hammerstein's 1959 musical *The Sound of Music,* and the book's theatrical theme gave the members of Pam Grover's Middle School Book Club at the Smoky Hill Public Library in Centennial, Colorado, an opportunity to take center stage. Grover selected a script adapted from *Sideways Stories from Wayside School* by Louis Sachar (Follett, 1978) on Aaron Shepard's Readers Theatre Page (www.aaronshep.com/rt/), a site that provides free original and adapted scripts of children's novels. The script Grover chose called for nine actors and took about twelve minutes to perform. Grover says that she sometimes borrows a video camera, tapes the kids acting, and then lets them watch their performances while eating popcorn.

Grover also showed a short clip from the film version of *The Sound of Music.*

Topics Discussed

- If you would want to attend a school similar to the Creative Academy
- The merits of homeschooling versus traditional education
- If the parents in the book were acting selfishly
- If you believe that Jake could change in such a short time

ASK IT!

Do you think Jake is a "bad kid," as he's been labeled by school officials, teachers, and even other kids? Are labels ever good?

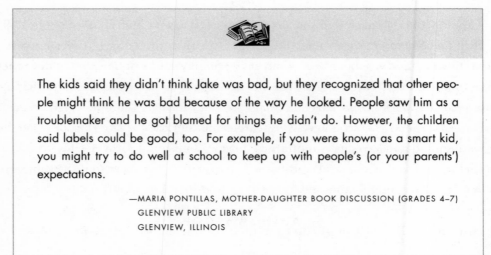

The kids said they didn't think Jake was bad, but they recognized that other people might think he was bad because of the way he looked. People saw him as a troublemaker and he got blamed for things he didn't do. However, the children said labels could be good, too. For example, if you were known as a smart kid, you might try to do well at school to keep up with people's (or your parents') expectations.

—MARIA PONTILLAS, MOTHER-DAUGHTER BOOK DISCUSSION (GRADES 4–7)
GLENVIEW PUBLIC LIBRARY
GLENVIEW, ILLINOIS

Grades 5–8

The View from Saturday

E. L. Konigsburg

Simon & Schuster, 1996
128 pages
Also available in paperback from Simon & Schuster
Fiction

Mrs. Olinski chooses four unlikely students to represent the Epiphany Middle School's sixth grade in the Academic Bowl, and her team has made it into the finals of the New York state competition. As Noah, Nadia, Ethan, and Julian take turns narrating their own stories, they reveal the reasons they were chosen for the team and the secrets of their success—as teammates and friends.

AUTHOR SCOOP

- Before writing children's novels, E. L. Konigsburg studied chemistry and taught science in a private girls school. She says she changed careers after becoming "more interested in what was going on inside my students' heads than what was going on inside the test tubes."

- Konigsburg began *The View from Saturday* by writing a story about Ethan Potter and Julian Singh meeting on a bus. At that point, she stopped writing and took a walk on the beach—where ideas for books often come to her. She says:

> When I write a book, I start a movie in my head, and there I was, walking along the beach, doing a rerun of what I had written. When I got to where Julian was telling Ethan about the B-and-B, I remembered that I had a story in my files—my mixed-up files—about a young man named Noah whose mother insists that he write his grandparents a bread-and-butter letter, a B-and-B letter. Then I remembered another short story I had about a dog named Ginger that plays the part of Sandy in the musical play *Annie*. And that led me to another story about an Academic Bowl team.
>
> Before I had finished my walk, I realized that these short stories were all united by a single theme. Taken together, they reinforced one another, and the whole became more than the sum of the parts.
>
> I knew that kids would love meeting one character and then two and three, and I also knew—because I had learned it from them—that they would enjoy fitting all the stories together as part of the adventure.

- Experiencing kindness, as the four sixth-graders in her novel do, is a critical developmental point for children, says Konigsburg. "A person must experience kindness to recognize it," she says. "He must recognize it in order to develop it. And just as there is a critical age by which we must speak in order to speak, there is a critical age by which we must experience kindness to be kind. And that critical age is before adolescence. That critical age is the cruelest year—grade six."

Watercress-Cucumber Tea Sandwiches

When we asked E. L. Konigsburg for a recipe, she respectfully declined. In her words:

I have developed a bad attitude toward the kitchen. Since my retirement from cooking, I sometimes assemble a meal from ready-to-eat products that come in easy-to-open cartons and which may or may not require microwaving. Please excuse me from supplying a recipe; I just noticed that my stove needs dusting.

In light of her feelings about cooking, we thought E. L. Konigsburg would enjoy this recipe featuring ready-made ingredients.

Just as Julian formally invited his team, The Souls, to tea, the members of the Kinloch Park Middle School Book Club of Miami, Florida, sent one another written invitations for their after-school *The View from Saturday* tea party and book discussion. In the style of The Souls' afternoon teas, they sampled finger sandwiches, pastries reflecting different cultures, such as rugelach and baklava (see our recipe, p. 356), and tea served with cream and sugar cubes. The assortment of sandwiches included watercress, cream cheese, and cucumber, as well as egg salad (see our recipe, p. 71).

NOTE: For these sandwiches, the bread should be thin. Our testers preferred Pepperidge Farm's very thin-sliced bread, but you can experiment with different varieties.

If preparing in advance, cover the sandwiches loosely with wax paper, drape a damp kitchen towel over the wax paper, and refrigerate to prevent them from drying out. Prepare the sandwiches as close to serving time as possible.

½ cucumber, peeled and thinly sliced

½ teaspoon salt

½ bunch watercress leaves (stems completely removed), finely chopped

4 ounces cream cheese, softened

8 slices best-quality white bread, preferably thinly sliced (see note)

1. In a bowl, place the cucumbers with the salt. Let stand for 30 minutes. Pat dry with paper towels.
2. In a bowl, combine the watercress and cream cheese.
3. Spread one side of 4 slices of bread lightly with the cream cheese mixture. Top with the sliced cucumbers and then another slice of bread.
4. Trim the crusts off sandwiches with a sharp knife, and cut each diagonally into quarters.

YIELD: 16 TEA SANDWICHES

TRY IT!

Calligraphy

Intrigued by references to calligraphy in *The View from Saturday*, Nicole Chase-Iverson, a librarian with the Sullivan Free Library in Chittenango, New York, introduced the art of decorative handwriting to her middle school book group. Chase-Iverson purchased some inexpensive calligraphy kits (available at crafts or discount stores) before the meeting and had books on calligraphy on display for the group to browse. She printed pre-lined sheets along with examples of uncial handwriting, a script with rounded capital letters, and highlighted pen strokes to demonstrate proper letter formation, which she downloaded from a calligraphy website (www.studioarts.net).

Chase-Iverson says uncial can be a challenging style for beginners, as it demands complex strokes to make letters authentic, and suggests choosing an easier alphabet, such as italic, for those trying calligraphy for the first time. She adds that there is a trick to learning calligraphy. "The pens are specially made with fine and thick tips, and pressure has to be applied just so for the lettering," she says. "After the group realized it would take practice before letters would look terrific, they enjoyed trying out all the letters and getting a feel for the tips of the pens."

MATERIALS

Calligraphy pens with ink, one per member

Instructions for using pens

Prelined sheets for practice, several per member

Examples of uncial handwriting with strokes highlighted

Distribute pens, ink, prelined sheets, and handwriting examples to group members. Review instructions and tips for forming letters. You might want to read Noah's tips on calligraphy from *The View from Saturday* during your meeting. Ask the group to practice letters on prelined sheets.

TRY IT!

Have a Tea Party

Carol Peckins, coordinator of Miami's Kinloch Park Middle School Book Club, read Chapter 7, "A Mad Tea Party," from Lewis Carroll's *Alice in Wonderland* (1865) during the group's *The View from Saturday* meeting. This chapter was "the first clue given for the invitation to Julian's tea party," says Peckins. Because it includes riddles, the students and teachers decided that a riddle would be the price of admission to the tea party, and each brought a riddle to share. "It was a huge success," says Peckins. "When students connect a book to their own experiences, to the world around them, or to another story they have read, they will experience comprehension at a deeper level."

A Character Web

"The characters and stories in *The View from Saturday* were so interwoven," says Carol Peckins. To help the group keep track of the different characters and their relationships, her members created a character web, in which students identify traits of characters in the story and organize them in a graphic format, borrowing an idea from Lori Licciardo-Musso's *Teaching with Favorite Newbery Books: Engaging Discussion Questions, Vocabulary Builders, Writing Prompts, and Great Literature Response Activities* (Scholastic, 1999).

Hold an Academic Bowl

You can hold an Academic Bowl to culminate your discussion of *The View from Saturday*, and explore the idea of how individuals can work successfully as a team. Form two teams and ask each team to search for answers to the Fifteen Questions with Thirty-six Answers at the end of the novel, using reference sources or the Internet. Allow each team time to share answers with the other team. Then discuss how each team became a team: What were the members' responsibilities, and how did they organize themselves?

You might focus your Academic Bowl on a particular theme or topic. Vickey Long, a librarian with the Basehor (Kansas) Community Library, chose to focus her book club's Academic Bowl on sea turtles and calligraphy, two topics presented in the novel. After sharing books on the topics, Long gave her club members questions on sea turtles, along with websites where the answers could be found (the club met in a computer lab, so they could find the answers during the meeting). Members of the club also had to learn how to write their names in Chinese calligraphy (see *Chinese Cinderella*, p. 268).

Topics Discussed

- How it feels to be compared with an older sibling who was a model student
- How it feels to be embarrassed by your parents' or grandparents' dress or actions, or the things they say
- How real estate development is affecting the life cycle of sea turtles in Florida
- How The Souls found acceptance by their peers and how they bonded as teammates

Why did the team come up with the name The Souls?

We explored why this name was chosen, how the group became a team, and what the benefits of the team membership were to the individuals.

—NICOLE CHASE-IVERSON, FAMILY LITERACY PROGRAM (FLiP) (GRADES 6–8)
SULLIVAN FREE LIBRARY
CHITTENANGO, NEW YORK

Walk Two Moons

Sharon Creech

Joanna Cotler, 1994
Available in paperback from HarperTrophy
288 pages
Fiction

Companion book: *Absolutely Normal Chaos* (Joanna Cotler, 1995)

Thirteen-year-old Salamanca Tree Hiddle, known as Sal, has spent the past year in Euclid, Ohio, where she reluctantly moved with her father after leaving behind her beloved home in Kentucky. Sal's mother has left and is not returning, so during the summer, Sal drives with her grandparents toward Lewiston, Idaho, to visit her. Along the way, Sal relates the story of her imaginative new friend in Euclid, Phoebe Winterbottom, who believes a lunatic lives in the neighborhood. As Phoebe's story unfolds, and as the cross-country trip continues, Sal's own tale of loss and displacement emerges.

AUTHOR SCOOP

- Sharon Creech set *Walk Two Moons* in places she had lived or visited, such as Euclid, Ohio, where Creech lived when she was in kindergarten and where Sal moves with her father, and Quincy, Kentucky, where the Creech family often used to visit relatives on their farm near the Ohio River, and which became the fictional town of Bybanks, Kentucky.

- When Creech was eleven, her family drove from South Euclid, Ohio, to Lewiston, Idaho, a trip that inspired Sal's cross-country journey in *Walk Two Moons*. The spectacular sights of that trip stayed with Creech, along with the souvenir she was allowed to purchase at an Indian reservation: leather moccasins.

- After finding the name "Salamanca" on a map of New York, Creech gave her character the full name Salamanca Tree Hiddle, which sounded Native American to her. As a child, Creech had been intrigued when a cousin told her she had a Native American ancestor, so she decided to make Sal partially Native American and curious about her roots, as she herself had been.

- Creech had submitted the manuscript of *Walk Two Moons* to her publisher twice, and both times had been told the story seemed unfinished. While struggling to strengthen the story line, one day Creech dug from her purse a crumpled fortune she had received at a Chinese restaurant. The message on the fortune—"Don't judge a man until you've walked two moons in his moccasins"—reminded Creech of the cross-country trip she had taken with her parents, the moccasins she had purchased, and her supposed Native American heritage, elements that she then incorporated into *Walk Two Moons*.

Author website: www.sharoncreech.com

Blackberry Pie

Watching Phoebe Winterbottom's mother make a blackberry pie awakens in Sal a memory of the time she and her own mother picked blackberries in Bybanks, Kentucky, and her mother announced that the berries set at "people height" on the vine were meant for people. That memory prompted another reminiscence of a time when Sal's mother left small dishes of blackberries as gifts for Sal and her father. "It's surprising all the things you remember just by eating a blackberry pie," she concludes.

Most commercial production of blackberries in the United States takes place in Oregon and Washington, but blackberries grow wild throughout the country on thorny bushes, called brambles, and ripen into plump, dark berries from May to August. Sharon Thompson compiled her favorite blackberry dishes in *Recipes from a Kentucky Blackberry Patch* (Windstone Farms, 1993), in which she recalls picking berries with her father in a briar patch in rural Kentucky—where Sal and her mother picked berries together.

The flavor of ripe blackberries stands on its own, but if you'd like an accompaniment, serve this pie with vanilla or cinnamon ice cream or sweetened whipped cream.

FOR THE PIE DOUGH

3 cups sifted all-purpose flour

2 tablespoons sugar

¼ teaspoon salt

1 cup solid vegetable shortening

6–8 tablespoons ice water

FOR THE FILLING

1 cup sugar

3 tablespoons quick-cooking tapioca

¼ teaspoon salt

6 cups fresh blackberries, washed and picked over, and divided

1. To make the pie dough: In a medium bowl, combine the flour, sugar, and salt. Cut in the shortening using a pastry cutter or fork until a pea-size coarse meal forms. Sprinkle with the ice water while mixing gently with a fork until the mixture forms a dough. The dough should not be wet but should form a ball when pressed together. A little more water may be added if needed.

2. Divide the dough in half. Form the dough into two flat discs. Cover with plastic wrap and refrigerate for at least 30 minutes, or until ready to use.

3. Preheat oven to 400° F.

4. To make the filling: In a medium saucepan, combine the sugar, tapioca, and salt, stirring well to remove lumps. Add 3 cups of the berries and mix well. Cook over very low heat about 7 minutes, until sugar melts, stirring constantly. Increase the heat to medium and cook about 6 minutes, until mixture just starts to boil.

5. Remove from the heat, stir in the remaining berries, and let cool.

6. Place one ball of dough on a lightly floured work surface (you will need a surface at least 15 inches square). With a lightly floured rolling pin, roll from the center outward into a circle roughly 14 inches in diameter. Carefully fold the dough in half, then again to form a triangle. Place the dough in an ungreased 9-inch pie plate, positioning it so the point of the triangle is in the center of the pie plate. Gently unfold. Trim the edges to within 1½ inches or so of the rim.

7. Pour the cooled berry mixture into the shell. Roll the remaining ball of dough in manner described above. Lay the rolled pastry over the filling, and trim the edges to within 1½ inches or so of the rim. Roll the bottom and top edges of the dough inward, pressing lightly to seal; with your thumb, indent at regular intervals to form a single fluted edge. With the tip of a sharp knife, cut several vents in the center of the top.

8. Place a sheet pan on the shelf below the pie to catch any dripping juice. Bake 20 minutes, then reduce heat to 350° F. and bake an additional 30 minutes, or until crust is golden brown and the juice comes through the top crust. Cool the pie on a wire rack 2–4 hours, until it reaches room temperature or is just barely warm.

YIELD: 1 (9-INCH) PIE, 6 TO 8 SERVINGS

Draw Your Soul

When they discussed *Walk Two Moons,* Carol Peckins asked members of her Kinloch Park Middle School Book Club in Miami to "draw their souls," an exercise Sal's teacher, Mr. Birkway, assigned his class. Peckins was prompted to try this activity after reading about it in *Teaching with Favorite Newbery Books: Engaging Discussion Questions, Vocabulary Builders, Writing Prompts, and Great Literature Response Activities* by Lori Licciardo-Musso (Scholastic, 1999).

Peckins began by opening to the chapter in *Walk Two Moons* titled "Souls," and reading the first two paragraphs aloud to the group. In this passage, Mr. Birkway instructs his students to complete, quickly and without giving it much thought, the exercise he is about to assign. Then Peckins distributed pencils and paper, and told participants they had fifteen seconds to draw their souls.

When the drawings were complete, Peckins read the rest of the chapter to the group, which she says was "really cool because group members could compare themselves to the students in Sal's class." As in the book, participants had each drawn central shapes, including hearts, flowers, happy and sad faces, a fish, and a broken heart with a teardrop hanging off the end for their "souls." Peckins says group members agreed that the exercise worked because they had so little time to think about how they felt or, as one participant put it, "pretend to be something else."

Map Sal's Journey

Carol Peckins gave members of her book club maps of the United States so, as they read, they could chart the route from Kentucky to Idaho traveled by Sal and her grandparents. The activity helped reinforce the knowledge of United States geography the students had learned in sixth grade, says Peckins, and gave them a glimpse of the larger world. "The students were especially impressed with Old Faithful and by mapping it, they felt like they were seeing it along with Sal and her grandparents," Peckins says. "Most of my students have never been out of South Florida, and this exercise helped to widen their horizons."

Topics Discussed

- The meaning of the message "Don't judge a man until you have walked two moons in his moccasins"
- If you have ever taken a trip with your grandparents, as Sal does
- Why Phoebe and Sal become friends
- If Sal had known the truth about her mother all along

ASK IT!

Were Phoebe Winterbottom's phobias realistic?

After Phoebe's mother left, Phoebe went overboard with her phobias, and this question led to a discussion of the clues Phoebe's mother left to indicate she was unhappy. The kids gave several examples of events in the story that showed how the mother was unappreciated. And they noticed that, as soon as the mother was gone, family members missed her terribly, and all their love for her was revealed.

—MARY SCHRADER, DIMOND BOOK CLUB (GRADES 4–7)
OAKLAND PUBLIC LIBRARY, DIMOND BRANCH
OAKLAND, CALIFORNIA

The House of the Scorpion

Nancy Farmer

Atheneum/Richard Jackson Books, 2002
Available in paperback from Simon Pulse
400 pages
Science Fiction

In a futuristic land named Opium, located between the United States and what was once known as Mexico, drug lord El Patrón presides over a powerful family dynasty, and creates clones of himself to extend his life. One of these clones, Matt Alacrán, grows up in a small cabin in the poppy fields, reared by Celia, the family cook. Matt inspires in El Patrón affection and nostalgia for his own youth, but is despised by members of the Alacrán family for his favored position with the patriarch, and shunned by a society that equates clones with livestock. When Matt's life is threatened, escape—with the help of Celia and Maria, his one ally in the Alacrán family—is his only chance of survival.

AUTHOR SCOOP

- Nancy Farmer grew up in the 1950s in Yuma, Arizona, a small town on the Mexican border, the setting for *The House of the Scorpion*. She lived in the hotel her father managed, and worked at the front desk from the age of nine, an experience she says helped prepare her for a life of writing because she heard so many stories from truck drivers, cowboys, and railroad workers. "My father took me to the American Legion hall on bingo night, and I heard a lot more stories there," she has said. "People were able to spin tales back then, and they taught me a lot."

- Farmer frequently draws upon her background as a scientist—she taught chemistry and biology while in the Peace Corps in India, and later worked as a freelance scientist in Mozambique and Zimbabwe—for ideas for her novels. Her curiosity about cloning inspired the theme of *The House of the Scorpion*. "I was intrigued by the cloning of Dolly the sheep and knew it was only a matter of time before someone tried cloning humans," she says. "To produce Dolly, the scientists had first created more than two hundred fifty failures, which died or were destroyed. My question in *The House of the Scorpion* was this: What do you do with two hundred fifty failed babies?"

- Many of the characters and places depicted in *The House of the Scorpion* were inspired by Farmer's childhood. As she told us:

  Celia's room was the bedroom of the mother of a friend. She, too, had a glow-in-the-dark crucifix and newspaper clippings glued to the wall. Celia is a portrait of her. Mr. Ortega is based on a music teacher who was completely deaf, but who could detect my mistakes by placing her hands on the piano. El Patrón has certain similarities to my mother, which is why Matt's emotions in the room full of sawdust are so realistic.

- To describe the setting of *The House of the Scorpion* more accurately, Farmer attempted to visit the Quitobanquito oasis on the Mexican border. This is the oasis described many times in the book and the setting for Matt's escape. Farmer had seen it as a child, but wasn't sure she remembered it.

  On Christmas Day, 2002, Farmer drove south from Ajo, Arizona, with her husband, Harold. As the road began to deteriorate into deep sand, Farmer noticed a man lying in the road. She cautiously approached, and discovered that the man—whose name, she learned, was José—was suffering from extreme thirst and cold. He had been part of a group of eight being led across the Mexican border by an illegal guide who had abandoned the group when the border patrol attacked in the middle of the night. She tells the story:

Now came the problem of what to do with him. There we were and there was José. We couldn't leave him behind to die. We couldn't take him back to Mexico because the road beyond disappeared under a sand dune. I made a quick decision. I loaded him into the backseat and Harold drove back to Ajo, swearing at me most of the way for getting him into this mess.

We left José at the edge of town with a bottle of water, a chocolate bar, and twenty dollars. I'm sure the border patrol found him quickly, because he didn't look remotely like a U.S. citizen. The next day, I asked a park ranger what we should have done. He said we should have left José with water and phoned the border patrol. We didn't have a cell phone, however, so that advice wouldn't have done us any good.

Harold refused to take me back out into the desert in case we met the seven other men. So I never did get to Quitobanquito Oasis and had to make up the description.

Nancy Farmer recommends:
The Devil's Highway by Luis Alberto Urrea (Little, Brown, 2004), which she calls "an absolutely accurate account of people crossing the Arizona desert from Mexico. This book is for people age twelve and up. The subject matter is too intense for younger children."

BOOK BITES

Mexican Red Salsa

Salsa, Spanish for "sauce," is a fresh or cooked mixture of tomatoes, onions, and chiles. Used as a dip or a condiment to main courses, salsa is extremely common in Mexican and Tex-Mex cooking, and is among the many traditional Mexican foods that Celia prepares for Matt in *The House of the Scorpion.*

Our salsa recipe, with lots of fresh tomatoes and one hot chile, makes a concoction with a mild kick, suitable for children's palates. Of course, feel free to adjust the amount of chiles according to your group's taste. The fresh lime juice and garlic give the salsa a robust flavor, and our testers (including the kids) couldn't get enough of it.

Serve this salsa with burritos (see p. 140), tacos (see p. 311), or as a dip with corn chips.

NOTE: To reduce the heat in the salsa, remove the seeds from the chile before chopping.

Whenever handling chiles, wear plastic or rubber gloves to protect your skin from the oil in them. Avoid direct contact with your eyes, and wash your hands thoroughly after handling.

3 large ripe tomatoes (about 2 pounds), cored and finely chopped

1 medium white onion, finely chopped

½ cup cilantro leaves, finely chopped

1 serrano chile or any fresh, hot green chile, cored, seeded (if desired), and finely chopped (see note)

1 medium garlic clove, minced

⅓ cup fresh lime juice (from about 3 medium limes)

Salt

In a medium bowl, mix all ingredients, including salt to taste. Cover and refrigerate at least 1 hour and up to 5 days, to blend flavors.

YIELD: 4 CUPS

Book Link: An Idea from Nancy Farmer

LISTEN TO CLASSICAL MUSIC

Both Matt and El Patrón enjoy classical music, and Farmer suggests that listening to the works of Mozart, Puccini, and Joaquín Rodrigo can provide insight into the aspirations and qualities of these characters.

I certainly had the following pieces of music in mind when I wrote the book. When I visualize a scene, I experience all the physical aspects of it—the heat, the smells, the sounds, the feel of things. I take music very seriously. Therefore, I would not recommend listening to only one section of a piece. The shape of a composition is as important as the plot in a novel.

For Matt: Listen to any Mozart sonata.

Both Matt and El Patrón are intensely musical, but only Matt was exposed to music early enough for it to have humanized him. Matt doesn't see music as an expression of power, but as something beyond his existence that can somehow redeem him. He loves Mozart for his orderliness and joy. What Matt senses in music—and El Patrón does not—is duende. *This Spanish word is difficult to translate: it means beauty, deep seriousness, and a sense of mortality.*

For El Patrón: Listen to Joaquín Rodrigo's *Concierto de Aranjuez* for guitar and orchestra.

Rodrigo was blind from early childhood, but received musical training in Valencia and Paris. The concierto is meant to portray a sixteenth-century Spanish nobleman.

It has the grandeur of someone who is not only brave and powerful, but courtly as well. El Patrón has wanted to be such a person his whole life.

Listen to the chorus from Puccini's *Madama Butterfly*.

At El Patrón's funeral, a choir of eejits [people with blunted intelligence and chips implanted in their brains] perform the humming chorus from Madama Butterfly. *This is an intensely moving piece of music full of* duende. *The joke is, neither the eejits nor El Patrón was capable of understanding it.*

All of the recordings may be available at local libraries.

Topics Discussed

- The current state of animal and human cloning, and how closely current conditions resemble the cloning described in the book
- If the cloning described in the book is likely to occur in the future
- Matt's strengths and weaknesses as a character
- The way characters of various nationalities, such as Irish and Mexican, are portrayed in the book

What really makes us human?

We discussed how clones like Matt are just as human as anyone else. Matt is capable of thinking for himself and feeling emotion, two qualities that are essential in our humanity. Although humans make mistakes, they are capable of learning from them, and we discussed how Matt learns from his mistakes. Finally, we talked about how our relationships with others make us human, and Matt clearly showed his humanity through his relationships with Celia and Maria. By the end of the novel, even they have trouble believing that he is less than human.

—DEBBIE BLUM, HOWARD COUNTY MIDDLE SCHOOL BOOK CLUB,
GIFTED AND TALENTED EDUCATION PROGRAM
ELLICOTT CITY, MARYLAND

Chinese Cinderella: The True Story of an Unwanted Daughter

Adeline Yen Mah

Delacorte, 1999
Also available in paperback from Laurel-Leaf
224 pages
Memoir

Companion books: *Falling Leaves: The Memoir of an Unwanted Chinese Daughter* (Wiley, 1998; adult version of *Chinese Cinderella*); *Chinese Cinderella and the Secret Dragon Society* (HarperCollins, 2004)

Adeline Yen Mah describes her childhood in China in the 1940s—years marked by pain, exclusion, and discrimination. When her mother dies two weeks after giving birth, Adeline is seen as bad luck. Shunned and mistreated by her siblings, father, and her father's new wife, Niang, Mah finds solace in her schoolwork, stories, and in her relationship with her devoted Aunt Baba.

- After she won an international writing competition at the age of fourteen, Adeline Yen Mah's father sent her to study in England, where she stayed to complete her medical degree. While practicing as an anesthesiologist in California, Mah wrote *Falling Leaves: The Memoir of an Unwanted Chinese Daughter,* an account of her painful childhood and the events following the deaths of her father and stepmother. The success of *Falling Leaves* convinced Mah to give up medicine in 1995 for a full-time writing career.

- After hearing from several young readers of *Falling Leaves,* Mah decided to craft a new memoir for a younger audience, which she hoped would comfort other unwanted children. She recalls:

> *At first, I was surprised that children would be reading* Falling Leaves, *let alone writing to me. When I read their letters, I realized that there are thousands of children out there who feel neglected and abandoned by their family. I wrote* Chinese Cinderella *and dedicated it to the unwanted child. I imagine them opening the pages of my book and meeting me as a ten-year-old in Shanghai. And I shall welcome each and every one of them with a smile and say, "How splendid of you to visit me! Come in and let me share with you my story, because I understand only too well the rankling in your heart and what you are going through."*

- Children with doting parents have told Mah her book helps them appreciate what they have, and Mah hopes *Chinese Cinderella* continues to help people recognize the good in their lives. She told us:

> *Unfortunately, all of us take the good things in life for granted. I want my readers to compare their childhoods with mine; and to recognize the importance of parental love in a person's life. I tell the children to throw their arms around their loving parents and express their appreciation. Many of us are not so lucky.*

Author website: www.adelineyenmah.com

Adeline Yen Mah's Pork and Chive Dumplings

When, during a family discussion of the next day's dinner menu, Aunt Baba proposes replacing the usual rice with pork dumplings, pandemonium erupts.

Those yummy dumplings were stuffed with pork, chives, and spring onions and were absolutely delicious! Big Brother shouted that he could eat fifty of them at one sitting. Second Brother immediately claimed sixty and Third Brother wanted sixty also. Big Sister ordered seventy. Big Brother told her she was already too fat. She screamed at him to shut up and they started to argue.

When you taste Mah's recipe, passed down by the cooks in the family, you'll understand what the fuss was about. These traditional Chinese dumplings are easy and fun to make, and disappear quickly. Mah often ate these delicious dumplings for dinner as a child growing up in Tianjin, and continues to enjoy them today. She reveals that, in spite of her brothers' and sister's inflated demands, they would eat between ten and twenty dumplings apiece; for the average person, the portion is eight to twelve.

NOTE: Although Mah provided instructions for making wrappers from scratch, she assures us that store-bought wrappers are just as delicious. "Homemade skins are usually thicker and more chewy than store-bought skins," she says, "but you can't really tell the difference in the taste." Mah recommends round *gyoza* (Japanese dumpling) wrappers, but round or square wonton wrappers, although thinner than *gyoza* wrappers, may also be used.

Chinese chives have a strong, garlicky flavor and their stems are flat and skinny rather than hollow, like regular chives. They are available at Asian markets. If Chinese chives are not available, an equivalent amount of Napa cabbage may be substituted. You may substitute ground chicken, beef, or tofu for the pork. Use extrafirm tofu and press the liquid out of it before crumbling.

Instead of boiling, you may steam dumplings in a steamer for ten minutes. Make sure to separate the dumplings in the steamer to avoid sticking.

Dumplings may be frozen before cooking. To freeze: Arrange in single layers on cookie sheets lined with wax paper, and place in freezer. After dumplings are frozen, they may be transferred to plastic freezer bags. To cook frozen dumplings: Bring a large pot of water to a boil. Place the frozen dumplings in the water and bring to a boil a second time. Add two cups of cold water and bring everything to a boil for a third time. Remove dumplings with a slotted spoon.

FOR THE FILLING

½ pound Chinese chives (see note)

½ pound minced pork

1 large egg white

½ teaspoon minced fresh ginger

½ teaspoon minced scallions

3 tablespoons light soy sauce

1 teaspoon dry sherry or Chinese rice wine

1 tablespoon sesame oil

FOR THE DIPPING SAUCE

1 tablespoon light soy sauce

2 tablespoons white vinegar

2 tablespoons grated fresh ginger

FOR THE WRAPPERS

2 cups sifted all-purpose flour

¼ teaspoon salt

½ cup boiling water

1. To make the filling: Bring a medium pot of water to a boil. Add the chives and blanch 30 seconds. Plunge the chives into an ice water bath, then drain.
2. Place the chives in a thin cotton cloth or several layers of paper towels and wring the water out of them. Mince finely.
3. In a medium bowl, mix the chives with the pork, egg white, ginger, scallions, soy sauce, sherry or rice wine, and oil. Stir to blend. Cover and refrigerate while preparing the dipping sauce and wrappers.
4. To make the dipping sauce: Combine ingredients in a small bowl.
5. To make the wrappers: Place the flour in a mixing bowl. Add the salt and boiling

water. Stir well, then turn out onto a floured surface and knead about 10 minutes, until dough is smooth.

6. Cover the dough with a damp cloth and let rest for another 10 minutes.

7. Roll the dough into a long round tube about 1 inch in diameter. Cut into 24 equal pieces. Roll each dough piece into a circular shape about 3¾ inches in diameter. The center should be thicker than the sides.

8. To assemble the dumplings: Place 1 tablespoon of filling in the center of each wrapper. Using your fingertip, moisten the edge of the wrapper with water. Fold the wrapper in half and pinch edges together to seal tightly. Repeat to form 24 dumplings.

9. Bring a large pot of water to a boil. Place the dumplings in boiling water and allow water to return to a boil. Add 1 cup of cold water and return to a boil. Remove the dumplings with a slotted spoon. Serve immediately with dipping sauce.

YIELD: 24 DUMPLINGS, 2 TO 3 SERVINGS

TRY IT!

Chinese Calligraphy

The art of calligraphy figures prominently in Chinese culture, and also in *Chinese Cinderella*. When, as a girl, Mah proclaims the study of Chinese language a waste of time, her grandfather Ye Ye rebukes her with detailed examples of "the wisdom and beauty" of the character-based language. Mah peppers the text of her book with Chinese characters, explaining in her Author's Note that "Chinese calligraphy evokes a greater emotional response than the same word lettered in alphabet."

Give members of your book club a chance to try their hand at Chinese calligraphy. Purchase inexpensive felt-tip calligraphy pens and calligraphy paper at an art-supply store. (See "Calligraphy," p. 250, for more ideas.) Visit a Chinese calligraphy website. Ask group members to find how their names are spelled in Chinese characters, and use the calligraphy pens to copy their names on the paper.

Bites from the Book

In addition to Chinese egg rolls and tea, Gale Ree served lychee fruit to members of her Mother-Daughter Book Club at the Palatine (Illinois) Public Library. Ree says the lychee fruit was the closest equivalent she could find to the dragon's-eye fruit, or longan, that Mah names as her favorite in *Chinese Cinderella*. Both lychees and dragon's-eye fruit are native to Southeast Asia, but lychees are more readily available in America, and can be purchased at many grocery stores. Dried dragon's-eye fruit can be purchased on the Internet.

Learn About Foot-Binding

If descriptions of Grandmother Nai Nai's bound feet spark the group's curiosity, bring information about the ancient Chinese practice of foot-binding to your meeting. *Aching for Beauty: Footbinding in China* by Wang Ping (University of Minnesota, 2000) is written for adults, but contains drawings and photographs related to foot-binding that young adults may find intriguing. Check your local library for other titles on the topic.

Topics Discussed

- Similarities and differences between Mah's story and the traditional fairy tale of Cinderella, and why Mah titles her book *Chinese Cinderella*
- How Chinese culture compares with your culture, especially around traditions of marriage

- Who could be deemed the "most despicable" person in the book, and how the various people in Mah's life contributed to her suffering
- How authors decide which events to include and exclude when writing a memoir

ASK IT!

What similarities and differences do you notice between Chinese culture as depicted in Chinese Cinderella *and your own culture?*

The Hmong teens in our group were very engaged in the discussion because of the comparisons they made between the Chinese and Hmong cultures. They noted that, in Hmong culture, the youngest child is always respected the most, even spoiled, while the oldest gets scapegoated and blamed for everything. The teens thought that, as the youngest child, Adeline might have been treated very differently if her mother hadn't died.

—NONG LEE, HMONG TEEN BOOK CLUB
HENNEPIN COUNTY LIBRARY
MINNETONKA, MINNESOTA

Eragon (Inheritance Trilogy, Book One)

Christopher Paolini

Alfred A. Knopf, 2003
Also available in paperback from Alfred A. Knopf
544 pages
Fantasy

Sequel: *Eldest* (Alfred A. Knopf, 2005)

Deep in a forest in the land of Alagaësia, a farm boy named Eragon finds a shiny rock that soon hatches into a beautiful blue-scaled dragon, Saphira. Unbeknownst to Eragon, Saphira has waited to hatch until her chosen Rider has arrived. As Saphira grows and Eragon learns to ride on her winged back, they begin to read each other's thoughts and their loyalty and affection deepen.

Galbatorix, the self-declared king of Alagaësia, learns of Saphira's birth and dispatches his men to kill Eragon, whose powers threaten his rule. Eragon flees, together with Saphira and Brom, the village storyteller. Traveling through lands of dwarves and vicious Urgals, monsters faithful to the king, and finally arriving in the mighty elven city of Tronjheim, Eragon matures as a warrior and struggles to understand his past and his destiny.

- Christopher Paolini was homeschooled by his mother, and wrote the first draft of *Eragon* at age fifteen, after earning his General Educational Development (GED) degree and before attending college. Paolini says he had no intention of publishing his story, but after many revisions decided to self-publish the book. The stepson of author Carl Hiaasen (see *Hoot*, p. 217) bought a copy while vacationing in Montana, and Hiaasen liked it enough to bring it to the attention of his editor at Knopf, who published *Eragon*.

- Paolini says that *Eragon* was inspired by an image in a book by the fantasy novelist Bruce Coville. He recalls:

> *It was the image—inspired by* Jeremy Thatcher, Dragon Hatcher *by Bruce Coville—of a dragon egg appearing before a young man deep within a dark pinewood forest. I knew nothing beyond that, only that I empathized with that nameless youth and that I wanted to, no, needed to find out what happened to him next.*

- Paolini was enthralled with imagining the details of a dwarf culture in *Eragon* and *Eldest*. He says:

> *One of the most enjoyable parts of writing the Inheritance trilogy has been exploring my dwarves' culture. In many fantasy stories, dwarves are only minor characters. I wanted to find out more about their history and customs and discover what their homes, family, women, and children are like. Thus, in* Eldest *readers learn how dwarves make their bows out of horn; visit Celbediel, the dwarves' most important temple; hear several dwarf riddles, and see more of their race. I will revisit the dwarves in the final book of the trilogy.*
>
> *In fact, I like the dwarves and the language I invented for them so much, I told my mom that if I could live in Alagaësia, I know exactly what I would do: I would make my home in the city-mountain of Tronjheim and write dwarf operas!*

- Paolini created three languages for Eragon, using Old Norse as the basis for his Elven language, and inventing all the Dwarf and Urgal words himself.
- Paolini lives in Paradise Valley, Montana, where the huge Beartooth Mountains inspired the scenery—including the ten-mile-high Beor Mountains—in *Eragon*.
- While he was writing *Eragon,* Paolini often listened to classical music by Beethoven, Mahler, and Wagner. He composed the final battle scene with *Carmina Burana*, a thrilling cantata by German composer Carl Orff, playing in the background.
- Paolini drew the map of Alagaësia and sketched the dragon's eye that appears inside the hardcover edition of the book.
- Paolini says he created the character of Angela the herbalist to lampoon his sister, Angela. The character turned out to be so interesting that Paolini decided to include her in the other two books of the trilogy.

Author website: www.alagaesia.com
Film adaptation:
Eragon (Fox, 2006), rated PG, 103 minutes

BOOK BITES

Talita Paolini's Honeyed Carrots

During his travels, Eragon eats so much meat that he eventually craves vegetables. According to Paolini:

When Eragon traveled with Brom, they lived primarily on fresh and dried meat; Brom packed a good supply of both beef and deer jerky to sustain them on their journey. How-

ever, by the time they arrived at the coastal city of Teirm, Eragon was so sick of meat, he considered any kind of fruit or vegetable a delicacy, even boiled cabbage.

When we asked Paolini to suggest a vegetable dish Eragon might like, he contributed a recipe for his mother Talita Paolini's heavenly honeyed carrots. Christopher Paolini says, "When Eragon visited the elves, he was served a delicious dish of sweetened carrots. Replicating the subtle floral essence that the elves' honey imparts to the dish is impossible in our world, but this recipe comes close."

1 pound carrots, peeled and sliced into ½-inch rounds

¼ cup water

1 tablespoon butter

1 tablespoon brown sugar

2 tablespoons honey (or more to taste)

Pinch salt, or to taste

Place all ingredients in a pot, cover, and bring to a boil. Boil 6 minutes, or until just tender. Uncover pot and boil off excess liquid, stirring occasionally, until a syrup coats the carrots, 15–20 minutes.

YIELD: 4 SERVINGS

TASTE IT!

Dragon Snot (Sherbet and Soda)

At her *Eragon* party, held at the Wright Memorial Public Library in Dayton, Ohio, librarian Jennifer Sommer served "dragon snot," a scoop of lime or lemon sherbet topped with a yellow-colored soda. Sommer served her "snot" in individual cups, but it can also be served in a punch bowl. Yum!

Book Link: An Idea from Christopher Paolini

IMAGINARY EGGS

Christopher Paolini suggests that book club members create imaginary eggs, write about them, and share their stories when they meet to discuss *Eragon*.

Distribute blank sheets of paper and markers or crayons, and ask each child to draw an imaginary egg. Then, place the pictures facedown, mix them, and let each child select from the pile at random. Ask participants to write a short story or poem about the egg they have "found," and what the egg becomes when it hatches. The stories and poems can then be shared, or saved to discuss at the next meeting.

MAKE IT!

Dragon Beanbags

Jennifer Sommer, teen librarian at the Wright Memorial Public Library in Dayton, Ohio, asked students in grades six through twelve to bring the most fantastical fabric they could find to the library's *Eragon* party. Sommer made and distributed cardboard patterns of dragons (to make the patterns, Sommer traced a dragon shape from Accu-Cut, a producer of die-cutting machines for schools and libraries, but any dragon pattern will do), which each child used to outline and cut their fabric into two copies of the same dragon shape. Participants then glued around the edges of the two dragon shapes using hot-glue guns, stuffed them with rice, and finally glued them shut.

Although open to all children in grades six through twelve, this library celebration attracted only boys. "The boys started throwing their beanbags around the room as soon as they were done!" Sommer recalls.

Discover Your Dragon's Color

Readers intrigued by the relationship between Eragon and Saphira can discover what qualities their own companion dragons might possess. Ask book club members to take an online interactive "dragon color" quiz (www.shurtugal.com, click on "Fun Stuff") to reveal the color—and qualities—of their companion dragons. Then ask them to draw their dragons.

Topics Discussed

- The struggle between good and evil in the book, in our society, and around the world
- Eragon's strengths and weaknesses, and whether you would have made similar decisions
- Whether, if you were given the chance to know your fate, you would choose to hear it, as Eragon did
- Whether you believe that some people have a destiny to fulfill or a special reason for living

How do you think being a Dragon Rider would feel?
Would you like to become a Rider?

The kids thought it would feel scary, exciting, strange, and even humbling. Some felt the responsibility of being a Rider would be too great. Others thought the benefits would outweigh the heavy responsibilities. It would never be boring, and it would be great to have magical powers and to talk to dragons. Some wanted to be a rider just for a while and then go back to normal.

—ANN NELSON, NEWTON SENIOR HIGH SCHOOL BOOK CLUB
NEWTON, IOWA

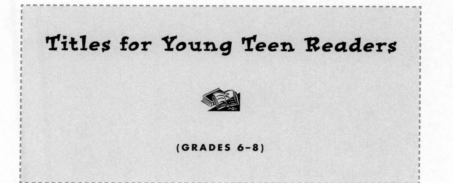

Titles for Young Teen Readers

(GRADES 6–8)

Al Capone Does My Shirts by Gennifer Choldenko

Flipped by Wendelin Van Draanen

The Skin I'm In by Sharon G. Flake

Kira-Kira by Cynthia Kadohata

The Outsiders by S. E. Hinton

Tangerine by Edward Bloor

Ender's Game by Orson Scott Card

The Giver by Lois Lowry

Monster by Walter Dean Myers

The Sisterhood of the Traveling Pants by Ann Brashares

Stuck in Neutral by Terry Trueman

Al Capone Does My Shirts

Gennifer Choldenko

Putnam, 2004
Available in paperback from Bloomsbury
240 pages
Historical Fiction

When his father takes a job as a prison guard in 1935, twelve-year-old Moose and his family relocate to Alcatraz Island, home of the federal penitentiary for notorious convicted criminals such as gangster Al Capone. Moose must care for his sister, Natalie, who has autism, try to meet his parents' demanding expectations, and contend with the trouble-seeking prison warden's daughter, Piper.

AUTHOR SCOOP

- A newspaper article in the *San Francisco Chronicle* about children who grew up on Alcatraz Island inspired *Al Capone Does My Shirts*. After reading the article, Gennifer Choldenko, who lives in the Bay Area, immediately signed up to work on Alcatraz. Her job was to give tours of the island, answer visitor questions, and help with crowd control. While on Alcatraz, she conducted research on all aspects of life on the island in 1935. Choldenko describes her research experience:

> *I interviewed people who grew up on the island, read handwritten records of inmates, guards, and kids who lived on the island. I went to an Alcatraz Island Alumni Day, where I heard dozens of old Alcatraz residents (from both sides of the bars) speak. I hobnobbed with several of the many Alcatraz heads, who know every arcane fact about the place. I read dozens and dozens of books and spent countless hours roaming the island imagining how it would feel to be Moose.*

- According to Choldenko, the title for the book was one example of many "bizarre coincidences" that occurred in the course of her research:

> *One day I'd come up with an incredible wacky idea, and a few days later I'd discover something remarkably similar actually happened. . . .*
>
> *Al Capone's first job on Alcatraz was working the mangle in the laundry facility that serviced all of the people who lived on Alcatraz, including the guards, their wives, and children. And so I figured if I were a kid living on Alcatraz I'd tell my friends, "Al Capone does my shirts." When the manuscript was finished, one of the historians we used to vet* Al Capone Does My Shirts *asked me why I didn't use the real quote. "What real quote?" I asked. "Al Capone does my shorts," he said. Apparently World War II GIs sometimes used the phrase "Al Capone does my shorts" to indicate they were stationed in San Francisco.*

- Choldenko describes why her favorite characters are Theresa, Moose, and Piper:

> *I love Theresa because she reminds me of me when I was seven. I was quirky and pesty and I had to be included in absolutely everything. I like Moose because he has a funny way of seeing the world. He's kind and intelligent and he tries so hard to do the right thing. And I like Piper because she's never*

apologetic. She's clever, callous, and cunning, not to mention supremely self-centered. But she's also confident, extremely bright, and full of great ideas. What I like best about Piper is how much she loves Moose. Something about the relationship between Moose and Piper fascinates me. There's a magnetic attraction that brings both their personalities into balance somehow.

- The characters Moose and Natalie have roots in Choldenko's personal experiences. She explains:

  Like the main character Moose, I grew up with a sibling who had autism. And though I am not Moose and my sister is not Natalie, there's no doubt that this experience fueled the book.

  But the fact that this book is "close to home" gave it some additional baggage as well. It was extremely confusing and terribly frustrating to grow up with a sibling who had autism. I really wanted to reach out to other children who are the siblings of children with problems. It was very important to me that the book ring true to those kids.

Author website: www.choldenko.com

Gennifer Choldenko recommends:
Holes by Louis Sachar (Farrar, Straus & Giroux, 1998; see p. 160), which she calls one of her "all-time favorite" middle grade novels. "I wouldn't say it has similar themes, but both *Holes* and *Al Capone Does My Shirts* are about prisons," she adds.

BOOK BITES

Aunt Lora's Oatmeal Coconut Cookies

Gennifer Choldenko confesses to being a "cookie monster" (see "Natalie, Lemon Cake, and How Characters Are Born," p. 289) and shared one of her favorite cookie recipes from her cousin's wife, Lora, whom Choldenko's children affectionately call Aunt Lora. "Aunt Lora is the best cookie cook I know," Choldenko said, "and these are my favorite of all her many yummy recipes!"

NOTE: These cookies cook quickly and burn easily, so keep an eye on them. Baking cookies on parchment paper or a silicone baking mat placed on a baking sheet can reduce the cookies' tendency to spread, burn, and stick to the baking sheet.

½ cup (1 stick) unsalted butter, melted and cooled

¼ cup sugar

1 cup quick-cooking rolled oats, uncooked

¼ cup all-purpose flour

1 teaspoon baking powder

¼ cup macadamia nuts, chopped

½ teaspoon coconut extract

1 large egg

1. Preheat oven to 375° F. Grease a cookie sheet lightly with butter, or place parchment paper or a baking mat on an ungreased cookie sheet (see note).
2. Pour the melted butter into a mixing bowl. Add the sugar, oats, flour, baking powder, nuts, coconut extract, and egg, and mix by hand until blended.
3. Drop by teaspoonfuls onto prepared cookie sheet, spaced at least 2 inches apart, as the cookies spread while baking. Bake 5–8 minutes, or until cookies are lightly golden brown around edges.
4. Allow cookies to cool on baking sheet 5 minutes. Remove to wire rack to cool completely.

YIELD: APPROXIMATELY 2½ DOZEN COOKIES

Book Link: An Idea from Gennifer Choldenko

NATALIE, LEMON CAKE, AND HOW CHARACTERS ARE BORN

Gennifer Choldenko explained how she developed Natalie's character—and how Natalie came to love lemon cake.

I based the character Natalie on my sister, Gina, who had autism. When I say I "based" Natalie on Gina, what I mean is, I used some mannerisms Gina had and I "borrowed," as the terrific novelist Lorrie Moore once said, "a piece of Gina's soul." But that doesn't mean Natalie "was" Gina. She wasn't. A huge part of Natalie was simply made up.

In "making up" characters, I've discovered that I must "try on" names, addresses, clothes, hairstyles, personal characteristics, and food preferences. I know when I "try something on" a character that it's a good fit, because I can't take it off again. The right name, for example, "becomes" that character's name and then I couldn't dream of changing it. But if I can easily change a character's name from Herbert, say, to Ralph, that means I haven't found the right name.

I remember once I was in a critique group and I read a chapter of a novel that had a boy with a leg brace in it. One of my fellow writers suggested I change the character to a boy with an arm brace because the leg brace was getting in the way of the scene. I thought she was out of her mind. I could no more change a character's brace like that than I could have in real life. Characters are extremely real to me and I can't arbitrarily make changes to anything about them, simply because it may be more convenient to a scene.

Since Natalie was based on Gina, I started by giving Natalie Gina's food preferences. Gina's favorite foods were chocolate cake, eggs cooked sunny-side up, and strawberries. But when I "tried" Gina's favorite foods on Natalie, weird as this is going to sound, Natalie didn't like them.

Next I tried pralines, because my great-aunt Helen loved pralines, but they didn't quite work. Pralines didn't seem like Natalie. And then I thought of chocolate-chip cookies, peanut butter cookies, oatmeal cookies, and coconut cookies because I am a cookie monster and I simply love cookies. But alas, I am not Natalie. She didn't have a passion for any of those foods. Then one day, my son, Ian, who is a very picky eater, discovered he loved lemon cake, so I decided to try lemon cake. As soon as I tried lemon cake, everything fell into place. There was no doubt about it. Natalie loved lemon cake.

Try the Lemon Bundt Cake recipe on p. 296 for a taste of Natalie's favorite treat!

TASTE IT!

Bites from the Book

The fifth- and sixth-graders in the Charles E. Smith Jewish Day School Parent-Child Book Club in Rockville, Maryland, sampled foods they found in *Al Capone Does My Shirts* and created cards describing foods to place next to the dishes. Group facilitator Stacey Weinberg says members tasted a smorgasbord of characters' favorites: the lemonade Piper brought to Natalie's party; the lemon cake Natalie loved; the cheese sandwiches Moose ate during his raid of the fridge; the bread-and-butter sandwiches he would eat while reading; the graham cracker sandwiches Natalie ate (and fed half of to the birds); and even the leftover pancakes Moose ate while his mother talked to him.

Book Links: Ideas from Gennifer Choldenko

BUSINESS PLANS FOR PIPER

Below, Gennifer Choldenko suggests a few activities that book clubs might enjoy.

- *Draw the poster Piper might have used to sell the convict laundry service to the kids at school. Remember, the sign should be compact and portable, as Piper had to hide it in her book bag during class.*
- *What are some ways other than the laundry service that Piper might make money on Alcatraz? Devise several moneymaking ideas for Piper. Piper was a really fun character to write, because she had big ideas and she would do almost anything, so think BIG here.*

BUSINESS PLANS FOR PIPER

Members of the Charles E. Smith Jewish Day School Book Club had fun coming up with ideas and posters promoting Piper's next moneymaking venture. One poster advertised convict baseballs for fifty cents apiece; others were for "convict cooking" (you could get a meal cooked by an inmate for fifteen cents) or flowers or vegetables grown by prisoners. One member even suggested people give Piper pictures of themselves and choose a public enemy with whom they could have their picture taken. The posters provided decorations for the bare windows outside the school library.

Give Out Book-Related Favors

As a reward for reading the book and coming to the discussion, Stacey Weinberg gives favors to students in the Charles E. Smith Jewish Day School Book Club. For their *Al Capone Does My Shirts* meeting, Weinberg purchased beanbag baseballs that served as table decorations. Weinberg says because baseball was very important to Moose and there was a lot of interest in convict baseballs in the group, each child received a "convict baseball" to take home, along with a book of Sudoku puzzles, since Natalie is so involved with numbers in the story.

Topics Discussed

- What it would be like to be free when other residents of your community are in prison
- If it was fair for Moose's mother to give him so much responsibility for his sister's care, and if you have ever had to care for a sibling
- Who wrote the word "done"
- How your ideas about autism changed after reading this book

Would you like to have lived on Alcatraz during this time period?

I showed the book club participants slides taken during a trip to Alcatraz. Seeing pictures of the actual locations described in the book spawned an excellent discussion about what life on Alcatraz would have been like. They were intrigued by the prison cells and the path the guards' families would have taken to the ferryboat for excursions to the mainland. They also found it amazing that a prison, exercise yard, and fence could be stuck on a rock in the middle of San Francisco Bay.

—JOANNE ZILLMAN, BOOK BEAT BOOK CLUB (GRADES 4–8)
BATAVIA PUBLIC LIBRARY
BATAVIA, ILLINOIS

NOTE: Choldenko recommends the San Francisco Public Library's online historical photo archive for photos of Alcatraz.

Flipped

Wendelin Van Draanen

Alfred A. Knopf, 2001
Available in paperback from Alfred A. Knopf
224 pages
Fiction

Julianna Baker is smitten with Bryce Loski from the day he moves to the neighborhood. Bryce's brilliant blue eyes and winning smile inspire Juli to do whatever it takes to be near him, while Bryce dodges Juli's annoying advances. But as eighth grade draws to a close, Juli begins to question what lies beneath Bryce's good looks, and Bryce sees Juli—and his own family—in a new light.

AUTHOR SCOOP

- Like Juli, Wendelin Van Draanen developed a childhood crush on a classmate and struggled to gain his attention. She recalls:

When I was in kindergarten, I developed the biggest crush on a neighbor boy named Charlie. He was the cutest thing I'd ever seen. Dark hair. Brown eyes. And I just couldn't help it—I chased him around school and tried to lay kisses on him.

By fourth grade, I'd long figured out that the way to express your crush was not to run around trying to tackle him or kiss him. No, instead, you should beat him in sports.

Okay, okay. So by junior high I realized that approach was wrong, too. I mean, really, what you're supposed to do is toilet-paper your crush's house, right?

Looking back, Van Draanen understands why her "crush" didn't return her affections. "Now I look back and know why he ran—I was a total embarrassment!" she says. "But I also wonder why I had such an enormous crush on the guy. Sure, he was cute. And nice. But I was so over the top about him and, really, I didn't know much about him."

- A former high school computer science teacher, Van Draanen observed that her students also had tendencies to develop crushes. She says:

  When I became a schoolteacher, I recognized similar patterns of crushing in my students. And trying to tell them, "Honey, he is so NOT worth it," or "Buddy, she may be hot, but that's all she's got," didn't have any effect, because there's just an age at which you're convinced that adults do not, and cannot, understand what you're going through.

- Van Draanen explains why *Flipped* is not set in a specific time or place:

  I wanted Flipped *to feel contemporary, but not time- or location-specific. What these characters go through is not unique to any generation or any location, but I wanted the story to resonate with today's youth. I imagine the characters to be a hybrid of people I knew growing up, and teens that went through similar emotional turmoil while they were students of mine.*

- As a child, Van Draanen disliked "preachy" books and appreciated the use of humor. In her writing she tries to highlight the humorous side of difficult situations. She says:

Flipped *deals with some serious issues, and I felt it was essential to weave humor throughout the story to balance out the tone of the book. Growing up is quite a drama when we're in the middle of it, but if we can step back from it, we can see that it's also a comedy of errors.*

- Van Draanen hopes *Flipped* will convey her beliefs about happiness and courage to young readers.

Flipped *is my way of talking to kids; of showing them the merits of seeing someone for who they are instead of what they look like. It's my way of explaining what I believe to be the foundation of long-term happiness; of demonstrating how it may take time, but in the end being who you are and standing tall for what you believe will yield an inner strength that will guide you to the person who is truly right for you.*

Author website: www.wendelinvandraanen.com
Wendelin Van Draanen recommends:
Stargirl by Jerry Spinelli (Alfred A. Knopf, 2000)

BOOK BITES

Lemon Bundt Cake

In addition to egg sandwiches and chick-shaped sugar cookies, the Reading Maniacs of Los Angeles enjoyed a lemon Bundt cake during their discussion of *Flipped*. They were inspired by the scene in which Juli's mother welcomes the Loskis to the neighborhood with a warm lemon Bundt cake, covered with confectioners' sugar and "sending sweet lemon smells into the air."

In our search for luscious lemon Bundt cake recipes, we found a clear favorite in *Cook's Illustrated* (number 78, January/February 2006). This version gets its intense lemon flavor from lots of lemon peel and a delicious lemon-buttermilk glaze, and maintains a moistness that other cakes lack. We think it's fit to welcome newcomers—or a book club—to the neighborhood.

NOTE: For this recipe, even after the lemon peel is grated, it should be minced into little specks and then soaked in the lemon juice. This softens the peel and prevents fibrous strands in the cake.

To store, wrap the cake tightly in plastic wrap and keep at room temperature. If eaten on the day it is baked, the cake is light and fluffy; by the following day it will assume a denser texture, similar to pound cake.

Serve alone or with slightly sweetened berries.

FOR THE CAKE

Grated peel of 3 lemons

3 tablespoons fresh lemon juice

3 cups all-purpose flour

1 teaspoon baking powder

½ teaspoon baking soda

1 teaspoon salt

1 teaspoon vanilla extract

¼ cup buttermilk, preferably low-fat

3 large eggs plus 1 large yolk, at room temperature

18 tablespoons (2¼ sticks) unsalted butter, softened

2 cups granulated sugar

FOR THE GLAZE

2–3 tablespoons fresh lemon juice

1 tablespoon buttermilk

2 cups confectioners' sugar

1. To make the cake: Preheat oven to 350° F. Grease and flour a Bundt pan, or spray pan with a cooking spray that contains flour, such as Pam for Baking.
2. Finely mince the grated lemon peel and combine with the lemon juice (see note). Set aside to soften for 10–15 minutes.
3. In a large bowl, whisk together the flour, baking powder, baking soda, and salt. In a medium bowl, combine the lemon juice mixture, vanilla, and buttermilk. In a small bowl, gently whisk the eggs and yolk to combine.
4. In a medium bowl of an electric mixer, cream the butter and sugar at medium-high speed about 3 minutes, until pale and fluffy. Reduce to medium speed and add half of the eggs, mixing about 15 seconds, until incorporated. Repeat with the remaining eggs. Reduce to low speed. Starting and ending with the dry ingredi-

ents, add the flour and buttermilk mixtures alternately, mixing about 5 seconds, until just incorporated after each addition. Remove the bowl from the mixer and fold the batter once or twice with a rubber spatula to incorporate any remaining flour.

5. Scrape the batter into the prepared pan. Set on the lower-middle rack of the oven and bake 45–50 minutes, until the cake is golden brown and a tester inserted in the center comes out clean.

6. To make the glaze: While the cake is baking, whisk 2 tablespoons lemon juice, the buttermilk, and confectioners' sugar until smooth, adding more lemon juice gradually as needed until the glaze is thick but still pourable.

7. Cool cake in pan on a wire rack set over a baking sheet 10 minutes, then turn the cake onto the rack. Pour half of the glaze over the warm cake and let cool 1 hour; pour remaining glaze evenly over the top of cake and continue to cool to room temperature, at least 2 hours.

YIELD: 1 (10-INCH) CAKE, 10 TO 12 SERVINGS

TRY IT!

Book Links: Tasty Ideas from Wendelin Van Draanen

If you're looking for ideas for foods to serve with your *Flipped* discussion, you're not alone. Many book clubs enjoyed foods mentioned in the book or suggested by the book's poultry theme. Wendelin Van Draanen offers her own culinary inspirations below.

- Blackberry cheesecake and pecan pie, the desserts Mrs. Baker brings to the Loskis' house for the dinner party
- Flaky apple tart, a treat that appears in Bryce's basket for the basket boy auction
- Amazing deviled eggs that Juli's neighbor brags about making from Juli's chickens' eggs

The Silent Name Game

Connie Mathews, facilitator of the Girls Night Out Book Club at the Mt. Lebanon Public Library in Pittsburgh, asked book group members to get to know one another—without using words. "This game is a great way to introduce *Flipped*, since it shows players how easily information can be distorted or misconstrued," Mathews explains. Here's how to play the game, which Mathews found in *Win-Win Games for All Ages: Cooperative Activities for Building Social Skills* (New Society Publishers, 2002):

1. Ask players to pair up with someone they don't know well.
2. Give players five minutes to learn as much about their partners as they can while maintaining complete silence (they may use gestures and pantomime to communicate).
3. When the time is up, ask members to introduce their partners to the rest of the group. Partners then have the chance to approve or correct the information given.

TRY IT!

Watercolor Painting

Nathalie Harty, teen services librarian at the Wilmington (Massachusetts) Memorial Library, gave her Teen Book Club members a chance to try Juli's father's favorite hobby. She set up a canvas with watercolor paints and asked participants to paint their favorite scene in the book.

If you try this with your group, inspire creative expression by bringing pictures of chickens, landscapes (Mr. Baker's preferred subject), or sycamore trees, the object of Juli's admiration.

Topics Discussed

- Why Juli does not feel the same pressure as Bryce to conform to other people's expectations of her
- Bryce's choice to lie to Juli and his dad about the eggs, and if Juli should have forgiven him
- How Bryce changes as he compares himself with Juli
- If it's important to always be honest, even if it will hurt someone's feelings

ASK IT!

How does Bryce change over the course of the book?

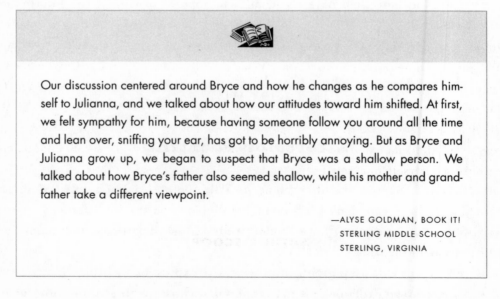

Our discussion centered around Bryce and how he changes as he compares himself to Julianna, and we talked about how our attitudes toward him shifted. At first, we felt sympathy for him, because having someone follow you around all the time and lean over, sniffing your ear, has got to be horribly annoying. But as Bryce and Julianna grow up, we began to suspect that Bryce was a shallow person. We talked about how Bryce's father also seemed shallow, while his mother and grandfather take a different viewpoint.

—ALYSE GOLDMAN, BOOK IT!
STERLING MIDDLE SCHOOL
STERLING, VIRGINIA

The Skin I'm In

Sharon G. Flake

Hyperion, 1998
Available in paperback from Jump at the Sun/Hyperion
176 pages
Fiction

Middle schooler Maleeka Madison is a good student, but her unstylish clothes and dark skin make her a target of constant teasing by her classmates. Charlese, leader of a popular, tough clique, allows Maleeka entrance into the group in exchange for Maleeka's homework services. When a new teacher, Miss Saunders, arrives at the school, Maleeka observes how Miss Saunders stands up to students' taunts. As the year progresses, Maleeka examines her feelings toward Charlese and Miss Saunders, and begins to see herself in a new light.

AUTHOR SCOOP

- Sharon Flake explains that her daughter was part of the inspiration for *The Skin I'm In*. Says Flake:

My daughter is dark-skinned, and since she was born I made up stories for her about beautiful, dark-skinned girls who fly, solve crimes, and are destined to succeed. Many times in the African-American community because of slavery and its focus on light skin being the hallmark of beauty, if you are dark-skinned people aren't so kind to you. Knowing this, I wanted my daughter to grow up loving the skin she's in, and valuing herself. The Skin I'm In *has taught me via my readers that other cultures struggle with the same skin-color issues, and young people from all cultures struggle with learning to love themselves just as they are.*

- Although her middle school experiences weren't anything like Maleeka's, Flake had similar feelings of self-doubt during her adolescence. She explains:

  Like Maleeka, I didn't like myself all that much in middle school. No one picked on me or chased me home. It's just that during that time period, like many young people today, I'd look in the mirror and pick myself to pieces. Why am I so skinny? I'd ask. How come I'm not as pretty as my older sister Daphne? I was painfully shy, staying in the house much of middle school reading and watching old movies. If a boy looked at me I'd cross the street and head in the other direction. All I saw was what I wasn't. It's only in the last few years that I've begun to see what I am. I wrote The Skin I'm In *hoping that somehow it will help girls to see themselves in a better light much earlier in life.*

- Flake says black male adults and boys are not represented as positively as they should be in television, print, and on the radio, and she is committed to portraying them more positively in her work. She explains:

  No one is perfect. So I'm not seeking perfection with the male characters I create. But I am seeking more balance in the portrayal of black males when I write. I want to see my brothers and father, the man that lives up the street from me. That's why I have Caleb in The Skin I'm In *and Sato in* Money

Hungry. *These are two loving, warm young men, whom young girls gravi-tate toward when they read my books. Beyond these characters, I have Maleeka's dad in* The Skin I'm In. *He's dead, yet he has left her a legacy of poetry and beauty that act as healing balms for her even in his absence. Imagine a black father writing poetry to his daughter. It happens, yet you won't read about that on the six-o'clock news. There are other wonderful boys and men in my books, and some villains as well. Life is positive and negative, the yin and yang. When it comes to inner-city communities, how-ever, people seem to forget the good stuff.*

- Flake is thrilled to hear from readers that they "find themselves" in her novels. She says:

Girls often say that they didn't like themselves and then they picked up The Skin I'm In *and something clicked. One girl's mother wrote to tell me that after reading the book her daughter began to encourage her friends to like themselves better as well. She also created a board game based on the book, hoping to build the self-esteem of her friends and other girls. Some girls write telling me they hated to read until they came across my work. The book has wings and seems to help young people fly. That's not my doing so much as it is the magic of literature.*

Author website: www.sharongflake.com
Sharon Flake recommends:
Heaven by Angela Johnson (Simon & Schuster, 1998)
Tough Tiffany by Belinda Hurmence (Doubleday, 1980)
The Legend of Buddy Bush by Shelia P. Moses (Margaret K. McElderry, 2004)
Dear America: Look to the Hills: The Diary of Lozette Moreau, a French Slave Girl by Patricia McKissack (Scholastic, 2004)

Desda Darling's Delicious Double-Dutch Chocolate-Chip Cake

In *The Skin I'm In*, Maleeka's schoolmate, Desda, has won a Pillsbury Bake-Off Contest for her Double-Dutch Chocolate-Chip Cake. Sharon Flake told us she imagined Desda's cake as a chocolate layer cake with chocolate chips in both the cake and the icing, and rich with chocolate pudding. We think this version would live up to Desda's baking talents.

The recipes for Darn Good Chocolate Cake and Chocolate Pan Frosting have been adapted from *Chocolate from the Cake Mix Doctor* by Anne Byrn (Workman, 2001).

NOTE: We adapted this recipe to fit two 9-inch layer pans, but you may also use a Bundt pan and bake 58 to 62 minutes. The frosting is best applied when warm. If frosting has cooled, you can gently reheat it on the stove top or in the microwave before icing the cake.

FOR THE CAKE

1 (8.25-ounce) package plain devil's food or dark chocolate fudge cake mix

1 (3.9-ounce) package chocolate flavor instant pudding & pie filling

4 large eggs, at room temperature

1 cup sour cream, at room temperature

½ cup water

½ cup vegetable oil

1½ cups semisweet chocolate morsels

FOR THE FROSTING

12 tablespoons (1½ sticks) unsalted butter

½ cup unsweetened cocoa powder

½ cup whole milk

5½ cups confectioners' sugar, sifted

1. Preheat oven to 350° F. Lightly grease and flour two 9-inch cake pans, or spray with a cooking spray with flour. Set aside.

2. To make the cake: In a large mixing bowl, blend the cake mix, pudding mix, eggs, sour cream, water, and oil with an electric mixer on low speed 1 minute. Stop the machine and scrape down the sides of the bowl with a rubber spatula. Increase the mixer speed to medium and beat 2–3 minutes more, scraping the sides down again if necessary. The batter should look thick and well combined.

3. Use a spatula to fold in the chocolate morsels, making sure they are well distributed throughout the batter. Pour half of the batter into each prepared pan.

4. Bake 28–32 minutes, until the cakes spring back when lightly pressed with a fingertip and just start to pull away from the sides of the pans. Remove the pans from the oven and place them on a wire rack to cool 20 minutes. Run a long, sharp knife around the sides of each cake and invert them onto the rack to cool completely, 20 minutes more.

5. To make the frosting: In a medium saucepan, melt the butter over low heat, approximately 2–3 minutes. Stir in the cocoa powder and milk until the mixture thickens and just begins to boil. Remove the pan from the heat.

6. Stir in 5 cups of confectioners' sugar, adding more as needed until the frosting is thickened and smooth (similar to the consistency of hot fudge sauce).

7. To frost the cakes: Place one cake right side up. Spoon warm frosting on top and spread to cover cake. Place second cake right side up on top of the first layer and frost the top and sides.

YIELD: ONE TWO-LAYER CAKE, 16 SERVINGS

Book Links: Ideas from Sharon Flake

NOTE: Sharon Flake's activities are designed for girls' book clubs only.

THEY DON'T KNOW ME

This exercise is designed to help girls break the silence about the negative words spoken so freely about themselves and others, and to encourage girls to give voice to their strength, beauty, and talent, no matter where they live. Six girls (minimum) sit in a circle with their backs to one another. Holding hands, one by one they shout out the hurtful words that other children call girls at their schools or in their neighborhoods. After each girl is finished speaking, they all clap and shout, "They don't know me. They don't know you. They don't know us!"

After the girls have taken several turns, they rearrange the chairs so that they face one another, but remain seated in a circle. An adult selects one girl who will tell the group two things that she loves about herself. Her statement must include at least one quality that shows how smart, talented, or brave she is. After she speaks, she is to clap her hands and shout, "They don't know me. They don't know you. They don't know us!" After this statement, she points to a girl of her choice who tells something wonderful about herself, claps, shouts the above statement, then points to another girl in the circle who will continue the scenario. This goes on until each girl has told the group several times how special, bright, and wonderful she is.

After the activity, the girls should further bond by making and sharing a meal or dessert together, painting nails and/or giving one another facials, or engaging in any activity that includes everyone and requires the participation of the group to make the activity a success.

SERVING UP BEAUTY

This activity encourages girls to take care of one another and to see the beauty in their sister friends.

Gather a group of girls together to make Desda Darling's Delicious Double-Dutch Chocolate-Chip Cake (see p. 304). While the girls are mixing, preparing, and cooking, an adult can start a conversation about how strong and wonderful the girls are, ensuring that each girl talks about her own strengths as well.

While the cake is baking, the girls sit around a table with art supplies (the more the merrier) to create art poems. They can write poems about themselves, or a girl or woman important to them, and then create artwork that reflects their poems. Encourage the girls to give their poems "personalities" by adding to their artwork the physical traits of a person (hair, lips, eyes), or simply create an abstract art interpretation of the poem. Use anything around the house: colorful beads, paint, buttons, shoestrings, or lace. The poems should celebrate each girl's uniqueness. After the poems are complete and the cake is cooled, each girl helps to set the table (including folding napkins and setting silverware). Once the girls are seated, then one by one they may serve one another.

TRY IT!

Lovin' the Skin We're In

Robin Hickman, an independent television and film producer, was inspired to create the "Lovin' the Skin We're In" Club in St. Paul, Minnesota, after reading *The Skin I'm In*. Hickman asked the middle school girls she mentors from local youth programs to read Flake's novel. "It was overwhelming to see the impact of the book on the girls," she says.

Hickman devised a variety of activities involving literature, media, and art to reinforce the book's theme and address "the historical origins of negative legacies within our community, as well as the impact of images and stereotypes in the media."

For one project, the girls researched a contemporary or historic African-American woman who they feel "loves the skin she's in"—who loves herself and has the courage to make a difference. The girls then dress as the women they are researching, e.g., Sojourner Truth, Madame C. J. Walker, Zora Neale Hurston, Rosa Parks, Shirley Chisholm, or Oprah Winfrey, and present their "herstories" to the group and at community events.

Historic research is an important part of the exercise, emphasizes Hickman, and the concept of poor self-image among girls of color has historic roots. "During slavery, blacks were separated by skin color, and issues about skin color, hair, and complexion still pose serious conflicts among young people," she says. "Some girls have expressed frustration when they are criticized about these same issues by other girls, and it's quite disheartening."

For another activity, Hickman gave the girls disposable cameras and notepads and asked them to become photojournalists. Their assignment: to interview African-American women and girls they know and ask them if they "love the skin they're in." In the end, says Hickman, the group created a beautiful exhibit of powerful images and words.

CHECK IT OUT!

Harriet A. Jacobs's
Incidents in the Life of a Slave Girl

As a companion to *The Skin I'm In*, the Wired for Youth Teen Book Club at the Austin (Texas) Public Library distributed copies of Harriet A. Jacobs's *Incidents in the Life of a Slave Girl* (Penguin, 2000), the book that Miss Saunders gives to Maleeka in *The Skin I'm In*. Jacobs's narrative parallels Maleeka's fictional journal about being a slave girl, and plays an important role in Maleeka's life and schoolwork. Facilitator Joanna Nigrelli says she wanted to connect the two stories, and for book club members to know that Jacobs's book, although mentioned in a fictional story, actually exists.

Topics Discussed

- The meaning of the book's title
- If Miss Saunders was a good teacher when she arrived at the school
- If someone other than a relative, such as Miss Saunders, has inspired you or made an impact on your life
- If the darkness of your skin makes a difference in how you are treated

ASK IT!

Why does Maleeka choose Charlese to be her friend?

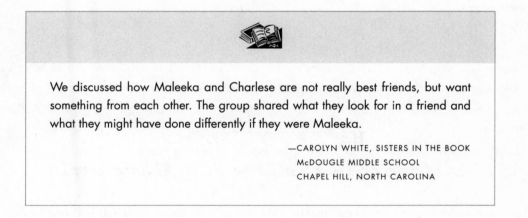

We discussed how Maleeka and Charlese are not really best friends, but want something from each other. The group shared what they look for in a friend and what they might have done differently if they were Maleeka.

—CAROLYN WHITE, SISTERS IN THE BOOK
McDOUGLE MIDDLE SCHOOL
CHAPEL HILL, NORTH CAROLINA

Grades 6–9

Kira-Kira

Cynthia Kadohata

Atheneum, 2004
Also available in paperback from Simon & Schuster
256 pages
Fiction

Katie Takeshima is a kindergartner in the 1950s when her family moves from Iowa to a Georgia town with a small Japanese community, where her parents work long hours in a poultry plant and hatchery under grueling conditions. Katie worships her older sister, Lynn, who teaches her how to see what is beautiful and glittering—or "kira-kira"—in the world. When Lynn becomes ill, Katie struggles to find strength by adopting Lynn's "kira-kira" view of life.

AUTHOR SCOOP

- Cynthia Kadohata was born in Chicago, but like the Takeshima family in *Kira-Kira*, Kadohata's family relocated to Georgia, where her father worked as a chicken sexer, separating the male from the female chicks at a poultry hatchery. The family later moved to Arkansas, where they lived until Kadohata was almost nine.

- There were many inspirations for *Kira-Kira*, explains Kadohata. An editor and friend suggested Kadohata write a children's novel and liked Kadohata's idea for the story. "I was very sad over the illness of someone I knew," she adds, "so it seemed like the time to write that particular story."

- Kadohata explains that she changed the book's title from *I Wish* to *Kira-Kira*. "When I was finished, it was clear that the title was *Kira-Kira*," she explains. "It was just what the title had to be because it was about hope and acting on that hope. It was about living the 'kira-kira' life, not about wishing, though a book about wishing would be nice too."

- Details of *Kira-Kira* are autobiographical, says Kadohata. "The hospital staff in Arkansas really did stop by to see my brother when he was born because they had never seen a Japanese baby before," she says, "and I did have a younger brother and older sister, and my older sister was my best friend."

Author website: www.kira-kira.us

Cynthia Kadohata recommends:

Bridge to Terabithia by Katherine Paterson (HarperCollins, 1977)

Let Us Now Praise Famous Men: Three Tenant Families by James Agee, photographs by Walker Evans (Houghton Mifflin, 1941)

BOOK BITES

Cynthia Kadohata's Tacos

Cynthia Kadohata explains her passion for tacos and how they became part of the story line of *Kira-Kira:*

When I lived in Arkansas, there was only one Mexican restaurant that we knew of in town. We used to go there as a special treat. I was crazy for tacos and used to beg

my mother to make them. I remember my parents asking me kiddingly which I liked
better, the restaurant tacos or my mother's tacos. I don't remember what I said, but I
do remember that they both laughed after I answered.

Of course, we always had giant bags of white rice around, which we ate with any
kind of meat or made rice balls out of. Rice was central to our daily diet, but tacos
were what I begged for.

Then I went through a period when I was a teenager when I always insisted on
making my own dinner: tacos. For weeks, I would eat them every day for dinner.

The main character of Kira-Kira eats five tacos at once in a restaurant in Georgia. I often ate five tacos at a sitting, but my record was six.

At some point my family converted to health foods, but I still love tacos.

Kadohata first made these tacos more than twenty years ago, adapting a recipe for tostadas in Frances Moore Lappé's *Diet for a Small Planet* (Ballantine, 1971) and folding the hot tortillas to make tacos. If you've never tried homemade tacos—or even if you have—you're in for a treat!

NOTE: Kadohata suggests simmering the tomato sauce while preparing the beef and garnishes, removing the sauce from the heat, and briefly reheating before serving. She prefers the tortillas on the crispy side, but others like them softer. The instructions below are for frying the tortillas, but you can also heat them for several minutes in the oven until warmed. You can mix the beef and tomato sauce together, or keep them separate for those who prefer vegetarian tacos.

Kadohata prefers to put the cheese in the warm tacos so it melts, and then adds the ground beef. "If I have guests, then they put them together the way they want—most people like to sprinkle their cheese on top," she says. "And being Japanese, I don't like to use four of anything because it's bad luck, so I will use either three or five very thin slices of onion." (This applies to other recipe ingredients as well, such as tomatoes.) She then adds more cayenne pepper for spice, followed by stewed tomatoes and vegetables and herbs, and some extra avocado slices by the side.

Kadohata sets the chopped vegetables and herbs on one big plate for guests to sprinkle on their tacos. She alternates colors to separate the greens from one another, but you can also put them in separate bowls. She uses organic corn tortillas and fries them in coconut oil, but any cooking oil will do. She prefers home-grown tomatoes: "They're so delicious, you want to just pop them into your mouth like candy. I'm kind of picky about tomatoes because the difference in taste between most store-bought tomatoes and homegrown is so substantial," she says.

FOR THE SAUCE

3 or 5 ripe tomatoes, organic if possible, peeled, seeded, and chopped (see note)

1 small onion, finely sliced

1 tablespoon cider vinegar

1 clove garlic, finely chopped

1 tablespoon chili powder

1 teaspoon salt

⅛ teaspoon cayenne

FOR THE GROUND BEEF

1 pound ground beef

½ teaspoon salt

FOR THE GARNISHES

2 avocados, sliced

1 onion, finely chopped

½ bunch cilantro, chopped

2 tomatoes, organic if possible, chopped (see note)

3 cups shredded romaine lettuce

2 cups grated cheddar or Monterey Jack cheese

FOR THE TACOS

1 dozen corn tortillas (see note)

Oil for frying

1. To make the sauce: Simmer the tomatoes, onion, cider vinegar, garlic, chili powder, salt and cayenne in a medium saucepan over low heat until the tomatoes and onions are soft. Remove from heat.
2. While the sauce is simmering, brown the ground beef in a skillet. Drain fat and add salt.
3. To prepare the garnishes: Arrange the avocado, onions, cilantro, tomatoes, and shredded romaine on a plate, or place in individual bowls.
4. To make the tacos: Heat a few tablespoons of oil in a small skillet. Fry the tortillas for 1–2 minutes, turning once.
5. Drain the tortillas on paper towels and fold over to form a taco shell.

6. To assemble the tacos: Place the cheese, meat, and sauce in taco shells (in preferred order) and add the garnishes.

YIELD: 12 TACOS

BOOK BITES

Cynthia Kadohata's Onigiri (Rice Balls)

Kadohata suggested making *onigiri*, or rice balls, the food Katie makes and eats in *Kira-Kira*, as a fun recipe and activity to go along with a discussion of her novel.

Onigiri, popular Japanese snacks, were a staple of Kadohata's childhood—and of Katie's in *Kira-Kira*. Kadohata recalls that "there was something very satisfying to me about shaping the rice," which she would take on picnics with her family. "I felt like I was doing something important," she adds.

While Kadohata always shaped *onigiri* into triangles, a friend told her she ate round or cylindrical *onigiri* as a child, so different shapes are possible. There are molds that make perfectly shaped *onigiri*, adds Kadohata, but "when I was young we just wet our hands and added salt, and I think that gave us more satisfaction than a mold would have."

In *Kira-Kira*, Katie's mother made fancy triangle-shaped *onigiri* with seaweed and pickled plums, but Katie knows only how to make basic *onigiri*. "Someday, when I got older, I would have to learn to make fancy *onigiri*, too, or nobody would marry me," Katie says.

NOTE: *Onigiri* are best eaten fresh, just after they have been prepared. Kadohata says:

The rice should be freshly cooked, and just cooled off enough for you to handle. When shaping the onigiri *keep in mind the shape should be lovely, since the Japanese are very much interested in the aesthetics of their food. Shapes such as a long cylinder are common, and if you use this shape you would decorate it with a piece of* nori, *black processed seaweed, on the outside, by cutting it into a strip and wrapping it around the cylinder.*

Kadohata enjoys *umeboshi* (picked plums with or without seeds) in the center but cautions that some find the taste quite salty. She also suggests using cooked meats or eggs inside the *onigiri*. "There are other possibilities for the middle," she adds. "The sky's the limit!"

Nori and *umeboshi* are available in specialty stores.

Salt

Cooked short-grain rice, approximately ½ cup for each rice ball (see note)

Fillings, such as umeboshi, *cooked meat, or eggs (optional; see note)*

Nori *(optional; see note)*

1. To make *onigiri*, wash your hands and cover your palms with salt (you can also dip your hands in a bowl of salty water before forming the ball). Grab a handful of rice and shape it into a round or triangular shape, pressing with both hands.
2. If you are filling *onigiri*, make a hole in the top of the rice ball with a chopstick or your finger, and then push approximately 1 teaspoon of filling inside the rice. Fill the hole with rice and reshape. If using *nori*, cut into a thin strip and wrap around the cylindrical shaped *onigiri*.

Enjoy!

TRY IT!

Share Family Stories

The Chautauqua Institution, a center for the arts, religion, education, and recreation in Chautauqua, New York, sponsored a program that highlighted the "family" theme of *Kira-Kira* for its Summer Young Readers' discussion of the novel. Program director Jack Voelker encouraged youngsters to bring older relatives who would share a memory of a family story, vacation or holiday celebration, or a lesson about overcoming a family hardship, as did the characters in *Kira-Kira*. After the adults told stories, some of the children wanted to share stories about their parents. Voelker says the group had a very moving and introspective conversation about how they define family.

Topics Discussed

- How being Japanese affects the characters' lives
- If Katie feels there is "kira-kira" in her future at the end of the book
- How all the characters' family roles change from the beginning of the story
- How it feels to be bullied because you are different

ASK IT!

What did Katie know about her sister's condition?

We tried to understand why Katie knew so little about her sister's illness. We worked backwards, recalling the details of Lynn's condition and when they were mentioned to Katie. We then discussed the parents' point of view in trying to protect Katie from the truth.

—NICOLE MIKESELL, PIZZA AND A PAPERBACK (GRADES 6–8)
CAMERON VILLAGE PUBLIC LIBRARY
RALEIGH, NORTH CAROLINA

The Outsiders

S. E. Hinton

Viking, 1967
Available in paperback from Puffin
192 pages
Fiction

Companion novel: *That Was Then, This Is Now* (1971)

After the deaths of their parents in the 1960s, fourteen-year-old Ponyboy Curtis and his two older brothers live on their own, counting on their loyal friends—"greasers" with slicked-back hair and hardscrabble lives—for companionship, guidance, and support. The rich Socs (short for "Socials"), a rival gang, aggravate the greasers with insults shouted from their passing cars and occasional attacks. When a rumble between the two gangs spins out of control and leads to a series of tragedies, Ponyboy turns to his pen to make sense of the violence.

- S. E. (Susan Eloise) Hinton began writing *The Outsiders* when she was a fifteen-year-old high school sophomore in Tulsa, Oklahoma. Hinton received her publishing contract on the day of her high school graduation, and the book was released in the spring of Hinton's freshman year at the University of Oklahoma, when she was eighteen years old.

- While in high school, Hinton craved fiction that explored difficult issues facing teens. Upon finding that most teen novels at the time dealt with lighter topics, such as attending the prom, Hinton decided to pen her own novel. *The Outsiders,* one of the first gritty, realistic novels for teens, revolutionized the genre of young adult literature.

- The feud between the greasers and the Socs in *The Outsiders* is based on similar group rivalries at Hinton's high school. As a high school student, Hinton hated the way the greasers at her school were treated. It was the beating of a friend on his way home from school that gave her the idea to write a book. "I was angry about the incident and began a short story about a boy who was beaten up on his way home from the movies," Hinton says.

- Hinton and her publisher, Viking, feared that boys might not read the book if they knew it was written by a female, so they replaced "Susan" with the genderless "S. E." Many readers still assume the book was written by a man. Hinton says she enjoys having public and private names.

- Soon after the book's publication, its popularity spread. Hinton began to hear from teenagers across the country who related to the situations depicted in the book and were grateful to read about other "outsiders." She continues to hear from fans today. "*The Outsiders* sells as well today as it ever has, only now I'm getting letters from parents who are giving their teens their own favorite teen book," Hinton says. "The in-group and the out-group will always be a fact of teenage life."

- All of Hinton's books, including *The Outsiders,* are written from the male perspective. Hinton says she has tried to write from a female point of view but has found it impossible. "I grew up as a tomboy, most of my friends were guys, and I couldn't identify with what the female culture was at that time," she explains.

Author website: www.sehinton.com
Film adaptation:
The Outsiders (Zoetrope, 1983), rated PG-13, 121 minutes

BOOK BITES

S. E. Hinton's Curtis Family Chocolate Cake

When we asked S. E. Hinton for a recipe, she sent us a description of "the gang"—the Curtis brothers and Two-Bit—making her family recipe for chocolate cake, rich, delicious, and simple to prepare. Hinton's grandmother, aunts, and mother used the recipe, and Hinton remembers eating the cake for holidays or as an after-school snack. "Nowadays, I only make it on special occasions like my husband's or son's birthday," she says. "It is the only thing I actually bake."

It's no wonder that in *The Outsiders*, the Curtis brothers—Darry, Sodapop, and Ponyboy—always keep chocolate cake on hand, and Sodapop "cooks one up real quick" when they run out.

Like her three characters, Hinton prefers her chocolate cake in the morning. "I loved it for breakfast, growing up, and thought if I had my way it would be breakfast every day, which didn't happen for me, but I made it happen for the Curtis family," she says. "In fact, my original manuscript still has chocolate smears on it."

Hinton suggests book clubs try the following activities based on her "Breakfast at the Curtis House" dialogue and chocolate cake recipe:

Write your own "Breakfast at the Curtis House" story in dialogue only.
OR
Have some friends over, bake the cake, assign one another character names, and role-play the "Breakfast at the Curtis House" scene.
And don't forget to clean the kitchen.

NOTE: Because this recipe appears in dialogue form, have at least two people on hand to bake it: one (or more) to read the dialogue aloud, and another to perform the steps.

This cake serves 14 to 16 people.

Darry: "The first thing you do is get all your ingredients together. That way you won't get halfway into it and find out you're out of something."
Soda: "That only happened once! Well, maybe twice."
Darry: "Sure. Anyway, to make this cake you'll need:

2 cups all-purpose flour	*2 large eggs, at room temperature*
½ cup unsweetened cocoa powder	*1 cup buttermilk, at room temperature*
½ teaspoon salt	*2 teaspoons baking soda*
2 cups granulated sugar	*1 cup hot water*
½ cup (1 stick) unsalted butter, softened	*1 teaspoon vanilla extract*

Ponyboy: "First, shift together . . ."
Two-Bit: "*Shift?* The kid thinks he's a chef."
Ponyboy: "Okay, *mix.*"

Darry: "You're forgetting something, actually two things, kiddo."

Ponyboy: "What? Oh, yeah, preheat the oven to 350. Or it'll turn into a big mess."

Soda: "And prep your 9 by 13-inch cake pan by rubbing butter all over the bottom and sides, then tossing a couple of tablespoons of flour around in it till it's coated."

Ponyboy: "I was going to say that. THEN you MIX the flour, cocoa powder, and salt into one bowl. In another, big mixing bowl, mix the sugar and the butter. Mom used to do this with a wooden spoon, but we use an electric mixer. Add eggs one at a time and beat till smooth."

Two-Bit: "Be sure and taste it."

Darry: "NO!"

Soda: "Then you add a little of the cocoa-flour mix, mix it in, then a little of the buttermilk, mix it in, then keep alternating the buttermilk and flour and beat till it's smooth."

Ponyboy: "Okay, at this point you dissolve your baking soda—not your brother, Soda—in the cup of hot water, add the vanilla, and gently beat this into your batter."

Soda: "Gently, and not too long, or your cake will be tough."

Two-Bit: "This cake is tuff."

Ponyboy and Soda: "SHUT UP."

Soda: "Pour it into the cake pan. It'll look a little runny, but that's the way it's supposed to look."

Ponyboy: "Then slide it into the PREHEATED oven for 35 to 40 minutes. Our oven underheats a little, but you can test for doneness by sticking a toothpick or a piece of uncooked spaghetti in the middle and if it comes out clean, it's done."

Two-Bit: "Or use your finger."

Soda: "Yeah, sure Two-Bit, stick your finger in a blazing-hot cake. That's real smart."

Two-Bit: "Okay, okay. Be sure and use oven mitts or something when you're handling the cake pan."

Darry: "And no wrestling around or jumping off countertops in the kitchen while it's baking, or it'll fall."

Ponyboy: "I guess that's it."

Soda: "Are you crazy? You're leaving out the most important part."

Soda and Two-Bit: "THE ICING!"

Darry: "Let the cake cool off for a while. You'll need:

> 2 cups confectioners' sugar
>
> 4 tablespoons (½ stick) salted butter, softened
>
> ½ teaspoon vanilla extract
>
> 3–4 tablespoons milk, or buttermilk if you have some left over
>
> 2–4 tablespoons unsweetened cocoa powder

Soda: "Do NOT soften the butter by sticking it in the oven. Trust me."

Ponyboy: "I keep the wrapper on the butter and put it in a bowl of hot water for a little while. Or get it out of the fridge real early. If you can remember."

Darry: "Then you beat the confectioners' sugar, butter, and vanilla together for a couple of minutes, scraping the bowl often, adding a little milk at a time for a thinner consistency."

Soda: "This is where we get creative. We add cocoa, which will make it too thick, then a little more milk, which will thin it out, and keep doing this until the icing is as chocolate as we like. Darry likes it real dark, but me and Pony like it a little lighter."

Ponyboy: "And be careful with the milk. Add just a little at a time or it'll get runny."

Two-Bit: "A shot of Kahlúa makes a good thing better."

Darry: "NO."

Two-Bit: "I'm just sayin'."

Soda: "Then put the icing on the cake and lick the bowl."

Ponyboy: "And the spoon."

Two-Bit: "And the mixer beaters."

Darry: "And don't forget to clean the kitchen."

Ponyboy, Soda, and Two-Bit: GROAN.

MAKE IT!

A Family Celebration Collage

Pam Grover, facilitator of the Middle School Book Club at the Smoky Hill Public Library in Centennial, Colorado, asked members to create a collage of pictures representing families of all types. "We discussed the substitution of gangs for families in

The Outsiders," says Grover, "and wanted to show what different kinds of families, or what people might consider a family, look like." Participants cut out pictures from old magazines and glued them onto poster board. "The kids found pictures that represented families of all types, including moms and kids, dads and kids, and many other types," Grover says.

TRY IT!

Acrostic Poem

Pam Grover asked students in her book club to compose an acrostic poem—a poem in which the first letters of each line form a word related to the poem's subject—using the letters of two gangs depicted in *The Outsiders*: GREASERS and SOCS. "In our discussion, we focused on the cliques the kids see at school," explains Grover. "Then, based on what we learned from the book, we came up with words that described the two cliques in *The Outsiders,* such as *grease, grungy,* and *gang* for the letter *g,* and *rumble, reputation,* and *rivalry* for the letter *r.*"

TRY IT!

Caricatures

To explore the various personalities depicted in *The Outsiders,* LeAnn Kunz's teen book group at the Washington (Iowa) Public Library drew caricatures. "The girls each chose their favorite male character," says Kunz. "One girl really liked the 'bad boy' image of Dally, and another liked the sensitive nature of Johnny." The girls then drew pencil sketches of the characters, emphasizing their special qualities: Dally had exaggerated muscles to represent toughness, for example, and Johnny was shown holding a book because he liked reading aloud.

Topics Discussed

- Whether or not you would convict Johnny of murder if you sat on a jury
- The importance of Robert Frost's poem "Nothing Gold Can Stay" to *The Outsiders*, and if Ponyboy will stay "gold"
- The problems that occur when rich and poor kids live near one another and form cliques
- The cliques you find at school and how they treat each other

ASK IT!

Why was the gang in The Outsiders *such an important part of each of the character's lives?*

We noticed that many of the greasers had incomplete or dysfunctional families, so they needed one another for emotional support. The relationship among these boys was very much a brotherhood: They were loyal to one another, no matter what. We talked about how the gang gave them the unconditional love they didn't get from their regular families.

—LeANN KUNZ, BOOK-BY-BOOK (GRADES 6–9)
WASHINGTON PUBLIC LIBRARY
WASHINGTON, IOWA

Tangerine

Edward Bloor

Harcourt, 1997
Available in paperback from Scholastic
304 pages
Fiction

Paul is adjusting to life as a seventh-grader after his family moves to the strange town of Tangerine, Florida, where tangerine groves have been replaced by upscale housing developments. Legally blind from an accident of which he has no memory, Paul is passionate about soccer and determined to find a way to play goalie. As he gradually recalls the event that damaged his eyesight and discovers disturbing facts about his older brother, Erik, Paul finds the courage and determination to speak out about some awful truths.

AUTHOR SCOOP

- Edward Bloor lives in Florida. He says the idea for *Tangerine* came to him while driving to work, when he observed the citrus groves around him being destroyed and noticed the impact of this destruction on local residents and the economy. "I passed miles of citrus groves that, over a very short period of time, got plowed up and turned into miles of walled housing developments with British-themed names," says Bloor. "I wanted to write a novel that included both the people who were moving into this place and the people who were getting pushed out of it."

- Bloor says his childhood experiences playing soccer helped to "fuel the soccer-as-more-than-a-game strand in *Tangerine*." He recalls:

  When I was eight years old, I started playing on a soccer team in Trenton, New Jersey, in a league that was dominated by emigrant teams from Eastern Europe. Every week, my homegrown team would face teams with names like the Ukrainian-American Club and the Polish-American Club. These teams arrived accompanied by parents who were absolutely rabid, venting their rage not only over soccer calls, but over issues that went back centuries in Europe.

- Bloor, who has lived in Florida over half of his life, explains that Paul, the hero of *Tangerine*, and he both look at Florida as outsiders:

  My parents moved from Trenton, New Jersey, to Hollywood, Florida, when I was in college in New York. I made brief visits, but I did not live there for several years because I really didn't like it. The weather, the economy, the news—just about everything seemed inferior to their counterparts in the North. When I finally did start living down there, it was with a very critical eye, which is what Paul has. Nowadays, I should add, I love living in Florida for many of the same things that once seemed to be negatives.

- During his speaking engagements around the country, Bloor has been surprised when people who live in other states view *Tangerine* as a science fiction novel. "I have to explain to them that bizarre and violent acts of nature are the staples of our nightly news broadcasts and our morning papers," says Bloor. "They're just part of life here in Florida. They're the price we pay for not having to shovel snow. Instead, we have to nail tarps to our roofs following Category 5 hurricanes."

Author website: www.edwardbloor.net

Edward Bloor recommends:

Shattering Glass by Gail Giles (Roaring Brook, 2002), which he calls "a story that plays out like a modern *Frankenstein*. I'd recommend it for high school ages and above." He also recommends *Stargirl* by Jerry Spinelli (Knopf, 2000).

BOOK BITES

Edward Bloor's Tangerine Smoothie

Edward Bloor created this tropical tangerine smoothie for our book to complement a discussion of *Tangerine*. "I suppose you could use orange juice and just claim you used tangerine juice," adds Bloor. "That's a matter of individual conscience. In the context of the novel, Paul would go the extra mile to find real tangerine juice; Erik would substitute and lie about it."

NOTE: You can substitute piña colada frozen yogurt for the yogurt in this recipe, or a combination of ¼ cup of vanilla yogurt and ½ cup of coconut and/or tropical fruit sorbet. If you use frozen yogurt, you might want to omit the sugar, depending on how sweet you like your smoothies.

¼ cup crushed ice

¼ cup piña colada yogurt (see note)

1 cup orange-tangerine juice

½ cup nonfat milk

1 tablespoon sugar

Place ice in a blender. Add the remaining ingredients and blend until smooth.

YIELD: APPROXIMATELY 3 (8-OUNCE) SERVINGS

Homemade Orange Julius

Andrea Purdy gave her Teen Time Book Club members an opportunity to taste test several varieties of tangerines to kick off their *Tangerine* discussion at the East Regional Library in Knightdale, North Carolina. The group then concocted a homemade version of Orange Julius, the blended orange-juice drink, using a recipe Purdy found on the Internet. Purdy wanted to make a Florida-style drink and said the kids had never tasted Orange Julius, but they enjoyed making and drinking it together.

*1 (6-ounce) can orange-juice
concentrate, frozen*

1 cup milk (can be low-fat)

1 cup water

¼ cup sugar

1 teaspoon vanilla extract

8 large ice cubes

Place the first five ingredients in a blender and blend until smooth, adding ice cubes one at a time.

YIELD: 3 (8-OUNCE) SERVINGS

TRY IT!

Write a Diary Entry

David Shade's Plymouth Church Students Training and Equipping for Personal Success program (STEPS), an after-school book club in Whittier, California, read and discussed *Tangerine* over a two-month period. Shade says the kids quickly identified themes of stereotyping in the book. STEPS members thought it would be interesting to imagine what other characters thought of Paul and proposed writing diary entries from various perspectives. "They each picked one day's entry, and narrated the same experiences from another character's point of view," says Shade. Members shared the diary entries at the next meeting.

Topics Discussed

- The truth about why Paul's eyes were damaged
- The different ways Paul and Joey reacted to Tangerine Middle School
- If you have a sibling who has mistreated you or if you have ever mistreated younger siblings
- Real estate development in Florida and its impact on the land

How did Paul and Erik's parents treat them differently?

Group members were fascinated that when Erik had done something terrible to Paul, it was glossed over by the parents. The behavior of the parents toward Erik, the football star, drew a lot of comments. The students saw the unfairness in the parents' continued favoritism toward Erik. But it was Paul who could clearly see what was happening—that Erik had many problems, including being bigoted, cruel, and the worst sort of bully, while his parents didn't have a clue. This led to an interesting discussion of why Paul was not taken seriously by his parents, why he was largely ignored in the family dynamic, and why football is more popular than soccer at many American schools.

—ANN BASSETT, ONE BOOK–ONE ISLAND PROGRAM/MARTHA'S VINEYARD (GRADES 6–7)
EDGARTOWN, MASSACHUSETTS

Ender's Game

Orson Scott Card

Tor, 1985

Available in paperback from Starscape

384 pages

Science Fiction

Sequels: *Speaker for the Dead* (Tor, 1986); *Xenocide* (Tor, 1991); *Children of the Mind* (Tor, 1996)
Companion novels: *Ender's Shadow* (Tor, 1999); *Shadow of the Hegemon* (Tor, 2001)

In a futuristic world, alien "buggers" threaten to attack Earth for the third time, and military leaders are seeking a commander who can lead the human race to victory when the war begins. They recruit six-year-old genius Ender Wiggin, relocating him to the Battle School floating high above Earth, where he quickly learns to maneuver and fight in a zero-gravity environment. Ender moves up the ranks of command, mastering tactics and strategies usually reserved for soldiers twice his age. But his isolation from the family he left behind and the peers he constantly bests upsets Ender, even as it shapes him into the kind of leader the human race requires for survival.

- Orson Scott Card wrote poetry, short stories, and plays before trying his hand at science fiction. He says his "on-again, off-again" science-fiction reading prompted him to write and sell science-fiction short stories to pay off a debt. He succeeded almost immediately. *Ender's Game* originally appeared as a short story in the August 1977 edition of *Analog* magazine (the original story can be found on Card's website; see below), and was later expanded into a novel of the same name. Although best known for his many works of science fiction and fantasy, Card's body of work, numbering more than forty novels, includes historical and mainstream fiction, nonfiction, and numerous plays.

- Card is a devout Mormon and spent two years in Brazil as a missionary for the Church of Jesus Christ of Latter-day Saints. Although he says he tries to refrain from injecting his religious beliefs into his writing, Card's faith inevitably informs his fiction. As he explains:

  Without ever meaning to, I can't help but include my core beliefs in everything I write—not beliefs about particular doctrines, but beliefs about how the world works, what causes things to happen, why people do the things they do, and which actions are noble, which evil or despicable, etc. Since many of these beliefs derive from Mormon teachings and my experiences as a Latter-day Saint, then in that sense, without any effort on my part, some aspects of my faith are going to show up in my fiction.

- Card says he deliberately omitted mention of specific clothing, food, and music in *Ender's Game* because he thought these realistic details of futuristic societies would seem outlandish to contemporary readers. Foretelling clothing styles, for example, says Card, would "disgust" his readers.

  Think about it—if, in 1973, when we were wearing platform shoes and wide ties and bell-bottom pants, someone had shown us the grunge look of the nineties, we would have found the styles ridiculous and hilarious. But if some-one had shown people from the fifties—with their poky-out petticoats and poodle skirts and bobby sox and ducktail greased-back hair—what the styles of the seventies would be, well, they would have been just as disbelieving.

Author website: www.hatrack.com

BOOK BITES

Space Peanut Butter and Jelly Wraps

For *Ender's Game,* we selected recipes recommended by the National Aeronautics and Space Administration (NASA) to help familiarize kids with the cuisine of modern-day space travelers. Although intended for astronauts, we think they're good enough to eat here on Earth, too.

NASA published this recipe for peanut butter and jelly wraps to demonstrate how the culinary challenges faced by space travelers have been met. Refrigeration is impossible during space travel, so foods carried into space must be canned, freeze-dried, or capable of remaining fresh at room temperature—as are peanut butter and jelly. And crumbly food such as bread can be hazardous in a weightless environment: Crumbs can float around, contaminating the space-station environment. Tortillas make a good substitute for bread because they don't crumble, are easy to handle in zero gravity, and stay fresh longer.

Favorite peanut butter
Favorite jelly
Flour tortillas

Spread thin layers of peanut butter and then jelly on tortillas. Fold tortillas in half and enjoy!

Orange Space Drink

Powdered orange drink, which has powered generations of space travelers, is an ideal space drink. Space missions try to minimize the weight carried on their shuttles, since lighter loads require less fuel to launch, so a lightweight powder is preferred to liquid. And powder can easily be rehydrated in space because water, a by-product of a space shuttle's fuel cells, is readily available.

NOTE: Provide reclosable plastic sandwich bags and bendable straws so each child can prepare his or her own space drink.

3 teaspoons powdered orange drink mix, such as Tang
¼ cup water

1. Place the drink mix in a sandwich-size reclosable plastic bag. Add a straw to the bag. Add water and close the bag securely, pressing out as much extra air as possible.
2. Gently knead the bag until the drink mix is completely dissolved.
3. Carefully pop open one corner, pull out the straw, and enjoy!

YIELD: 1 DRINK

TASTE IT!

Freeze-Dried Ice-Cream Sandwiches

Card names ice-cream sandwiches as one of the foods he "can eat daily, forever." We thought book clubs would enjoy sampling freeze-dried ice-cream sandwiches to complement a discussion of *Ender's Game*. Freeze-dried ice cream requires no refrigeration and has been used by NASA since the early days of the Apollo space program. You can purchase freeze-dried ice-cream sandwiches on the Internet, or at museum or science stores.

TRY IT!

Book Link: An Idea from Orson Scott Card

VIEW WAR FROM DIFFERENT PERSPECTIVES

When asked to contribute an activity appropriate for his book, Orson Scott Card suggested that experiencing weightlessness might be impractical for book clubs, but imagining war from different perspectives is not.

It's unfortunate that a ride on the "vomit comet" airplane is probably beyond the means of most book clubs, so weightlessness will have to be imagined. And I doubt that most people would be interested in sending one of their children away to a tough boarding school for five years in order to see what Ender's parents went through— though some younger readers might approve of sending off a sibling.

Perhaps the most useful thing would be to look together at a globe. Imagine that you're one of the hive queens approaching this planet. You have no idea of any of those boundaries. You can see the lights of cities, so you know there's a technological civilization, but nobody talks to you as you approach. You look for a fertile, well-settled area and you act as you would if you were approaching the world of another hive queen who refused to talk to you: You assert yourself boldly, killing off a few thousand of the other hive queen's workers in order to get her attention and insist that she let you in on her thoughts. Surely, you can work out some way to share this world, if only as a way station for you on your way to colonize other planets.

Imagine your horror as your opponent, instead of talking, starts attacking your ship, refusing to allow you any space on the planet at all. What selfishness! Well, you have your main colony fleet right behind, and it is well armed. You'll clear away these pesky ships in no time, and then you'll just take whatever part of the world you want to use. Rude people like this forfeit some of their rights when they refuse to behave in a civilized manner toward strangers.

Now look at the world from the point of view of the humans who lift off the planet's surface in their spaceships, armed with weapons that are thrown together in a hurry. There has never been a war in space before; you've never had to arm the hodgepodge of shuttles and launch rockets and other spacecraft, and the most terrifying thing, to you, is that the only weapons that seem likely to accomplish anything are nukes. And if you use them too close to the atmosphere, the likelihood is that you'll kill as many humans as the invaders did.

Now you look down, as a human, and while you don't see the borders either, you know that they're there. Suppose that you're an American. Would it do you any good to try to defend only American airspace? You know that an attack on Uganda or a landing in Brazil would be every bit as dangerous to you as such an attack on Kansas or California. It isn't your country you're defending—it's the whole human race. Because if any part of our world is conquered, no part of our world will be safe. You are protecting everyone, and they are helping protect you. Last week, you might have been at war with some other country. But right now, it's as important to you to defend that former enemy as to defend your own land.

Nations are real, and boundaries matter—don't let anyone tell you otherwise. However, they aren't so important that they can't be ignored when the need is great enough.

Now step back a few yards from that globe. Look how small it is. Remember that breathable air is only slightly thicker than a fine layer of dust on the surface might be. We live on the shell of this globe. All of our weather is just a shimmering on the surface. All of our monuments are imperceptible from the distance of an approaching starship entering our solar system. Our art, our literature, our history—invisible. And yet it is precious to us, and our teeming billions are all human individuals with great value in our sight. Fragile and recent as our existence is, it is all we have.

Laser Tag

Ede Marquissee, sixth-grade teacher at Summit Middle School in Fort Wayne, Indiana, took the boys in her Strong Wild Action Team (SWAT) book club on a field trip to a laser tag facility after reading *Ender's Game.* "The book is about space battles and aliens," says Marquissee, "and laser tag is a game of strategy that's also futuristic."

At the multilevel laser-tag arena, full of connecting ramps and hiding places, the fifteen boys who attended the trip broke into two teams. Each team was assigned a "base" which they would protect, and the object of the game was to score enough "hits" on the opponent's base to render it inactive. As they were storming the base, players would contend with opposing forces trying to shoot them with their lasers. The boys were given weapons and strapped into harnesses with sensors to detect when they had been hit, and they were off to battle! The teams competed for forty minutes before the "crazy insanity" ended, says Marquissee, who came in second to last.

Marquissee claims that the excitement of the book discussion and field trip inspired several of the boys to continue reading the *Ender* series outside of the book club.

PLAY IT!

Battle-Room Freeze Tag

If it's impractical to bring your group to a laser tag facility, you can try Battle-Room Freeze Tag, an icebreaker activity Melissa Moeller's Teen Book Club enjoyed at the Orlando Public Library, part of the Orange County Library System in Florida.

Split your group into two teams. Set up two stars (groups of two chairs each). Have each group hide behind a star. Each group will gently toss small items at the other group. If you get hit in the head, back, or chest, you are completely frozen where you are, and you must remain there until the game is over. If you are hit on any other body part (such as an arm or a leg), that part is frozen until the game is over. The first team to completely freeze the other team wins.

Go on a Library Scavenger Hunt

Melissa Moeller created a scavenger hunt revolving around books when her group read *Ender's Game*. Moeller chose the activity as a way to interest teens through "something active that involves bodily kinesthetic functions," just as the characters in the book engaged through space battle maneuvers. Moeller adds that this type of activity also appeals to visual learners.

Moeller created clues related to *Ender's Game* that encouraged participants to use library resources—and participants' own creativity. Some of her clues included:

- The first army Ender was assigned to was Salamander. Find a book about salamanders.
- Ender went to Battle School on a space shuttle. Find a picture of a space shuttle.
- Ender's sister's name was Valentine. Create a Valentine's Day card.

For the final task, participants were asked to piece together a puzzle, bring it to Moeller, and claim their prize, a small bag of candy. "The teens especially enjoyed the active and creative aspects of this activity," says Moeller. "Plus, they got a refresher course on locating books!"

Topics Discussed

- If it was necessary for Ender to commit murder
- If it was fair for the adults to manipulate Ender to reach what they thought was an important goal
- Why children were chosen to be military leaders
- If genocide is ever justified

ASK IT!

How did you feel about the way Ender was treated by the adults?

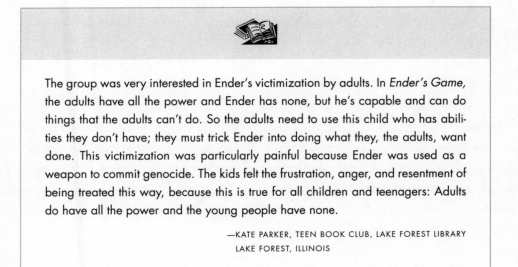

The group was very interested in Ender's victimization by adults. In *Ender's Game*, the adults have all the power and Ender has none, but he's capable and can do things that the adults can't do. So the adults need to use this child who has abilities they don't have; they must trick Ender into doing what they, the adults, want done. This victimization was particularly painful because Ender was used as a weapon to commit genocide. The kids felt the frustration, anger, and resentment of being treated this way, because this is true for all children and teenagers: Adults do have all the power and the young people have none.

—KATE PARKER, TEEN BOOK CLUB, LAKE FOREST LIBRARY
LAKE FOREST, ILLINOIS

Grades 6 and up

The Giver

Lois Lowry

Houghton Mifflin, 1993
Available in paperback from Random House
192 pages
Science Fiction

Companion novels: *Gathering Blue* (Houghton Mifflin, 2000), *Messenger* (Houghton Mifflin, 2004)

Jonas's futuristic world seems perfect: His community has eliminated disease, war, and all unpleasant feelings including pain and fear. At the age of twelve, when citizens are assigned jobs suited for them, Jonas is selected to be the Receiver of collective memories for his generation. Under the tutelage of the Giver, the last Receiver of memories, Jonas experiences the pain and pleasure that have been eliminated from his world—and begins to question his community's established ways.

- Lois Lowry says she deliberately tried to create a world that was safe and secure, to draw readers in to the community depicted in *The Giver*.

  I tried to make Jonas's world seem familiar, comfortable, and safe, and I tried to seduce the reader. I seduced myself along the way. It did feel good, that world. I got rid of all the things I fear and dislike; all the violence, poverty, prejudice and injustice, and I even threw in good manners as a way of life because I liked the idea of it.

- Readers often tell Lowry that they want a more definitive ending to *The Giver*. She says readers have offered many interpretations of the book's final scene, which she purposely left ambiguous. There isn't a right ending, according to Lowry: "There's a right one for each of us and it depends on our own beliefs, our own hopes."

- Lowry took the photograph of landscape and still-life painter Carl Nelson that appears on the cover of *The Giver* when she interviewed him for a magazine article at his Maine home in 1979. The image of Nelson's face haunted her, she says, and he was an inspiration for the story.

- While some of Lowry's books were inspired by specific events, she says *The Giver* "is a much more complicated book and therefore it comes from much more complicated places." Her interest in memory was one of many origins of the book, and she wanted to explore what might happen if memories were manipulated. Lowry believes it's important not to forget the past, and that memory is critical so that mistakes are not repeated.

Author website: www.loislowry.com

Perfect Apple Pie

Lois Lowry shared her thoughts on food in *The Giver* and why apples are an important part of her memories and her novel.

I think apples are the only food mentioned in my book The Giver, *which portrays a society so stark and colorless that interesting food preparation would not have been part of the people's lives. I suppose they ate something like frozen dinners: fairly nutritious but pretty dull fare.*

But suddenly the boy, Jonas, the main character in the book, sees something special about an apple.

I wonder why I, as a writer, chose an apple when that moment came. It could as easily have been an orange.

But my children grew up in a Maine farmhouse with an ancient orchard out beyond the barn. The apples were untended and misshapen. But every fall, using an antique cider press we had bought from an old farmer, we gathered those apples and ground them and pressed them into cider. Our horses always liked cider-making day because they got to eat the mushed-up remains, a real treat if you are a horse!

So apples play a large role in my memories, and probably that of my grown children as well.

I'm a good apple pie maker and apple pies are the best way, in my opinion, to use fresh apples in the fall if you live in New England, as I do.

We think you'll see something special about this delicious pie created by our friend the novelist and baker Eileen Goudge. The recipe is from her cookbook, *Something Warm from the Oven: Baking Memories, Making Memories* (Morrow, 2005). Goudge says she has served the pie to "foodies" from all over the world, including those who believe their mother's apple pie can't be topped, and it has never failed to garner raves. She has tweaked the recipe over the years, and says "it's about as close to perfect as an apple pie can get."

NOTE: You can make the pie dough with a combination of half lard and half butter. For a healthier alternative, Goudge suggests nonhydrogenated lard. If neither lard nor butter is available, Goudge recommends vegetable shortening such as Crisco stick shortening, either as a substitute for the lard or in combination with the butter.

The dough keeps well in the refrigerator for up to a week and in the freezer for several months. When thawing frozen dough, place in the refrigerator overnight, and then leave at room temperature for 30 minutes before rolling out.

Goudge prefers tart varieties of apples such as McIntosh, Jonathan, Greening, and Granny Smith for the filling.

She prefers to use Sucanat, dehydrated cane juice with all its vitamins and minerals intact, for its rich flavor. Sucanat has a light molasses flavor and is often used in place of brown sugar. It can be purchased at some grocery stores and many specialty or health food stores. You can substitute 1 cup dark brown sugar or 1 cup granulated sugar plus 1 tablespoon molasses for Sucanat in this recipe.

FOR THE NEVER-FAIL PIE DOUGH
(MAKES ENOUGH FOR A DOUBLE-CRUST 9-INCH PIE)

2 cups all-purpose flour

1 tablespoon granulated sugar

1½ teaspoons baking powder

¼ teaspoon salt

¼ cup chilled lard or unsalted butter, or a combination

1½ teaspoons cider vinegar

1 large egg, beaten

3½ tablespoons cold water

FOR THE FILLING

8 cups peeled, cored, and sliced apples (see note)

1 tablespoon fresh lemon juice

1 cup Sucanat, Demerara, or turbinado sugar (see note)

4–5 tablespoons all-purpose flour (depending on the apples' juiciness)

1 teaspoon ground cinnamon

⅛ teaspoon ground nutmeg

1 large egg

1 teaspoon water

1 tablespoon unsalted butter, chilled

FOR THE TOPPING

Granulated sugar

1. To make the pie dough: Place the flour, sugar, baking powder, and salt in a food processor and whir to combine. Add the lard in chunks. Whir for several seconds, then pulse until crumbly but not pulverized. Place the mixture in a large bowl. (Alternate method: Place the above ingredients in a large bowl and cut with a pastry cutter until crumbly.)

2. Whisk the vinegar and beaten egg in a small bowl with water. Add to the flour mixture all at once. Whisk vigorously with a fork just until the dough comes together (be careful not to overmix, as this will result in a tough crust). Shape into a ball. Divide in half, and gently shape each half into a ball. Wrap individually in plastic wrap and chill for at least 30 minutes.

3. To make the filling: In a large bowl, toss the apple slices with the lemon juice. Add the Sucanat (or sugar), flour, cinnamon, and nutmeg. With a large spoon or spatula, toss until the apples are coated.

4. Place one ball of dough on a floured work surface. Flatten by pressing down with the heel of your hand, shaping the edges to keep them from becoming ragged, until it forms about a 1-inch-thick round. With a rolling pin, roll (from the center outward) into a circle roughly 14 inches in diameter. Carefully fold in half, then again to form a triangle. Place in an ungreased 9-inch pie plate, positioning it so the point of the triangle is in the center of the pie plate. Gently unfold. Trim the edges to within 1½ inches of the rim.

5. Whisk the egg with water. Using a pastry brush, lightly brush mixture over the bottom and sides of the rolled dough. Spoon in the filling and pat it into a mound. Dot with the chilled butter.

6. Roll out the remaining ball of dough as described above. Transfer to the pie plate. With a sharp knife or kitchen shears, trim the overhang to within 1 inch of the rim. Roll the bottom and top edges inward, pressing lightly to seal; with your thumb, indent at regular intervals to form a single fluted edge. With the tip of a sharp knife, cut vents in the center of the top crust (such as a four-pointed star pattern).

7. Preheat oven to 375° F. Place the pie in the freezer for at least 15 minutes, until the dough is firm. Using aluminum foil cut into 2-inch strips, form a collar around the fluted edge of the dough to keep it from browning too quickly, crimping it to hold in place. Brush with the remaining egg glaze (you won't need it all). Sprinkle with granulated sugar (just enough to lend some sparkle).

8. Bake 15 minutes, then lower oven temperature to 350° F. and bake an additional 50–55 minutes, or until the filling is tender but not mushy (it should give way when the tip of a sharp knife is inserted in one of the vents). If the crust is browning too quickly, place a sheet of aluminum foil lightly over the top. Remove pie from oven and place on a wire rack to cool. When cool enough to handle, gently peel away the foil strips. Serve warm or at room temperature.

YIELD: 1 (9-INCH) PIE, 6 TO 8 SERVINGS

TRY IT!

Examine Language in *The Giver*

When citizens misspeak in Jonas's community, they receive lessons in "language precision." When Jonas asks his parents if they love him, his mother warns him that the "community can't function properly if people don't use precise language," and tells him to instead ask, "Do you enjoy me?"

Your group can come up with a list of euphemisms—words for which the community in *The Giver* has attributed other meanings. Then ask the group to find the definitions of these words in the dictionary. Compare the meaning of the words as used in the story with their dictionary definitions.

Test Your Memory

Danielle King played a memory game with her teen book club to launch their discussion of *The Giver* at the Orlando (Florida) Public Library. King placed twenty random items on the table, such as pencil toppers, books, paper clips, pictures, and small toys, making sure that some of them stood out more than others. King then removed the items, and asked teams to write down what they remembered seeing on the table. "In the book, memories are taken away from the people and only the Giver can have memories," says King. "The group members related how it felt when they could not remember the items, which led into a discussion of how they would feel if all of their memories were taken away."

TRY IT!

Pick a Profession

Jenne Laytham wanted her middle school book club at the Basehor (Kansas) Community Library to think about what their lives might be like if they were living in the community portrayed in *The Giver*. Just as Jonas and his peers were assigned occupations in the "Ceremony of the Twelve" in the novel, the middle schoolers received job assignments on slips of paper. Laytham had written down various occupations on slips of paper, and members discussed whether they were suited to the jobs they received, how they would feel being assigned jobs—and were given the chance to trade jobs with other members. "For fun, we went around the circle and said what occupation each person *should* have received," adds Laytham.

Create Your Utopia

Members of the Summer Young Readers Program at the Chautauqua Institution, a center for the arts, religion, education, and recreation in Chautauqua, New York, attempted to design a perfect place. Jack Voelker, the program director, asked the Summer Readers how they would construct a utopian community: What types of laws, rules, jobs, and activities would make up this community? Voelker then played devil's advocate. He asked, "If everyone receives free food, where does the food come from? Who pays for the seeds, the farm equipment, the trucks to bring it to market? What's in it for the farmer?" The members considered what made them uncomfortable about the perfect community they had created. "This led to an interesting discussion about the possible downside of utopias—the loss of personal freedoms, independence, and individuality," adds Voelker.

Topics Discussed

- What was most startling about Jonas's community
- Why books are banned in the community, and how this compares with banning books in our society
- The similarities and differences between our society and the society portrayed in the novel
- What it would take to make your life perfect

How did the book end?

I was surprised to discover how many people did not realize it was an ambiguous ending, and they were startled to hear other people had read different things into the end. In *The Giver,* the reader comes to care deeply about the main character and his journey, so passions rose as we discussed how people interpreted the ending. I noticed that how people interpreted the ending reflected a bit of their own outlook on life. People's views ranged from pessimistic to pragmatic to idealistic, and often their religious beliefs affected how they perceived the ending of the book. That simple question was all we needed to get a rousing discussion under way.

—KERSTIN WARNER
WESTPORT READS BOOK DISCUSSION GROUP
WESTPORT, CONNECTICUT

Monster

Walter Dean Myers

Amistad, 1999
Available in paperback from Amistad
288 pages
Fiction

Sixteen-year-old Steve Harmon is on trial, accused of acting as the lookout in the robbery of a Harlem drugstore that turned violent. The prosecution asks for a conviction of felony murder—and life imprisonment for Steve. The defense portrays Steve as a gifted student and loving brother, not the "monster" the prosecution has labeled him. Steve describes his ordeal through journal entries and, using a movie script, depicts his unfolding drama as it might be seen through the lens of a camera.

AUTHOR SCOOP

- Born in West Virginia and raised by his adoptive family in New York City's Harlem, Walter Dean Myers suffered from a severe speech impediment as a child, and often fought on the playground with classmates who teased him. He attended Stuyvesant High School in New York City, the same school his character Steve Harmon attends, but unlike Harmon, Myers dropped out at the age of fifteen. Myers says these tumultuous childhood years remain vivid, and ultimately inspired him to write literature for young adults.

- As part of his research on the criminal justice system for *Monster*, Myers interviewed prison inmates. He says:

> *The interviews were done in youth houses, halfway houses, and correctional facilities, adult and juvenile, in New York and New Jersey. I used the interviews extensively in planning the book. I also attended hours and hours of trials. My interview with a local assistant district attorney was useful, as was the enormously long trial transcript that I bought.*

- During these prison interviews, Myers began to recognize a pattern of denial among the inmates. He recalls:

> *I was interviewing an inmate at a maximum security prison in upstate New York when I heard the familiar excuse. The deaths, according to the man sitting across from me, were not his fault. Yes, he had held the gun and had pulled the trigger, but somehow I was to believe that the two victims caused their own demise. What was familiar was the mental process which excused the crime.*
>
> *In thinking about the interviews, trying to make sense of the often "senseless" crimes I encountered, I came to the conclusion that in many of these inmates what was lacking was an overall moral compass. Yes, they all knew right from wrong and legal from illegal, but in many instances the idea of "rightness" and "legality" were merely technical terms that they could manipulate in such a manner as to allow them to do whatever action was at hand. This was the case with most of the interviews I conducted. My ultimate conclusion was that, although there were people out there whom I considered just plain bad, there were far more whose foggy ideas of personal morality made up the bulk of criminal activity.*

- Myers explains how his prison interviews inspired the unusual screenplay format for *Monster*.

> *During the interviews, the inmates spoke in first person as they described their lives ("I lived in the South Bronx with my mom and older brother . . ."), but often switched to the third person when discussing the crime for which they were incarcerated ("There was a stickup about three in the morning and a guy was killed . . ."). In my mind they were again separating themselves from responsibility for their actions.*
>
> *Steve Harmon, in* Monster, *is bright, articulate, and known as a good young man. He also allows himself to tackle a crime opportunity in a highly technical manner, reminiscent of the inmates I had interviewed. To show how Steve separated himself from the crime, I used the movie scenario to discuss the crime and first person to discuss his personal life.*

Author information: www.harperchildrens.com

MAKE IT!

A Movie Storyboard

Kelly Czarnecki, Young Adult librarian at the Bloomington (Illinois) Public Library, asked members of the Young Adult Reads and Writes Book Club to create a storyboard, or a series of rough sketches showing the plot, action, characters, and setting of a film, when they discussed *Monster*. "The idea for the storyboarding activity came from the style and subject of *Monster*, in which Steve is an aspiring filmmaker," explains Czarnecki. "We talked about different camera angles, and close-up shots, and how these can be used to tell a story."

To educate and inspire participants, Czarnecki brought books about moviemaking and storyboarding to the meeting, including *Storyboarding 101: A Crash Course in Professional Storyboarding* by James Fraioli (Michael Wiese Productions, 2000), *Ex-*

ploring Storyboarding by Wendy Tumminello (Thomson Delmar Learning, 2004), and *Lights, Camera, Action! Making Movies and TV from the Inside Out* by Lisa O'Brien (Maple Tree Press, 1998).

Czarnecki also prepared a sample storyboard for the group involving a skateboarder who falls off his skateboard. "I tried to come up with a story that could be drawn with lots of good camera angles, like in *Monster* when the camera zooms in and out during the trial," says Czarnecki. For the activity, she distributed pencils and poster board with prepared grids of eight panels, and encouraged participants to use all eight panels or more, if need be. "I suggested they use a close-up shot, a long shot, and I challenged them to try an aerial view. Some brave folks tried it out!" she adds.

Participants drew stories based on their interests or events that happened in their lives. "I remember one girl storyboarded a short story about a car accident she had seen a few days prior to the project," says Czarnecki. "That one was hard to forget."

Topics Discussed

- -

- Whether Steve was innocent or guilty
- Whether the screenplay format of the book was effective
- Why Steve was called a "monster," and who the "real" Steve Harmon was
- How Steve, a "good kid," got to where he was, and how his situation could have been avoided

*What is the definition of a friend—someone to snitch you out
or someone to tell the truth in order to help you?*

We discussed what a friend means when you're in jail and in trouble. For a lot of the guys in the group, this is their first time in jail. When they first get here, they think they'll beat the system, they'll hang with the homeboys. But when they find their homeboys have rolled on them, all this camaraderie goes right out the window. We discussed how eventually you come to understand that a true friend is somebody who tells you whether you're right or wrong, somebody who won't close his eyes to your foolishness. It's somebody who's going to tell you the truth.

—JOHN RICHTER, LITERATURE AND LIVING BOOK CLUB (BOYS AGES 14–17)
ORANGE COUNTY JAIL YOUTHFUL OFFENDER PROGRAM
ORLANDO, FLORIDA

The Sisterhood of the Traveling Pants

Ann Brashares

Delacorte, 2001

Available in paperback from Delacorte

320 pages

Fiction

Sequels (all Delacorte): *The Second Summer of the Sisterhood* (2003); *Girls in Pants: The Third Summer of the Sisterhood* (2005); *Forever in Blue: The Fourth Summer of the Sisterhood* (2007)

Four teenaged best friends are preparing to separate for the summer when they discover a pair of thrift-shop jeans that magically fits each of them—although they all wear different sizes. Bridget, Carmen, Lena, and Tibby make a pact to take turns wearing the jeans, send them to one another, and write their most exciting and important summer adventures on the jeans. During their time apart the magic jeans keep the girlfriends connected as each of them embarks on new challenges and takes new risks.

- Ann Brashares was working as an editor when a colleague related a story about a pair of jeans her friends shared one summer. The story immediately gave Brashares many ideas and inspired *The Sisterhood of the Traveling Pants*.
- The idea for the traveling pants is related to another event in Brashares's life: choosing a wedding dress. Brashares had a photograph of the wedding dress she planned to buy, when an acquaintance, whose wedding hadn't worked out, asked Brashares if she would consider wearing the wedding dress she had purchased. After declining several times, Brashares decided to see the dress, which to her surprise matched the one in her picture. Brashares borrowed the dress and has since shared it with members of her own "sisterhood."
- Too many portrayals of teenage girls, says Brashares, involve "backstabbing and cruel social food chains." In *The Sisterhood of the Traveling Pants*, she wanted to explore the positive, rich friendships that constitute a huge part of teenagers' lives.
- Brashares has never traveled to Baja or Greece, two of the settings in her novel. As a child, she imagined visiting foreign countries and wrote letters from these imaginary trips. She says writing *The Sisterhood of the Traveling Pants* was somewhat of a continuation of these imaginary years.

Author information: www.randomhouse.com/teens/sisterhoodcentral
Film adaptation:
The Sisterhood of the Traveling Pants (Warner Brothers, 2005), rated PG, 119 minutes

Baklava

Paulette Clements and her daughter Stephanie, both of San Carlos, California, enjoyed reading about Lena's adventures in Greece, and prepared Greek refreshments for their mother-daughter book club's discussion of *The Sisterhood of the Traveling Pants*. "Being Greek made this very easy for us!" says Paulette, who made dolmades (stuffed grape leaves), and *kourabiethes* (sugar cookies) and baklava, the desserts Lena's grandmother prepares for the celebration of Koimisis tis Theotokou, the Assumption of the Virgin, in the novel.

The foundation of baklava, a popular Greek sweet, is phyllo (or filo) pastry, which is brushed with melted butter, layered with spices and chopped nuts, baked, and soaked in syrup. Clements's recipe originated from her great-aunt Alexandra "Aleka" Sperry, who immigrated to the United States from Greece. Clements received the recipe from her late brother, George Skofis, who loved to cook and took over the baking of baklava for family celebrations. Enjoy a taste of this Greek confection with your group.

NOTE: Phyllo dough is the ultrathin pastry often used in Greek cooking. Fresh phyllo can be found at specialty stores, and frozen phyllo is available in most supermarkets. To thaw phyllo, leave the box in the refrigerator overnight.

Phyllo dries out very quickly, so it is important to have a pastry brush and bowl of melted butter handy. As you're working, keep your stack of phyllo covered with plastic wrap. Removing one sheet at a time, brush the sheet well with butter, working from the edges in. Try to work quickly before it dries out.

If you are using the 9 x 14-inch sheets of phyllo commonly found in grocery stores, you may want to cut one inch off the sheets, so the phyllo measures 9 x 13 inches, the size of the baking pan called for in this recipe. Don't overtrim, since the dough shrinks as it dries.

For a slightly less "fruity" taste, you might cut back on the lemon juice in the syrup.

Clements makes this baklava with almonds, but says walnuts can be substituted. She recommends cutting individual pieces and placing them in paper or foil cupcake cups to keep the stickiness manageable.

FOR THE BAKLAVA

*1 pound (approximately 3 cups)
blanched almonds, coarsely
ground (see note)*

1 cup sugar

Peel of 1 orange, grated finely

2 cups (4 sticks) unsalted butter, melted

1½ pounds phyllo dough (see note)

FOR THE SYRUP

4 cups sugar

2 cups water

*1 tablespoon freshly grated
lemon peel*

*Juice of 1 lemon (about 3 tablespoons;
see note)*

1. To make the baklava: In a bowl, combine nuts with sugar. Add the orange peel and set mixture aside.

2. Brush a 9 x 13-inch baking pan along the bottom and sides with some of the melted butter.

3. Place 1 sheet of phyllo in the pan.

4. Brush the phyllo generously with the melted butter. Repeat, layering and brushing with butter 8 sheets of phyllo, working quickly (see note).

5. Sprinkle approximately ½ cup (more or less according to taste) of the nut mixture evenly across the top.

6. Layer 3 more phyllo sheets, brushing each sheet with melted butter. Then sprinkle nut mixture evenly across the phyllo. Repeat this step until you run out of the nut mixture.

7. After the last layer of nut mixture, layer 8 more sheets of phyllo, brushing each sheet with butter. Cover the pan and place in the refrigerator for approximately 1 hour.

8. Preheat oven to 300° F.

9. When the baklava is chilled, remove the pan from refrigerator. Using a long, very sharp knife, cut the baklava into small diamonds: First make 6 evenly spaced lengthwise cuts. Cut straight down until the tip of the knife touches the bottom of the pan, and keeping the knife straight, cut in a straight line all the way. Next, begin at the upper left end and cut diagonally across the lengthwise cuts to form

diamonds, starting in one corner and making cuts until you reach the opposite corner. You should have about 48 diamonds.

10. Bake 90 minutes, or until golden brown. Do not underbake: The phyllo should be crispy. While the baklava is baking, prepare the syrup, so it has plenty of time to cool.

11. To make the syrup: Mix the sugar and water in a medium saucepan. Add the lemon peel.

12. Bring the mixture to a boil. Reduce heat to low and simmer 15–25 minutes, until the syrup thickens. Remove from the heat and remove the lemon peel with a slotted spoon.

13. Add the lemon juice and stir. Set the syrup aside to cool.

14. Remove the baklava from the oven and spoon the cooled syrup evenly over the hot baklava.

15. Cover and allow to rest, at least several hours and preferably overnight, at room temperature, before serving.

YIELD: 48 (1½-INCH) DIAMONDS

MAKE IT!

Denim Locker Pockets

Members of the teen book club at the Wilmington (Massachusetts) Memorial Library used old jean pockets to create holders for pens and pencils to hang in their lockers. Facilitator Nathalie Harty found instructions for the activity in *Family Fun* magazine. The "pocket" making was so well received that Harty repeated the activity when the film version of *The Sisterhood of the Traveling Pants* was released.

MATERIALS (FOR ONE POCKET)

Scissors

Old pair of jeans

Decorations, such as iron-on patches, puffy and fabric paints, buttons and sequins

Tacky or craft glue

Cloth tape or colored duct tape

4 adhesive-backed magnets, each at least ⅛ inch thick

1. Cut the back pocket from the jeans. Make sure to include the material to which the pocket is attached when cutting the pocket. Cut closely around the three sewn edges of the pocket, leaving an extra inch of material on the back piece above the pocket opening.
2. To begin decorating, attach any iron-on patches according to the package directions. After ironing, decorate with fabric and puffy paints and glue on buttons and sequins.
3. When paint is dry, turn the pocket facedown. Fold the flap of material along the pocket's top edge and secure it against the back of the pocket with the tape.
4. Affix a magnet to each corner of the pocket (you may use glue to make it adhere more securely). When it is dry, the pocket is ready to hang in a school locker or on a refrigerator.

MAKE IT!

Traveling Pants

LeAnn Kunz's teen book group at the Washington (Iowa) Public Library decided to create a pair of pants that would travel among members as they discussed *The Sisterhood of the Traveling Pants* over several meetings. The teenagers selected two pairs of jeans at the local Goodwill store to use as their "traveling pants." Two book club members took the pants for the week, and returned with a short description of their week inscribed on the pants with fabric markers. Two other members took the pants for the following week, and by the time the group had completed the book, the group had two pairs of pants, personalized by all members of the group. "Every girl wanted to take them home," says Kunz, who had a raffle for the first pair of jeans, and displayed the second pair in the library.

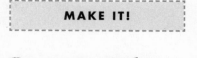

Decorated Jeans

Danielle King's teen book group at the Orlando (Florida) Public Library decorated paper pants with words, drawings, and expressions reflecting themselves, without letting anyone else in the group see the result. King then collected the paper pants and asked group members to guess who created each pair. An exchange about how members view themselves, and whether others view them the same way followed. King says the group loved the activity, and the library displayed the pants after the meeting.

TRY IT!

Dress Like a Sisterhood Member

The daughters of the mother-daughter Reading Maniacs of Los Angeles arrived dressed as one of the four girlfriends of the "Sisterhood." Bridget arrived in a soccer uniform, along with three Lenas in blue jeans and cute tops, several Tibbys with smocks, name tags, and false piercings on their noses, and one mother dressed as Carmen in her daughter's jeans. The girls shared their reasons for choosing their characters and explained whether they related to or admired them. Mom Nancy Zimble says dressing up was great fun for the girls and a wonderful way to entice them into the discussion.

Topics Discussed

- How the four girls deal in different ways with their problems that summer
- What each girl learns over the summer
- Which character you most identify with or are most like
- What makes the girls' bonds with one another so strong

*Is there a scene in the book that you found
memorable or that raised questions?*

The girls in our group were fixated on Lena being caught skinny-dipping in the lake, and how fast she could really put her jeans on when they were inside out and dripping wet. Two of them got so involved in the discussion that they decided to test it. After barricading the door and closing the window shades, they ducked behind chairs, shucked off their jeans, turned them inside out, and then put them back on again as fast as they could, which turned out to be pretty fast indeed.

—MIRIAM NEIMAN, PAGETURNERS BOOK CLUB (GRADES 9–12)
WELLES-TURNER MEMORIAL LIBRARY
GLASTONBURY, CONNECTICUT

Stuck in Neutral

Terry Trueman

HarperCollins, 2000

128 pages

Available in paperback from HarperCollins

Fiction

Sequel: *Cruise Control* (HarperCollins, 2004)

Fourteen-year-old Shawn McDaniel is trapped in his own body. His cerebral palsy has ravaged his nerves and muscles, leaving him unable to walk, talk, communicate, or control his bodily functions. No one knows that Shawn is a "secret genius" with a rich inner life, understanding and processing everything that happens around him. Shawn begins to suspect that his father, who believes Shawn suffers terribly from his condition, might attempt to kill him as an act of mercy. Through his narrative, Shawn conveys his fear and powerlessness to save his own life.

- Terry Trueman invented the character Shawn, but the inspiration for *Stuck in Neutral* is Trueman's son, Sheehan, who has cerebral palsy and cannot communicate. Trueman says that Sheehan, like Shawn, is misperceived by the world around him. Through Shawn's character, Trueman wanted to explore what life might be like for Sheehan. Living through this "worst thing that ever happened to me" experience, explains Trueman, "gave me insights into the story that I would not have otherwise had."

- Trueman says the response he has received to *Stuck in Neutral* has been incredibly gratifying. "One of the most rewarding things for me as the author of *Stuck in Neutral* is seeing the ways that it has changed readers' views of people with developmental disabilities," says Trueman. "Many teachers have used *Stuck in Neutral* in their classes and tied the book to activities outside of the classroom, such as visits to group homes and other facilities for people with special needs. I think this is amazing and wonderful."

- Trueman says he prefers writing stories in the first person, present tense "because anything can happen at any time the reader is going through the experience with the main character right as the experience unfolds."

Author website: www.terrytrueman.com

Terry Trueman's Favorite Teriyaki Don (Chicken)

Terry Trueman says he would rather write than cook. "In fact," says Trueman, "when I'm writing and it's going well, I often completely forget about eating for hours and hours at a time."

Trueman lives in Spokane, Washington, but when he's visiting his native Seattle, he always stops in at Hana restaurant on Seattle's Capitol Hill for teriyaki don, his favorite dish. Trueman says when he takes time away from writing, he makes his own version of the dish. Hana's owner, Ken Wada, was kind enough to share the recipe, so you can try one of Trueman's favorites at home.

NOTE: You may substitute prepared chicken broth for the homemade broth, and canola or peanut oil for the soybean oil.

At Hana, chicken is boned and prepared with the skin on. However, you may skin the chicken, if you prefer.

To prepare homemade chicken broth: Place 2 pounds of chicken bones in a large pot and cover with water. Simmer 6 hours, skimming occasionally. Remove the bones and strain liquid through cheesecloth.

FOR THE MARINADE

1½ cups hot water

⅓ cup low-sodium soy sauce

⅓ cup sugar

FOR THE CHICKEN

8 chicken thighs (about 2 pounds), or 4 small chicken breast halves (about 2 pounds), boned (see note)

FOR THE TERIYAKI SAUCE

1½ cups homemade chicken broth (see note)

1 cup low-sodium soy sauce

¼ cup sugar

1 teaspoon grated garlic

1¼ teaspoons grated fresh ginger

ACCOMPANIMENT

Japanese short-grain rice, cooked (approximately ½ cup per person)

GARNISHES

2 scallions, thinly sliced

1. To make the marinade: Mix the water, soy sauce, and sugar. Pour over the chicken, cover, and marinate in refrigerator 2 hours.
2. To make the teriyaki sauce: Combine all sauce ingredients in a large saucepan. Bring to a boil and simmer 45 minutes, until reduced by about 20 percent. Remove from the heat and set aside.
3. Preheat oven to 400° F. Remove the chicken from marinade and discard marinade. Place chicken on a rimmed baking sheet and bake 15–25 minutes for thighs (10–20 minutes for breasts), until chicken is tender and no longer pink.
4. Brush a large griddle or skillet with oil. Place the chicken on the hot griddle or skillet, and heat 4 minutes per side, until skin is browned. (If skin is on the chicken, place chicken skin side down and heat until skin is browned and crispy.)
5. Reheat teriyaki sauce over low heat in a large skillet. Place chicken directly in pan with sauce; increase heat to high 1–2 minutes, until sauce boils. Slice chicken on the diagonal into ½ inch slices and serve immediately on a bed of rice. Spoon sauce over chicken and garnish with thinly sliced scallions.

YIELD: 3 TO 4 SERVINGS

TRY IT!

Promote Disability Awareness

When the Messalonskee Middle School in Oakland, Maine, chose *Stuck in Neutral* for its schoolwide reading program, literacy coordinator Lisa Savage planned a Disability Awareness Day to complement the reading and discussions. Savage says the goal was to raise awareness of the challenges faced by a range of disabled people in the world, from those who are completely unable to communicate or move, like Shawn, to those who can participate more fully.

For Disability Awareness Day, college students studying Special Education at the University of Maine at Farmington set up stations to demonstrate various approaches to using adaptive technology. The experiences were eye opening for students, says Savage. Your group can easily re-create several of these activities.

Students had the opportunity to try to type on conventional keyboards—something they consider an easy, everyday task—wearing ski gloves. "They quickly found out how difficult it was," says Savage. "The exercise showed them keyboarding could be horrendously difficult, if not impossible, if you didn't have the motor skills that you take for granted," she adds.

Eating a potato chip without chewing was also tremendously challenging for the middle schoolers, but they got the sense of what it was like for Shawn, whose favorite treat in the book was the occasional potato chip that his brother would feed him: Shawn couldn't chew the chip but had to let it dissolve in his mouth until his swallowing reflex kicked in. Students found out how long it takes to dissolve a potato chip and gained an understanding of what it would be like if this was how they had to eat all of their food, says Savage.

The students also toured their school with an eye to the challenges of navigating the building in a wheelchair.

You might inquire at the special education department of a local college or university or an organization devoted to the disabled about demonstrating adaptive technology to your group. For the Messalonskee Middle School's Disability Awareness Day, a special smoothie maker was very popular. The machine had a communication device that allowed kids to order a smoothie without speaking; the attendant then poured their smoothie order into a cup. The student also had a chance to use Cheap Talk 8, a device that allows users who cannot otherwise communicate to record eight phrases. The students were engaged by the idea of which messages they would choose if they were limited to eight. Is there room for "I love you"? was a point of discussion at this station as students considered how to prioritize communications to their families, says Savage. A variety of adaptive scissors for people with different motor skill issues pointed out how difficult it could be to cut even the simplest shapes.

Topics Discussed

- If Shawn's fear of his father is justified
- Which one of the characters is closest to believing Shawn isn't just a "vegetable"
- How the book changed the way you look at mentally disabled people
- The pressures involved in parenting a special-needs child

ASK IT!

How can you judge the happiness of someone who can't communicate?

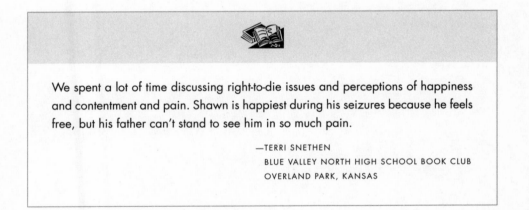

We spent a lot of time discussing right-to-die issues and perceptions of happiness and contentment and pain. Shawn is happiest during his seizures because he feels free, but his father can't stand to see him in so much pain.

—TERRI SNETHEN
BLUE VALLEY NORTH HIGH SCHOOL BOOK CLUB
OVERLAND PARK, KANSAS

Titles for Older Teen Readers

(GRADES 9 AND UP)

The Curious Incident of the Dog in the Night-Time by Mark Haddon

The First Part Last by Angela Johnson

The Gospel According to Larry by Janet Tashjian

Speak by Laurie Halse Anderson

To Kill a Mockingbird by Harper Lee

Persepolis: The Story of a Childhood by Marjane Satrapi

The Curious Incident of the Dog in the Night-Time

Mark Haddon

Doubleday, 2003
Also available in paperback from Vintage
240 pages
Fiction/Mystery

Fifteen-year-old Christopher Boone lives in Swindon, England, with his father. He suffers from Asperger's syndrome, a form of autism. Although Christopher thinks logically, he processes information literally, and has little comprehension of human emotions or social nuances. Patterns and rituals—solving math problems, eating red but not yellow or brown foods—help Christopher maintain order and calm. When a neighbor's dog is killed, and Christopher attempts to solve the mystery, he has to navigate a world that he finds alien and confusing.

- Mark Haddon shared with us these thoughts about his character Christopher and *The Curious Incident of the Dog in the Night-Time*:

  The words "autism" and "Asperger's syndrome" are never used in Curious Incident, *and for a good reason. I wanted people to react to Christopher as a human being first and foremost, not as a person with a specific diagnosis. Which is, I believe, the way we should react to everyone. Ignore the labels. Talk to the person.*

  Of course, the novel is now known, almost universally, as a book about Asperger's syndrome. I have come to accept that. And I know, from the many letters I receive, that it has been of great use to some people with Asperger's syndrome and to their parents and friends and caregivers.

  But, as a good friend of mine once said, "It's not a book about someone with Asperger's. It's a book about a young mathematician with some behavioural issues."

  And that's the way I prefer to see it. Not as a novel about a syndrome. But as a novel about difference, and empathy, and prejudice. And maths. And space. And families.

  It is also a novel about reading. One of the peculiar effects of the stripped-down writing style is that readers have to supply a lot of the information themselves. When you come to the end of the book, you will have done at least half the work imagining that world. And that, I suspect, is why so many readers feel so attached to it. Because it belongs to them in a way that many books do not.

- Haddon says the literary work that most influenced him when writing *The Curious Incident of the Dog in the Night-Time* was Jane Austen's *Pride and Prejudice*. Austen, according to Haddon, wrote about "boring people with desperately limited lives" who "were bound by iron rules about what they could do, where they could go and what they could say." Yet, says Haddon,

Austen writes about these humdrum lives with such empathy that they seem endlessly fascinating. And her first act of empathy is to write about them in the kind of book these women would themselves read—the romantic novel.

This was what I was trying to do in Curious Incident. *To take a life that seemed horribly constrained, to write about it in the kind of book that the hero would read—a murder mystery—and hopefully show that if you viewed this life with sufficient imagination it would seem infinite.*

- As a young man, when the term "autism" wasn't widely used, Mark Haddon worked with adults and children with physical and mental handicaps, who might now be diagnosed as autistic. Haddon emphasizes, however, that he is not an expert on autism, nor did he research the topic to create Christopher's character for his book, "because I wanted Christopher to work as a human being and not as a clinical case study."
- Haddon did not set out to write a book about a young man with autism. He began with an image of a dog stabbed with a fork, because he was looking for a way to draw readers into his novel on the first page. He explains that it was then easy for him to find Christopher's voice.

I realised that if you described [the dog's murder] in a flat, emotionless, neutral way it was also (with apologies to all dog lovers) very funny. So I had the voice. Only after using that voice for a few pages did I work out whom it belonged to. Having done that, the difficult thing was to work out a believable way for Christopher to construct a novel given that he is utterly unaware of the reader's emotional responses to what he is writing. Having Christopher simply copy his hero, Sherlock Holmes, by borrowing the format of the murder mystery was the solution to this problem.

- Haddon says he and Christopher share a love of math, and that most of the math problems included in the novel came "straight out of my own head." "If you enjoy math and you write novels, it's very rare that you'll get a chance to put your math into a novel," says Haddon. "I leapt at the chance."
- As a children's book author and illustrator, Haddon has been "doodling" on

his computer for years. When he realized his computer-generated art were the types of illustrations that Christopher might use in his mystery, "it was one of those glorious moments when something on which you have stupidly wasted many months of valuable time suddenly becomes useful." Haddon says he believes "the book could have worked without them, but Christopher has a very graphic, visual imagination and the pictures are a very efficient way of sharing that with the reader and a very efficient way for Christopher to get across some of the complex things he wants to say."

Author website: www.markhaddon.com

BOOK BITES

Pink (Raspberry or Strawberry) Milk Shakes

Christopher's favorite color is red, and he prefers red foods, such as red licorice laces, pink wafers, and strawberry or raspberry milk shakes. When we asked Mark Haddon about Christopher's color preferences, he explained:

Christopher hates the colours yellow and brown. He hates yellow because it is the colour of custard (which he dislikes) and bananas (which turn brown) and double yellow lines (which mean you can't park your car) and yellow fever (which is a deadly disease) and sweet corn ("because it comes out in your poo and you don't digest it, so you are not really meant to eat it, like grass or leaves"). He hates brown because it is the colour of dirt and poo and gravy (which he dislikes) and wood (which is not as modern as metal and plastic), and because there is a girl at his school called Melissa Brown (who tore his big astronaut painting into two pieces).

Christopher does, however, like the colour red. One of his teachers tells him that this is silly. And Christopher agrees, to an extent:

"Because it is sort of being silly. But in life you have to take lots of decisions and if you don't take decisions you would never do anything because you would spend all

your time choosing between things you could do. So it is good to have a reason why you hate some things and you like others."

NOTE: You might need to make the milk shakes in batches, depending on the size of your blender.

1 cup fresh whole raspberries or sliced strawberries

2 cups milk

4 teaspoons sugar

4 scoops (2 cups) good-quality vanilla ice cream

Puree the berries in a blender. Add the milk and sugar, and blend. Add ice cream, and blend until smooth.

YIELD: 4 (8-OUNCE) SERVINGS

THINK ABOUT IT!

Discover How Sherlock Holmes— and Christopher—Solve a Case

"*The Curious Incident of the Dog in the Night-Time* is a terrific choice for a community reading program because it addresses the issue of differences and how we can function together," says Beth Avery, a coordinator of the One Book, One Valley community reading program in Gunnison, Colorado. In the novel, Christopher enjoys Sir Arthur Conan Doyle's Sherlock Holmes stories, because the puzzles in the mysteries appeal to his scientific mind. For their program, One Book, One Valley sponsored an intergenerational Sherlock Holmes tea where William Dorn, a Sherlock Holmes expert, engaged the group in a discussion of Holmes's problem-solving methods, and how Christopher used these same techniques in *The Curious Incident of the Dog in the Night-Time*.

Dorn introduced several types of logic, most notably deduction and retroduction (or abduction) to the group. Deduction, explains Dorn, is the approach Sherlock Holmes says he uses, but seldom does. Deduction is based on facts and is the process detectives use when they start with a few clues and use them to solve a mystery. For example, a detective might see a jar that contains only white beans. If the detective sees a man take beans from the jar, then he can conclude that the beans in the man's hand will be white beans. That is an example of deduction. Deduction is certain: There can be no doubt that the detective's conclusion is correct.

However, suppose that what the detective sees is another man who is standing near the jar and who has white beans in his hand. Can the detective conclude that the man took the beans from the jar? Of course, he cannot. The beans might have come from any one of a number of places, such as a store. On the other hand, the jar with white beans is very close by, so the detective may still say, "It is quite likely that the beans came from the jar." Although not certain, this is a pretty good guess (some people call it an educated guess). This line of reasoning, which is always risky, is called retroduction, and this is the method, says Dorn, which Sherlock Holmes—and Christopher—use most frequently.

TRY IT!

Deduction or Retroduction?

William Dorn contributed an exercise that demonstrates Christopher's problem-solving approach in *The Curious Incident of the Dog in the Night-Time*. In Chapter 107 of the book, Christopher refers to the book *The Hound of the Baskervilles* and says, "Two of Sir Henry Baskerville's boots go missing . . ." From this he concludes that someone took Sir Henry's boots. Was Christopher using deduction or retroduction? It is possible that someone took the boots, but it is also possible that Sir Henry simply misplaced them and could not find them. Therefore, Christopher was using retroduction.

Of course, detectives usually know some other things as well as the particular clues they are considering. Perhaps Christopher knew that Sir Henry was very neat and kept all of his things in order. Then it would be more likely that someone took the boots. But that is still not certain. Perhaps someone who worked at the hotel was busy cleaning and polishing the boots. Christopher's conclusion is still risky, although not as risky as it was before he learned about Sir Henry's neatness. He is still using retroduction.

Dorn launched a competition among members of the group, giving examples of Christopher's statements from the book and asking members to determine which logical method Christopher was using by analyzing each statement. The answers, cautions Dorn, are not always obvious. In the end, the group had a much clearer understanding of Christopher's thought processes and different ways to solve a problem, Dorn says. "They understood that most of the time you use deduction when you have all the facts, but in solving crimes, you often don't have all the facts."

TRY IT!

Learn About Autism

In Wake County, North Carolina, Wake Reads Together, a community reading program, forged a partnership with the local autism society for a program around *The Curious Incident of the Dog in the Night-Time*. The Autism Society of North Carolina asked parents of children with autism to attend each of the eighteen book club discussions planned as part of the community-wide program. Jill Hinton Keel, executive director of the Autism Society of North Carolina, says the organization wanted the community to understand that all children with autism are not exactly like Christopher in the book. "The parents who attended the book discussions explained that autism is a spectrum disorder," says Keel, "and Christopher was on the upper end of the spectrum in terms of his verbal ability and comprehension. It would be easy to see how children who have even less comprehension than Christopher would be overwhelmed in some of his situations."

The society demonstrated interactive music therapy for individuals with autism, and Creative Living, a local program for adults with autism and developmental disabilities operated by the Autism Society of North Carolina, brought examples of artwork created by people with autism, including pottery and paintings. For people with autism who have more difficulty in social situations, music and art are a way to promote communication, says Keel. She adds that through the Society's involvement with the reading program, the group was able to help local citizens better understand autism, and demonstrate that people with autism can make valuable contributions to their communities.

Topics Discussed

- How Christopher's mind works, and how he views the world
- How the diagrams and drawings in the book help you understand Christopher
- The different approaches to parenting taken by Christopher's mother and father
- Whether you know someone like Christopher

Why did Christopher's father keep secrets from him?

We discussed why the father kept secrets from Christopher. We thought it was possible that the father was secretive because he didn't think that his son could handle any real-life dilemmas or complications because of his autism.

—MORGAN McMILLIAN, TEEN BOOK GROUP
POLITICS AND PROSE BOOKSTORE
WASHINGTON, D.C.

The First Part Last

Angela Johnson

Simon & Schuster, 2003
Available in paperback from Simon Pulse
144 pages
Fiction

Companion novel: *Heaven* (Simon Pulse, 2000)

Sixteen-year-old Bobby's life changes dramatically when he finds out his girlfriend, Nia, is pregnant. Throughout Nia's pregnancy and after the birth of his daughter, Bobby struggles to balance life as an average urban teenager—doing his schoolwork, hanging with his buddies, and getting along with his parents—with his determination to be a good father.

AUTHOR SCOOP

- *The First Part Last* is a prequel to Angela Johnson's book *Heaven*, in which the character of Bobby first appears. In *Heaven*, says Johnson, Bobby is a secondary "but very solid" character, who struggles to raise his young daughter. Johnson was inspired to write *The First Part Last* after her editor donated copies of *Heaven* to the Manhattan School for Children. She explains:

> *The students overwhelmingly loved and were intrigued with the character of Bobby, and they wanted to know more about him. My editor asked if I would be interested in writing Bobby's story. At first I declined, but then changed my mind when, on a trip to New York City, I saw a young man (about fifteen years old) on the train in the middle of the day with an infant.*

- Teenage readers of *The First Part Last* tell Johnson they can identify with the characters in the book, although some criticize the behavior of Bobby's mother. "Almost all of them knew someone who is under eighteen, pregnant, or about to become a teen father," Johnson reports. "Interestingly enough, the only problem any of them ever has with the book is that they think Bobby's mother is not loving enough because she doesn't take over raising the baby."
- *The First Part Last* was Johnson's first attempt at writing in a male voice, a task she calls "a stretch." She explains:

> *Though many of my minor characters are men and boys, I worried that I would not be able to find a voice that rang true. My brother helped me out by telling me if I was indeed being faithful to the language of a male teen— as he himself had been one. . . . After the language obstacle, Bobby became just another character, acting and reacting to his life.*

Author information: www.visitingauthors.com
Angela Johnson recommends:
Make Lemonade by Virginia Euwer Wolff (Henry Holt, 1993)
The Dear One by Jacqueline Woodson (Delacorte, 1991)

Angela Johnson's Favorite Chili-Cheese Fries

In *The First Part Last*, Bobby's father, Fred, owns a restaurant and nurtures his son by cooking favorite foods, including cheese fries. When Bobby visits Fred, he knows Fred's apartment will smell like chili-cheese fries—"just for me."

Angela Johnson was thrilled to discover chili-cheese fries—a dish featuring some of her favorite foods—in college.

Three of the first foods that I ever cooked by myself were chili, homemade French fries, and toasted cheddar cheese sandwiches. I was brilliant at the creation of all three by the time I was in seventh grade. Most afternoons, this was what my brothers and I ate during summer vacation while my parents worked. They were also the three foods I could have lived on forever. I decided they were their own food group, and there was no need for veggies or anything else that didn't contain these three things. But I never thought to combine any of them.

But something happened when I went off to college—salad and buffet bars. So the first week I was away from home and feeling a little homesick, there they all were—just sitting in vats and metal trays waiting to come together for me: crisp, crinkly fries; thick, chunky chili; and buttery, tangy cheese. And for one minute in the dining hall of my dorm I was twelve again and just as happy as my brothers had been when I dished my three best, and only, dishes out to them.

So now, anytime I travel and want a bit of home I search for chili-cheese fries on restaurant menus. Some things never change!

Johnson enjoys the chili-cheese fries at Mike's Place in her hometown of Kent, Ohio. Owner Mike Kostensky generously contributed his recipe for Johnson's favorite dish, which his menu lists as California curly fries. Kostensky first tasted these fries in Redondo Beach, California, and created a recipe to include a crispy burrito shell basket. You can also serve the fries and toppings on a plate.

Kostensky says his servings are so generous that groups generally buy one order of fries to share. Although Johnson enjoys her fries without sour cream, Kostensky serves up his fries with sour cream on the side. He also suggests varying the recipe by sprinkling raw diced onions on top.

1½–2 pounds frozen seasoned curly fries

1 (15-ounce) can prepared chili

Oil for deep frying

2 (8-inch) flour burritos

1 (8-ounce) package process cheese, such as Velveeta

2 tablespoons shredded cheese mix (provolone-mozzarella or cheddar-mozzarella)

1. To make the fries: Prepare the fries according to package directions.
2. Empty the chili into a small saucepan and heat over low heat. While the fries are cooking and the chili is heating, make the burrito shells.
3. To make the burrito shells: Fill a large saucepan with oil to a depth of about 5 inches. Heat oil to very hot (around 350° F.). Fold the burrito around a glass jar or metal can (an empty 28-ounce can of tomatoes works well). Using metal tongs, hold the burrito in place around the can and dunk it into the hot oil. Fry 20–30 seconds, until golden brown. Remove from the oil, flip the burrito over on some paper towels, and let drain. (Be careful not to burn hands, as hot oil can hide in pockets.) Repeat with second burrito.
4. Cut the process cheese into cubes. Place the cubes in a microwave-safe bowl and heat on high power 5 minutes, stirring after 3 minutes, or until the cheese is melted. Or, heat the cheese in a saucepan over low heat until melted, stirring occasionally.
5. Fill each burrito shell with half of the fries. Spoon half the chili on top of each serving of fries, followed by half of the melted cheese. Sprinkle each serving with 1 tablespoon shredded cheese. Serve immediately.

YIELD: 2 FILLED SHELLS, ABOUT 8 SERVINGS

Egg Babies

When considering an activity to connect with the parenting theme in *The First Part Last* for her middle school book club at the Southwest County Regional Library in Boca Raton, Florida, Karyn Dombrosky recalled the egg babies she made as a child. "I wanted the teens to gain an understanding of the life Bobby chose, and I felt making egg babies, which are so delicate and must be named and protected, would allow them to connect a little with Bobby's situation," says Dombrosky.

Dombrosky found instructions for making egg babies on the Internet. First, she "blew out" eighteen eggs by poking holes in the ends of each egg and blowing through one end to force out the contents. Then she dipped them in a vinegar solution to clean them and remove any odors and set them back in their cartons to drain and dry. Dombrosky started four or five days in advance of the meeting to check the stability of the eggs over time, but she says the process could be done the day before the meeting, as long as the eggs are completely drained out and dry. At the meeting, she set out decorating supplies, including markers, sequins, and bows, and participants drew faces on and decorated their "babies."

To make carriers for the babies, Dombrosky found small plastic containers, but she says other objects, such as small empty berry cartons, could be used. Participants made handles for the carriers by punching holes in the sides of the containers and threading pipe cleaners through. As a finishing touch, kids made "blankets" for their babies out of pieces of felt. Dombrosky says the project was a big success. "Even several days after the program, I saw teens carrying their egg babies with them. I was happy to see that no one regarded it as just a silly egg, but as something to take care of," she says.

NOTE: Bring the eggs to room temperature so the insides liquefy and will be easier to blow out. Prepare the eggs at least one day in advance of your meeting so they have time to dry.

MATERIALS

Raw eggs, 1 per person (see note)

Large sewing needle or safety pin

2 mixing bowls

Vinegar

Water

Markers

Glue

Googly eyes

Decorations (ribbons, lace, buttons, sequins, cotton balls, macaroni, feathers, glitter, fabric, yarn, or jewelry)

Small containers (optional)

Pipe cleaners (optional)

Felt (optional)

1. To prepare each egg: Wash and dry the egg. Use the needle or pin to puncture a small hole at the small end of the egg.

2. Puncture another hole at the large end of the egg, and use the needle or pin to enlarge the hole to about ⅛ inch in diameter. Try to puncture the egg yolk by swirling the needle or pin around in the hole.

3. Hold the egg gently over a mixing bowl with the large hole facing down, and blow firmly on the other hole until the insides have all come out.

4. In another mixing bowl, make a solution of half vinegar and half water. Immerse the egg completely in the solution, and allow the inside to fill partway. Shake the vinegar solution around in the egg, and blow it out. (Vinegar will fade brown eggs. If you'd like to lighten the color of your eggs, let them sit in the vinegar solution for a few minutes. Make sure to completely immerse the egg in the solution or you will end up with rings on the egg where the air and the mixture meet.)

5. Set the egg back in the egg carton with the large hole facing down. Allow to drain and dry for one day. Repeat steps 1–5 for all eggs.

6. To make the "babies": Set out markers, glue, and art supplies. Allow participants to decorate their "babies."

7. If desired, make baby carriers out of small containers, attach pipe cleaners for handles, and cut "blankets" out of pieces of felt.

Realityworks Infant Simulators

Angela Johnson suggests an improbable scenario to accompany a discussion of *The First Part Last*. "I would want each teen who's read *The First Part Last* to have to spend one week out of the school year to raise an infant full-time," she says. "No breaks after school, no breaks on the weekend, no parental interference. I can think of no movie, book, or music that could speak as loudly as this."

Others have had the same thought. To help teens understand the responsibilities of parenting, Mary and Rick Jurmain of Eau Claire, Wisconsin, invented the original Baby Think It Over infant simulator in 1994. Now used as part of the RealCare Parenting Program, the realistic, life-size, computerized "doll" cried at random intervals and required holding and comforting for the approximate duration needed to feed, bathe, or diaper an infant. Newer models utilize bottles and diapers with wireless technology and require constant head support, just like a real baby. Instructors can program infant care schedules from fifteen minutes to six hours and choose from cranky, normal, or easy-to-care-for baby modes. If the parent allows the infant to cry for more than one minute or throws, hits, or shakes the baby, the simulator will register that the baby has been abused. Data can be downloaded from the baby to evaluate the results of a simulation, which typically takes place over a weekend for maximum effect.

According to Rebecca Dienger, marketing communications manager for Realityworks, the company that produces the simulator, the purpose of the RealCare Parenting Program is to teach "responsibility, proper infant care skills, and what it takes to nurture a dependent being, including the physical, emotional, social, and financial impact a baby has on one's life." Since the simulator's creation, it has been used as part of comprehensive pregnancy prevention programs in schools, churches, and community centers in fifty thousand American schools and thirty-five different countries. Some educators have reported up to a fifty percent drop in teenage pregnancy in their schools after instituting the Baby Think It Over or RealCare Parenting Program, and the program continues to be researched extensively for its effectiveness.

Although the high price of the simulator makes it an unlikely choice for individual book clubs, you can find out more about the product at www.realityworks.com or contact your community's middle or high schools to find out if they are being incorporated into parenting education or child development classes.

Topics Discussed

- How Bobby's decisions are shaped by his new role as a single parent
- How Bobby's relationships with his buddies change after he becomes a father
- The different ways in which Bobby's buddies support him
- How one action can affect every aspect of your life

ASK IT!

In your opinion, how realistic is the portrayal of Bobby as a father?

When Nia gets pregnant, Bobby assumes his and Nia's parents will deal with the baby, but that isn't the case. Bobby's parents force him to deal with the harsh realities of child care on his own. The girls in our group were impressed with how well Bobby handled being a dad. They also thought it was very romantic and not necessarily realistic, because they don't know any single fathers like Bobby in real life.

—CYNTHIA RIDER, GIRLS' PROGRAM BOOK CLUB (AGES 14–18)
HILLCREST JUVENILE HALL
SAN MATEO COUNTY, CALIFORNIA

Grades 8 and up

The Gospel According to Larry

Janet Tashjian

Henry Holt, 2001
Available in paperback from Dell
192 pages
Fiction

Sequel: *Vote for Larry* (Henry Holt, 2004)

Seventeen-year-old Josh Swensen wants to change the world. Using the pseudonym "Larry," Josh creates a website that features his sermons on consumerism, photographs of his seventy-five possessions, and suggestions for teen activism. When thegospelaccordingtolarry.com captures national attention—and Larry's following swells to include Josh's best friend, Beth—it becomes more difficult for Josh to remain anonymous. He must determine when to reveal the truth and how to keep his cherished beliefs from becoming compromised.

• Janet Tashjian explains the origins of *The Gospel According to Larry*:

> *I wanted to write about consumerism and teens; it's a subject I feel very strongly about. (I think Abercrombie & Fitch should be paying kids for all the free advertising instead of the other way around.) I also wanted to experiment in format by trying to blur the line between fiction and nonfiction—the easiest way to do that was to put myself in the story. One of the best novels I've ever read was* The Things They Carried *by Tim O'Brien. The book was so amazing, I literally quit my job the next day to become a writer. O'Brien also plays with what's real and not real in his story.* The Gospel According to Larry *is very much an homage to him.*

• Tashjian describes how two features of the novel—Josh's footnotes describing details of the story and photographs of his possessions—became a part of her novel.

> *The footnotes are there because Larry is writing his story the way he'd write a term paper. But it also gave me a place to put statistics, jokes, and sidebar information. I can have a pretty short attention span and that kind of "doodling in the margins" is a way to keep me on track. Needless to say, the typesetter at my publisher wasn't too happy!*
>
> *Originally, I took all the pictures of Larry's possessions myself. The photos were terrible! My friend Mark Morelli, an amazing professional photographer, mercifully bailed me out. I was very fortunate that my editor, Christy Ottaviano at Henry Holt, didn't freak out when I handed her a manuscript full of footnotes and photos. She's perennially patient—all my books are filled with sticky notes, lists, crossword puzzles, anagrams, drawings . . . mostly because they're enjoyable for me to do. One of my basic theories of writing is this—if I have fun writing a book, my readers will have fun reading it.*

- Tashjian says she is often asked if Larry is like her. She describes their similarities:

> We have some similar traits—we both do yoga, are politically active, and are supercurious about the world. He is much more computer literate than I am and kicks my butt in both math and tree pose. His "faster, faster!" attitude about life is very much drawn from my son.
>
> I framed Larry's tale with "real" people like me. As I wrote, other people jumped into the book—most notably, Bono of U2.

Author websites: www.janettashjian.com
www.thegospelaccordingtolarry.com

Janet Tashjian recommends:

No Logo: No Space, No Choice, No Jobs by Naomi Klein (Picador, 2000), and *Branded: The Buying and Selling of Teenagers* by Alissa Quart (Perseus, 2003). Tashjian says these are "two good nonfiction books dealing with consumerism." She also recommends *The Things They Carried* by Tim O'Brien (Houghton Mifflin, 1990), which she says is "a masterpiece and on a lot of required reading lists for high schools," and any books by Henry David Thoreau, especially *Walden* (1854).

BOOK BITES

Janet Tashjian's Favorite Baked Chocolate Pudding

Tashjian suggests trying one of her favorite desserts, baked chocolate pudding, to complement your discussion of *The Gospel According to Larry*, and explains this choice:

> When I do school visits, students talk about Larry as if he's a real person; he certainly is to me. But the thing no one else knows about Larry is that besides being a

yoga practitioner, math whiz, and blogger, he's a massive chocoholic. This recipe comes from Jamie Oliver's cookbook Jamie's Kitchen *(Hyperion, 2003). It is one of my—and Larry's—favorite recipes on the planet. My sister Judi and friend Liz still talk about the night we made this for the first time—an occasion bordering on culinary rapture.*

Much of The Gospel According to Larry *deals with celebrity worship and Jamie Oliver can certainly be considered a celebrity chef. But here's what Oliver did with his fame: He chose to mentor fifteen disadvantaged youths and train them as chefs to staff a new restaurant. After much hard work, 15 is now one of the hottest restaurants in London. Jamie continues to hire, train, and mentor unemployed and homeless workers.*

One of the credos Larry lives by is that one person can change the world. Well, Jamie Oliver must believe that too, because his "Feed Me Better" program and documentary challenged the British government to put more money and effort into feeding British schoolchildren quality food. After working in school kitchens and getting people to sign petitions, Jamie got the British government to sign legislation giving 280 million pounds to upgrade the food served in school cafeterias. Almost half a billion dollars for the country's students to receive healthier food—that's what I call one person making a difference. This recipe is quite rich and should be savored on only the most special occasions—oh, I don't know, maybe a book club meeting.

NOTE: Janet Tashjian shares some thoughts about the recipe:

I usually don't bother with the hazelnuts, but that might have something to do with getting to the chocolate faster. Because this recipe uses rice flour, it's also gluten-free. Since the chocolate and coffee mixture needs to be frozen, make sure you do that first before you go ahead with the rest of the recipe. I also use decaf espresso instead of caffeinated. Like Larry, I have all the energy I need without additional stimulation! Enjoy!

One-cup custard or flan cups work well for baking the puddings.

Cake flour may be substituted for the rice flour.

The ground almonds can be omitted for a smooth-textured pudding.

1 pound best-quality bittersweet or dark chocolate (70% cocoa solids), divided

¼ cup hot espresso (or good strong instant coffee; see note)

9 tablespoons butter, plus extra for greasing

6 eggs, separated, at room temperature

1 cup plus 2 tablespoons sugar

Generous ½ cup (3.5 ounces) finely ground almonds (see note)

¼ cup rice flour (see note)

1 small handful chopped hazelnuts (see note)

1. In a saucepan, melt 4.5 ounces of the chocolate with the coffee. Pour into six small ice-cube molds and freeze 20–30 minutes, until hard.

2. Grease six 1-cup oven-safe cups or molds with the butter. Place in the refrigerator while preparing the pudding mixture.

3. Melt the remaining chocolate with the butter in a bowl set over a saucepan of boiling water. Set melted chocolate aside to cool. In a separate large mixing bowl, beat the egg whites with the sugar until stiff. Fold the yolks into the cooled chocolate mixture, then add the almonds and the flour. Carefully fold in the beaten egg whites.

4. Preheat oven to 375° F. Remove the molds from the refrigerator. Spoon a little pudding mixture into each one. Push a cube of frozen chocolate into the pudding mixture. Cover with the remaining pudding mixture so each ice cube is completely enveloped.

5. Bake 18–20 minutes. While the pudding is hot, remove carefully from molds (insert a knife around edges to loosen if necessary). Serve immediately, sprinkled with hazelnuts.

YIELD: 6 (1-CUP) SERVINGS

Book Links: Ideas from Janet Tashjian

GO BACK TO NATURE

Most of all, when I think about Larry, I think about nature. Unfortunately, I don't have a hole in the ground deep in the woods to sit and think the way Larry does. (It is one of my biggest regrets.) I do, however, spend a lot of time in the woods, just breathing in the fresh air and silence. Book club members can do a walking meditation in a nearby forest or park for a firsthand experience of what nurtures and feeds Larry's spirit.

TRY IT!

Go Back to Nature

Christine Durling, a media specialist at Bordentown (New Jersey) Regional High School, planned a trip to the great outdoors for her Ravenous Readers Book Club. The members, who embark on a field trip for each book discussion, visited the Historic Whitesbog Village in Burlington County, New Jersey, to discuss *The Gospel According to Larry*. Whitesbog Village, the birthplace of the cultivated blueberry (the official state fruit of New Jersey), was also the largest cranberry farm in New Jersey during the early 1900s. It is now part of the Pinelands National Reserve with nature and hiking trails. "Larry's environmental spirit would certainly be elevated by the beauty and serenity surrounding the crimson haze that embraces the cranberry fields," says Durling. "Had Larry been with us, I know he would have loved the cranberry picking."

BE AN AD WHIZ

Many schools and book clubs I've visited do lots of projects around the consumerism and advertising talked about in the book. Students have done amazing "ads" for companies that market to them; many have analyzed the barrage of advertisements they're exposed to in a day. I've also been a part of some great discussions where kids talk about whether the "news" we get on television is just another item being sold. Have book club members make original ads or ad parodies of companies that market to teens.

BE AN ACTIVIST

I've received many letters from kids who have made big differences in their schools by starting political clubs or banning junk food and sodas. Brainstorm in your book club about issues that can be addressed in your school and put together an action plan to effect positive change.

TRY IT!

Design a Website and a Commercial

Danielle King asked members of her teen book group at the Orlando (Florida) Public Library to imagine designing and posting a website while keeping their true identity hidden, as Larry did. King asked the group to consider how they would express their ideas and if they would write sermons like Larry or include photos on their websites. The members jotted their ideas down along with logos for their websites, and put the papers in a pile. Each member then picked a piece of paper and read or showed the imagined website.

King says teens enjoyed "Commercial Time," in which they worked in groups to develop a commercial for a product. After developing and acting out their commercial, they discussed how commercials influence viewers. "This was a nice icebreaker that led into the discussion of how Larry influenced people on his website," says King.

```
TRY IT!
```

Conjure a Larry-like Atmosphere

Nathalie Harty created a "Larry-like ambience" with music, books, movies, and food mentioned in *The Gospel According to Larry* when her teen book club at the Wilmington (Massachusetts) Memorial Library discussed the novel. Harty played songs by musicians mentioned, such as Kurt Cobain and U2. A volunteer created and displayed a mural-size "ticket" to Larryfest, the Woodstock-like musical festival in the novel. Books and movies mentioned—works by Ralph Waldo Emerson and Mark Twain, films about Woodstock, and other films, including *Groundhog Day* and *Pee-wee's Big Adventure*—were also available for browsing. Members snacked on "Larry" foods, including lasagna, peanut butter and apple slices, and Chinese takeout.

For a door prize, Harty filled a brown paper bag from Bloomingdale's department store, one of the book's settings, with copies of *The Gospel According to Larry* and *Vote for Larry,* M&M's, tarot cards, a Hindu statuette, a Wizard Hat, a U2 CD, a book about yoga, a copy of Henry David Thoreau's *Walden,* and other items mentioned in the story.

Topics Discussed

- The consequences of Josh's decision to withhold information on his identity and how he dealt with these consequences
- If Josh avoids taking responsibility
- If the Larryfest was hypocritical or went against Larry's principles
- The risks associated with creating websites

ASK IT!

Could you limit yourself to only a certain number of personal possessions?

I told the group that after reading the book, my daughter went through her personal items and whittled them down considerably. They thought Larry took this to extremes in the book, but they agreed with the principles of sharing CD collections and books. It was interesting to talk about what they could easily give up, what they absolutely couldn't give up, and the pressure here in America to have so much *stuff*.

—AMY KRAHN, BOOK CLUB FOR TEENS
SHOREWOOD PUBLIC LIBRARY
SHOREWOOD, WISCONSIN

Speak

Laurie Halse Anderson

Farrar, Straus & Giroux, 1999
Available in paperback from Puffin, 2003
208 pages
Fiction

After calling the police to break up a schoolmate's house party over the summer, Melinda Sordino begins her freshman year of high school as a social outcast. Traumatized by an event that occurred during the party, Melinda becomes increasingly alienated from her parents and peers and retreats into silence, struggling to face her fears and find the confidence to speak.

AUTHOR SCOOP

- Laurie Halse Anderson describes how the idea for *Speak* "was born out of terror": Melinda came to her in a dream during the winter of 1996, when she awoke to the sound of a girl sobbing.

Speak started in a bad dream for me. I heard a girl's voice crying and I got thinking about who she was and why she was in such pain. I leapt out of bed and dashed down the hall to check on my two daughters. Sound asleep, both of them, no tears on their pillows. They were fine. But I could still hear a girl crying, hysterical. She was in my head. It was a nightmare.

And so I had to write down the Crying Girl. She kept sobbing as I pulled on a robe and turned on my computer. Once the word processor blinked awake, she stopped. She made a tapping noise and blew into a microphone. "Is this thing on?" she asked. "I have a story to tell you."

That is how I met Melinda Sordino, the protagonist of Speak.

- Though *Speak* is not autobiographical, Anderson says that as with Melinda, loneliness and isolation marked her own freshman year of high school: She was an "outsider" in a new school district. She believes that "a culture that allows a kid to feel alone" is one of the worst aspects of high school. She explains:

My family went through some hard times as I entered high school, and some of Melinda's experiences reflect mine. It was hard to know which was worse: the idea that nobody knew I existed, or that they knew I existed and were choosing to ignore me, or maybe, talk about me and laugh at me behind my back. Even thinking about that year turns my stomach. Going to school every morning felt like walking into prison.

Spoiler Warning: Plot and/or ending details follow.

- Anderson says she is often asked if she was raped. She says :

The answer is yes. I was thirteen. It was under different circumstances than the rape in the book, but it's how I understand what Melinda felt like. I am also asked, "Was it really rape?" Shocking, but true. Kids today do not understand what the laws are regarding sexual assault. This might be a great research project. Boys need to know, too, or else they can wind up in jail for a crime they did not realize they were committing.

• Melinda's retreat into silence ultimately causes her more pain. Anderson explains that for teenagers, silence is common after a traumatic event such as Melinda experiences, and having an adult in whom they can confide is critical.

The point of adolescence is to separate (safely) from your parents, so you develop your own "family" of friends. That's cool. But let's face it, even the best friends in the world, which Melinda does not have, are not going to be able to help with everything. All kids need an adult who won't freak out if the kid is honest, and who will really listen when the kid speaks up. It can be a relative, a friend's mom, a teacher, guidance counselor, clergy-person, the guy who runs the bagel shop—whatever. As long as you can trust them.

Author website: www.writerlady.com
Film adaptation:
Speak (Showtime, 2005), rated PG-13, 93 minutes
Laurie Halse Anderson recommends:
I Know Why the Caged Bird Sings by Maya Angelou (Random House, 1969)
Inexcusable by Chris Lynch (Atheneum, 2005)
The Perks of Being a Wallflower by Stephen Chbosky (MTV Books, 1999)
What My Mother Doesn't Know by Sonya Sones (Simon & Schuster, 2001)

Book Links: Tasty Ideas
from Laurie Halse Anderson

LAURIE HALSE ANDERSON'S POPCORN

Laurie Halse Anderson contributed this recipe for popcorn, one of her favorite foods. It's a terrific accompaniment to the *Speak* movie and game (see p. 400).

You'll need one bag of microwave popcorn.

1. Put the bag in a microwave.
2. Start the microwave.
3. Stop the microwave before the popcorn burns.
4. Argue with self about the need for butter versus the need not to gain weight.
5. Flip a coin to decide on butter.
5a. While the butter is melting, grab paper towels.
6. Inhale the popcorn and drink a quart of lemonade.
7. Pat belly and moan.

Anderson also offered some menu suggestions for foods mentioned in *Speak*:

1. Ho Hos
2. Mashed potatoes
3. Powdered doughnuts
4. Pop-Tarts
5. Very bad turkey soup
6. Pizza
7. Applesauce

Book Links: Ideas from Laurie Halse Anderson

SPEAK MOVIE AND GAME

Anderson recommends watching the DVD version of the *Speak* film adaptation, which features a voice-over of the movie with comments from Anderson and film director Jessica Sharzer.

Many readers have held *Speak* movie parties, says Anderson, and she suggests your group play a game she devised while watching *Speak*. While watching *Speak*:

1. Count how many times Melinda speaks.
2. Watch for lines that came from the book.
3. Figure out which famous teen movie the director paid homage to in one of the cafeteria scenes.
4. Throw popcorn at the TV whenever IT shows up.
5. Figure out what scenes were NOT in the book.
6. Cheer when the author shows up on-screen.

LEARN ABOUT AND DISCUSS SEXUAL ASSAULT

Anderson suggests you research statistics about sexual assault before your book club discussion and visit the website for the Rape, Abuse & Incest National Network (RAINN), the nation's largest anti–sexual assault organization (www.rainn.org).

Anderson also recommends that you "have a discussion about what is hard to talk about." She explains:

Using hypothetical people, of course, discuss what topics teens really want to talk to their parents about but don't because they are afraid their parents would totally freak out. What kinds of problems are caused by this lack of communication? What should parents do differently so that their teens will be more open with them? How can a teen prepare her parents for a difficult conversation?

Topics Discussed

- If the "First Ten Lies They Tell You in High School" and the depiction of high school life in the book are realistic
- If Melinda's parents are actually removed and distant, or if this was just her perception
- If Melinda is a sympathetic character
- How friends can help someone who is silent

ASK IT!

Have you had a friend who changed over time—for better or worse? How did you notice those changes?

I ask members of my teen book clubs to look for hints of what Melinda, the main character, was like before she was speechless and how she had changed. We look at the clues given by her friends and parents. I want them to be able to spot if something tragic is happening to someone they know and to let them know they are not alone if something tragic is happening to them. As a comparison, I also introduce them to Maya Angelou's *I Know Why the Caged Bird Sings*.

—SHERELLE HARRIS, TEEN BOOK CLUB
SOUTH NORWALK PUBLIC LIBRARY
NORWALK, CONNECTICUT

Grades 8 and up

To Kill a Mockingbird

Harper Lee

1960

Available in paperback from Warner Books

336 pages

Fiction

Scout Finch recalls her childhood in small-town Alabama in the 1930s, when townsfolk knew one another by name and racial prejudices ran deep. Scout, her brother Jem, and their friend Dill spent lazy summer afternoons playing in the yard and summoning courage to approach the house of their mysterious, reclusive neighbor, Boo Radley. When Atticus, Scout's father and a local lawyer, is asked to represent Tom Robinson, a young black man falsely accused of rape, the trial electrifies the town, and the biases—and courage—of its citizens emerge.

- Harper Lee's character Scout Finch is largely autobiographical. Like Scout,

  - Lee was born in 1926, so she would have been exactly the same age as Scout during the time the novel took place.
  - Lee grew up in Monroeville, Alabama, a town in the Deep South.
  - Lee's father, Amasa C. Lee, was a small-town lawyer with an unusual first name.
  - The Lee family took pride in their descent from Confederate war general Robert E. Lee.
  - There was a dilapidated, boarded-up old house in Lee's neighborhood rumored to have been inhabited by a mysterious recluse named Sonny Boular.

- In 1950, Lee had quit her job as an airline reservation clerk in New York City to work on writing full-time when her father fell sick. Lee's trips back to Monroeville to tend to her father reawakened childhood memories of time spent with him at the courthouse, and sparked ideas for her book. *To Kill a Mockingbird* took Lee eight years—and many revisions—to complete, and remains her only published novel.

- Tom Robinson's case in *To Kill a Mockingbird* is based partially on the 1931 trial in Scottsboro, Alabama, of nine black men who were accused of raping two white women in the coal car of a train. As in Tom Robinson's case, there was very little physical evidence linking the men to the crime, and several of them had physical disabilities that would have made it impossible for them to commit the crime. In spite of the evidence, all the men were convicted and sentenced to death. (In the next six years, after a series of appeals, all but one man were freed or paroled.)

- Upon its publication in 1960, *To Kill a Mockingbird* became an instant success. The book earned Lee a Pulitzer Prize for Fiction in 1961, and an Academy Award–winning movie was produced in 1962. Lee disliked the fame and attention surrounding her success and, since the early 1960s, has refused most interviews. She announced in 1961 that she was working on a second novel, this one about eccentric characters commonly found in small southern towns, but the novel never materialized.

- It is widely acknowledged that the character of Dill was modeled after renowned author Truman Capote, a childhood friend of Lee's. During their adult years, Lee accompanied Capote to Kansas when he researched *In Cold Blood* (1966), a nonfiction account of multiple murders, which Capote dedicated to Lee. Capote recalls his childhood friend as a spirited girl who bullied boys—similar to Lee's depiction of the character Scout.

Film adaptation:

To Kill a Mockingbird (Brentwood Productions, 1962), not rated, 130 minutes

BOOK BITES

Cream Cheese Pound Cake

Harper Lee divides her time between New York City and Monroeville, Alabama, where tourists flock each season to see the local stage production of *To Kill a Mockingbird* and to view the courthouse that served as the model for the trial setting in the book.

The Courthouse Café stands on the far side of the square, in plain view of the courthouse building. Janet Sawyer opened the café in 2000 and serves lunch and dinner to locals as well as tourists. For her menus, she relies heavily on *Sumpthn' Yummy*, a cookbook of recipes contributed by residents of Monroeville County in the 1970s, when three local women self-published and sold the book as a fund-raiser for the high school band. Nan Williams, the book's editor, says residents contributed their "finest, finest recipes" to the project; the book sold out three times and continues to enjoy great popularity in Monroeville today.

Of all the recipes in *Sumpthn' Yummy*, Sawyer names Cream Cheese Pound Cake as a personal favorite. Pound cake, a timeless southern classic, gets its name from the original recipe, which called for a pound of butter, a pound of sugar, and a pound of flour. The addition of cream cheese in this recipe gives the cake a moist, rich consistency. It was the first cake she tried making at the Courthouse Café, and after several failed attempts (because she made the mistake of using self-rising flour) she perfected it. Now Sawyer claims to have made "a million" of these over the years, and when she bakes it for a lunchtime dessert, it flies off the counter.

This unusual pound cake cooks for two hours and, according to Sawyer, is distinguished by its crunchy top and "tiny ooey-gooey spot in the middle where the cream cheese and butter settle." Sawyer likes the cake cool, but says it's especially good straight out of the oven, topped with a scoop of vanilla ice cream. We liked it with strawberries, too.

This recipe was contributed to *Sumpthn' Yummy* (edited by Mrs. David Stallworth, Mrs. Harvel Deas, Jr., and Mrs. Albert Nettles, Jr., *The Monroe Journal*, ca. 1976) by Mrs. Dick Carter and Virginia Nettles.

NOTE: Sawyer says this cake tends to burn in a thin-sided tube pan because of its long baking time. She recommends using a heavy-duty, thick-sided tube pan. (A Bundt pan does not work well because the cake should not be turned over, but rather served with the crusty brown side facing up.)

The crusty top sometimes crumbles when the cake is sliced the first day, but will be easier to cut through on the second day.

For this recipe, do not preheat the oven. Turn the oven on *after* putting the cake in.

1½ cups (3 sticks) salted butter, softened (do not substitute margarine)

1 (8-ounce) package cream cheese, softened

3 cups sugar

6 large eggs, at room temperature

3 cups all-purpose flour

Pinch of salt

3 teaspoons vanilla extract

1. Grease and flour a 10-inch heavy-sided tube pan, or spray with nonstick cooking spray with flour.
2. In a large bowl, beat the butter and cream cheese with an electric mixer on high speed until combined. Add the sugar and beat well, scraping down the sides of the bowl. Add the eggs 1 at a time, beating well after each addition.

3. Stir in the flour and salt. Add the vanilla. Blend well.

4. Pour the batter into the prepared pan. Start in a cold oven, and bake at 300° F. about 2 hours, until the top is light golden brown and crunchy. (A toothpick stuck in the center should come out with batter on it—it will never come out completely clean.)

5. Cool the cake 15–20 minutes. Remove the cake from the pan onto a plate, then immediately turn onto a wire rack so cake is right-side up (this will allow the crust to develop on top). Be careful not to break the crispy brown top as you turn the cake out.

YIELD: 1 (10-INCH) CAKE, 10–12 SERVINGS

MAKE IT!

Soap Carvings

The soap carvings that Boo Radley leaves in the tree as gifts for the children inspired Elisa Carlson of the East County Regional Library in Lehigh Acres, Florida, to devise a soap-carving craft when the Lee County Library's One Book, One Community program featured *To Kill a Mockingbird.*

Soap carving—using simple, handmade tools to cut shapes and designs out of bars of soap—is a craft native to Appalachia, but Carlson says it has gained appeal in other parts of the country. A friend of hers from the North grew up carving soap. "This is a poverty craft," she explains. "This is something you can do with whatever you have around."

While soap carving sometimes means etching designs into the surface of the soap, Carlson's activity involved creating three-dimensional soap sculptures, as Boo Radley had done. To prepare for the activity, Carlson benefited from the guidance of an experienced soap carver in her community, and she highly recommends that the group leader practice carving soap before trying it with the group.

Before the meeting, Carlson made carving tools out of wooden craft sticks and gathered simple patterns. Participants traced their patterns onto the soap, then used the wooden tools to carve around the pattern, and to round the edges of the finished shape to remove its cube-like appearance. As a finishing touch, participants used the marking tool to make eyeholes, and placed shiny black beads in the holes.

NOTE: In advance of the meeting, make enough soap-carving tools for the group (see "To Make Soap-Carving Tools" on p. 408). Or ask participants to make the tools at the start of the meeting, but try to make one set in advance so you can estimate the time it will take. These tools work well carving soft soap, such as Ivory, and are safe for children ages five and up.

Unwrap bars of soap one day in advance to allow them to dry slightly.

For patterns, Carlson cut out photographs or drew outlines of simple, recognizable shapes: duck, whale, turtle, snowman. She suggests avoiding patterns with small details or narrow parts, such as the thin neck of an animal, as soap can easily break.

MATERIALS (FOR ONE SOAP CARVING)

Carving tools, such as a knife, chisel, shaping tool, marking tool (see note)

1 large bar of Ivory soap

Simple pattern (see note)

2–3 small black beads (optional)

1. Using a knife tool, scrape the lettering off the bar of soap.
2. Place the pattern on the soap and trace around it with the marking tool.
3. Use a chisel or shaping tool to cut away small pieces of soap until a basic shape is achieved. Cut clear through the bar, removing excess soap all the way around. Always cut small chunks, as soap can break if large chunks are removed. Leave a ¼-inch margin around the outline of the pattern to allow for mistakes and more detail work later.
4. After a basic shape is formed, use the knife tool to further refine the shape, carving in smooth, upward strokes.
5. If you like, use a marking tool to make eyeholes, and place black beads in the holes.

TO MAKE SOAP-CARVING TOOLS

A plane is useful in making these tools, especially if you plan to make several sets for your group, but rough sandpaper can also be used. Carlson recommends wrapping masking tape around the handles of the craft stick tools to create a gripping surface.

MATERIALS (FOR ONE SET OF TOOLS)

9 wooden craft sticks   *Glue*

1 wooden cuticle stick   *Plane tool or rough sandpaper*

Knife: Glue three wooden craft sticks together in a sandwich fashion, with the middle stick protruding 1 inch beyond the other two sticks to form the "blade" of the knife. Allow to dry. Using a plane or rough sandpaper, remove about ¼ inch off one edge of the middle craft stick to form a sharp, angled point.

Chisel: Glue three wooden craft sticks together in a sandwich fashion. Allow to dry. Using a plane or rough sandpaper, form one edge of the tool into an angled point.

Shaping Tool: Glue three wooden craft sticks together in a sandwich fashion, with the middle stick protruding about ¼ inch beyond the other two sticks. Allow to dry.

Marking Tool: Using a pencil sharpener, sharpen one end of a wooden cuticle stick. (Sometimes presharpened cuticle sticks can be purchased.)

Topics Discussed

- Why the book is considered a literary classic
- How the issues of rape and racism in the novel compare with those in John Grisham's *A Time to Kill*
- Whether you agree with the statement "All men are created equal," which Atticus uses in his closing argument
- Whether Tom Robinson was the only person on trial

What is the significance of the book's title?

The title interested the group because it refers to killing something whose sole purpose is to sing a beautiful song and please people. We discussed how this relates to Tom Robinson—he was so good, he was there to help Mayella, and he didn't do anything wrong.

—ELISE SHEPPARD, FRIDAY CLASSIC BOOK CLUB FOR HOMESCHOOLED TEENS
HARRIS COUNTY PUBLIC LIBRARY SYSTEM, CY-FAIR COLLEGE BRANCH
CYPRESS, TEXAS

Persepolis: The Story of a Childhood

Marjane Satrapi

Pantheon, 2003
Available in paperback from Pantheon
160 pages
Memoir/Graphic Novel

Sequel: *Persepolis 2: The Story of a Return* (Pantheon, 2004)

In comic-book format, Marjane Satrapi tells of her childhood in Iran. In 1979, an Islamic fundamentalist government replaced the ousted Shah of Iran, and many of the freedoms Satrapi and her family had enjoyed quickly vanished. Satrapi and her mother are forced to wear veils in public, and the family fears the police will detect their small, forbidden pleasures—wearing nail polish, listening to Western music, and drinking alcohol. As she learns of friends and family members tortured and killed by the repressive regime, Satrapi joins her parents in demonstrations, while she struggles for personal independence and an understanding of the violence around her.

- Marjane Satrapi grew up in Rasht, Iran, where the culture of graphic novels did not exist. She became interested in drawing comics when she moved into a studio apartment in Paris with several artists who demonstrated the process of cartooning. Satrapi began to realize that creating graphic novels fit her skills well, because, she says, "thinking with images is extremely normal" for her. She adds, "From the second I made the first page, I knew this is what I should be doing."

- By increasing understanding of life in Iran, Satrapi hopes *Persepolis* will promote tolerance of cultures throughout the world. "If people are given the chance to experience life in more than one country, they will hate a little less," she explains. "That is why I wanted people in other countries to read *Persepolis,* to see that I grew up just like other children."

- When she arrived in New York from Paris, where she now lives, to promote *Persepolis* in 2003, Satrapi was detained and questioned at John F. Kennedy Airport, and she fainted during the aggressive interrogation. She was questioned similarly while traveling to promote *Persepolis 2* in the fall of 2004, when she was called a liar and reduced to tears. Satrapi considers these experiences evidence of Americans' fear and misunderstanding of Iranian culture, which they tend to equate with fundamentalism.

- According to Satrapi, her parents reacted positively to *Persepolis* and found humor in the small criticisms they received in their daughter's book. Satrapi credits her parents with teaching her that it's all right to make mistakes, and with giving her "the most important thing—the freedom of thinking and deciding for myself."

Author information: www.randomhouse.com

Naan-Gerdooee (Persian Walnut Cookies)

Deborah MacInnis, a librarian at the Edgartown Public Library in Martha's Vineyard, Massachusetts, served these walnut cookies for the library's Evening of Persian Delights, organized in honor of *Persepolis*, the community's 2006 One Book–One Island Program reading selection.

Walnuts, a common ingredient in Persian cooking, have traditionally been a symbol of abundance and prosperity. In ancient times, the king of Persia reserved the fruit of the walnut tree solely for his own delight. When he made a present of some of his prized walnut trees to another ruler, the trees were similarly reserved for that ruler's enjoyment. Throughout history, Iranians of all social classes have prized walnut trees: The poor planted them for economic reasons, because a single walnut tree could support an entire family, and the rich lined the edges of their property with the trees as a sign of wealth.

MacInnis located this recipe on the Internet, where you can find many variations. She enjoyed the recipe's simplicity and ease of preparation, and we like the cookie's interesting appearance, rich nutty flavor, and pleasantly crunchy consistency.

NOTE: Keep the cookies small, using] no more than one teaspoon of batter per cookie, so they will bake up crunchy rather than chewy.

6 large egg yolks

½ cup sugar

1 teaspoon vanilla extract

3½ cups coarsely chopped walnuts

1. Preheat oven to 300° F. Place parchment paper on two ungreased baking sheets.
2. In a large bowl, beat the egg yolks, sugar, and vanilla with an electric mixer at high speed 4 minutes, until very thick and almost white. Add the walnuts and mix well.
3. Drop teaspoonfuls of the batter 2 inches apart on the prepared baking sheets.

4. Bake for 18–20 minutes, or until dry, firm, and golden brown. Cool the cookies completely on baking sheets before removing.

YIELD: ABOUT 5 DOZEN COOKIES

TASTE IT!

Iranian Tea

The prevalence of tea in Iranian society dates to the early decades of the twentieth century. For centuries before that, coffeehouses flourished throughout Persia, until the 1700s, when Middle Eastern rulers began to view coffeehouses as breeding grounds for dissent. More recently, the shah, who was also suspicious of activity at coffeehouses, attempted to convert coffee drinkers into tea enthusiasts by importing new strains of tea from China and banning games played in coffeehouses. His mission succeeded: today, coffee is confined to a morning beverage only, but tea is consumed throughout the day. And currently, tea is the only drink (besides soda) served in Iranian "coffeehouses."

Tea is an important part of the daily lives of most Iranians. Tea is served throughout the day in all Iranian homes, both wealthy and poor; in offices, tea accompanies every important business transaction. In *Persepolis*, like other Iranian families, Marji's family drinks tea in the evening, when they recall the day's events, and Marji's mother quickly offers tea to unexpected guests.

Although Iranian tea can be difficult to find in the United States, your book club can create tea with a similar flavor by combining Earl Grey and Darjeeling teas. Simply steep one of each type of tea bag in a mug of boiling water for several minutes.

In Iran, tea is served without milk or sugar, but Iranians put a sugar cube on their tongues and draw the tea through the cube as they drink. On formal occasions, the tea is flavored with cinnamon or garnished with crushed rose petals. Small plates of dried fruit, nuts, and assorted pastries, such as the Persian walnut cookies above, are traditional accompaniments to Iranian tea.

Draw a Cartoon

Since the mid-1990s the graphic novel—a story told through a combination of text, panels, and images—has gained tremendous popularity in the United States. Similar in form to comic books but longer, graphic novels go beyond traditional superhero subject matter and tackle a wide range of topics. Graphic novels appeal to people of different ages and genders.

Graphic novels demand different skills of the reader than prose, and in many ways, children and teens are uniquely suited to understanding this genre. Robin Brenner, a librarian at Cary Memorial Library in Lexington, Massachusetts, and an authority on graphic novels, explains that the visual literacy kids develop through technology gives them an advantage in understanding graphic novels. "When you read a graphic novel, you have to do the work of combining the panels into a story," she explains. "Kids who have grown up in a multimedia world—with CD-ROMs, the Internet, and video games—instinctively understand how to make sense of the visual sequence."

Several book clubs have tried cartooning during their discussions of *Persepolis.* Some groups have asked participants to compose a comic about a part of the *Persepolis* story they liked, while others have suggested drawing a comic about giving up a luxury, because Satrapi writes of the luxuries she and her family had to sacrifice after the Islamic Revolution. Either way, we suggest reading about graphic novels before asking your group to draw their own comics, and bringing examples of graphic novels to the meeting to inspire ideas (see "Understanding Graphic Novels," p. 416).

Before handing out materials—paper, pencils, black outline markers, and thin and thick colored markers—discuss with group members the following considerations:

What role will you play in creating the cartoon?

Brenner explains that, although *Persepolis* was written and illustrated by one person, graphic novels are typically composed by a writer and artist working together, and sometimes committees of up to twenty-five people are involved.

(These could include pencillers, who create the look and style of the art; inkers, who ink the lines; colorists; letterers, who complete the lettering by hand or computer; and editors, who steer the process.) Decide what role you want to play in creating your cartoon, and if you will work alone or with other people.

Should you include text bubbles?

Stories told without dialogue can have tremendous impact. Brenner refers to the scene in *Persepolis* where Satrapi draws an all-black panel after the death of her neighbors. "This is a strong emotional statement that would be hard to articulate in words," she says.

Will you include panels and, if so, what shape will they be?

Satrapi uses rectangular panels throughout *Persepolis*, but graphic artists often vary the shape of their panels (Japanese graphic novels, or *manga*, are characterized by the varied shape of the panels), use them intermittently, or leave them out entirely. Discuss the impact of panels on the comic and how you want to use them.

Will your comic be black-and-white, or will it include color?

Brenner points out that some graphic novelists, such as Michael Avon Oeming, the main artist behind the Powers series, use color to great effect, while others find color distracting. Discuss the impact of color versus black-and-white drawings and decide which you will use.

Consider the style of the characters.

Brenner says that Scott McCloud's book *Understanding Comics* (see "Understanding Graphic Novels," p. 416) explains why readers are more likely to identify with simple faces. "The less a face looks like a specific person, the easier it is for the reader to say, 'That could be me,'" explains Brenner. This theory explains why Mickey Mouse and a happy face are universally appealing. More complex figures, such as superheroes, encourage readers to distance themselves from the story.

UNDERSTANDING GRAPHIC NOVELS

Before asking book club members to try their hand at cartooning, you might want to consult these resources recommended by Robin Brenner:

Understanding Comics: The Invisible Art by Scott McCloud (Kitchen Sink Press, 1993), "for anyone who wants to understand how comics work."

Getting Graphic! Using Graphic Novels to Promote Literacy with Preteens and Teens by Michele Gorman (Linworth, 2003), a compact book that "gives you lots of information in a short amount of time."

Graphic Novels in Your Media Center: A Definitive Guide by Allyson A. W. Lyga (Libraries Unlimited, 2004)

Topics Discussed

- If the graphic novel format is effective for Marji's story
- What kind of person Marji is, and the nature of her relationship with God and with her family and friends
- How humor is used to expose the absurdities of politics and war
- The social and political issues highlighted in the book, such as religious freedom, gender inequality, and class differences

ASK IT!

*How does the religious government in Iran compare
with religious governments in other countries?*

Our discussion of repressive governments and freedom of expression was especially interesting because we have a regular participant who practices Orthodox Judaism and is an avid supporter of Israel. She shared quite a bit of information about the Israeli government, and how Israel works as a religious state. We talked about the similarities and differences among the governments of Israel, Iran, and the United States.

—AMY MARTIN, TEEN VOLUME BOOK DISCUSSION PROGRAMS
CHICAGO PUBLIC LIBRARY, SULZER BRANCH
CHICAGO

Notes

Introduction

Page xiv **According to a 2006 report sponsored by Scholastic, Inc.:** "The Kids and Family Reading Report™ Conducted by Yankelovich and Scholastic," www.scholastic.com/about scholastic/news/readingreport.htm, accessed June 16, 2006.

Page xiv **According to a 2004 National Endowment for the Arts study:** "Reading at Risk: A Survey of Literary Reading in America," www.arts.gov/pub/ReadingAtRisk.pdf, accessed June 22, 2006.

The Boxcar Children

Page 50 **As a child . . . watching and waving:** Mary Ellen Ellsworth, *Gertrude Chandler Warner and* The Boxcar Children (Morton Grove, IL: Albert Whitman, 1997).

Page 50 **She wrote . . . recuperating from bronchitis; "I decided to write":** *Something about the Author*, vol. 9 (Detroit: Gale, 1976), p. 196.

Page 50 **Warner rewrote *The Boxcar Children*:** Ellsworth, *Gertrude Chandler Warner and* The Boxcar Children, pp. 45–46.

Page 50 **"Perhaps you know":** www.kidsreads.com/series/series-boxcar-author.asp, accessed March 19, 2006.

The Hundred Dresses

Page 57   **poor but loving family:** Anita Silvey, ed., *Children's Books and Their Creators* (Boston: Houghton Mifflin, 1995), p. 226.

Page 57   **"In my writing, I like":** *Something about the Author*, vol. 7 (Detroit: Gale, 1975), p. 80.

Sarah, Plain and Tall

Page 63   **ancestor who was a mail-order bride:** David L. Russell, *Patricia MacLachlan* (New York: Twayne, 1997), p. 65.

Page 63   **"it keeps me centered":** www.audiofilemagazine.com/features/A1086.html, accessed March 20, 2006.

Page 63   **"It was a gift for all of us":** Maria B. Salvadore, Roger Sutton, and Kathleen T. Horning, eds., *The Newbery & Caldecott Medal Books, 1986–2000: A Comprehensive Guide to the Winners* (Chicago and London: American Library Association, 2001), p. 40.

Page 63   **"wrap the land and the people":** Ibid., p. 41.

Pages 63–64   **"words are limiting"** . . . **"It is often what is left unsaid":** Ibid.

Because of Winn-Dixie

Page 70   **"I did not know it":** *Something about the Author*, vol. 121 (Detroit: Thomson Gale, 2001), p. 75.

Half Magic

Page 76   **a family of three girls . . . in certain respects the prototypes:** *Something about the Author*, vol. 17 (Detroit: Gale, 1979), pp. 56–57.

Page 76   **"second-generation Nesbitian"; "I have not got":** Ibid.

Charlie and the Chocolate Factory

Page 82   **"chocolate-guzzling"; "When I was young":** Roald Dahl, "The Chocolate Revolution," *Sunday Magazine*, September 7, 1997, www.roalddahlfans.com/articles/choc.php, accessed April 15, 2006.

Page 83   **In an early draft of *Charlie*:** "Early Drafts of *Charlie and the Chocolate Factory*," www.roalddahlmuseum.org/discoverdahl, accessed April 15, 2006.

Page 83   **black pygmies from Africa:** Mark I. West, *Roald Dahl* (New York: Twayne, 1992), pp. 70–71.

Page 83   **he and his wife . . . planning to write a cookbook:** Felicity Dahl, *Roald Dahl's Revolting Recipes* (New York: Viking, 1994), "Introduction."

Frindle

Page 90   "Pulling a pen": www.frindle.com/faq.html, accessed January 21, 2006.

Page 90   "When I was a fourth-grade teacher": Kid Scoops, *Time for Kids*, "Meet Andrew Clements, Author," www.timeforkids.com/TFK/kidscoops/ story, January 21, 2006.

Page 90   "One of the things I love about Nick": www.frindle.com/faq.html, accessed January 21, 2006.

The Lion, the Witch and the Wardrobe

Page 102   The idea for *The Lion, the Witch and the Wardrobe*: Michael White, *C. S. Lewis: A Life* (New York: Carroll & Graf, 2004), p. 130.

Page 102   the dreams and "mental pictures": Ibid., p. 129.

Page 102   Lewis was a scholar at Oxford: Anita Silvey, ed., *Children's Books and Their Creators* (Boston: Houghton Mifflin, 1995), p. 405.

Page 102   no intention of writing a Christian allegory: White, *C. S. Lewis: A Life*, p. 133.

Page 102   "Everything began with images": C. S. Lewis, *Of Other Worlds: Essays and Stories* (New York: Harcourt, Brace & World, 1966), p. 36.

Page 102   Chronicles are best read chronologically: Silvey, *Children's Books and Their Creators*, p. 406.

Page 103   Turkish delight was first concocted: www.turkish-delight.com, accessed January 12, 2006.

The Phantom Tollbooth

Page 111   An architect who had received a grant: http:archive.salon.com/books/int/2001/03/12/juster/, accessed January 12, 2006.

Page 111   "seemed like a perfect, contemporary way": Ibid.

Page 111   simply eavesdropping on the characters: Ibid.

Chasing Vermeer

Page 120   "in part because you're never": http://teacher.scholastic.com/authorsandbooks/events/balliett/transcript.htm, accessed January 23, 2006.

Page 120   "with a little sprinkling": Ibid.

The City of Ember

Page 134   "What would it be like to live": http:www.jeanneduprau.com/faq.shtml, accessed June 30, 2006.

Freaky Friday

Page 149   "Since I had nothing to do": *Something about the Author*, vol. 130 (Detroit: Gale, 2002), p. 186.

Hatchet

Page 155   He wrote *Hatchet . . .* while training: Elizabeth Paterra, *Gary Paulsen* (Philadelphia: Chelsea House, 2002), p. 81.

Page 155   Readers have consistently asked: www.randomhouse.com/features/garypaulsen/new adventures.html, accessed January 3, 2006.

Page 155   watched a man die before his eyes: Gary Paulsen, *Guts: The True Stories Behind Hatchet and the Brian Books* (New York: Laurel-Leaf, 2001), pp. 1–6.

Page 155   "She made it personal": Ibid., p. 51.

Page 155   turtle eggs . . . tried to eat some: Ibid., pp. 132–134.

Holes

Page 161   "Anybody who has ever tried": www.louissachar.com/HolesBook.htm, accessed April 8, 2006.

Page 161   *Holes* is Sachar's favorite: Ibid.

Page 161   Creating the multilayered story: Ibid.

Page 161   It took Sachar a year and a half: Ibid.

The Watsons Go to Birmingham—1963

Page 181   While working at the auto factory: www.powells.com/authors/curtis.html, accessed March 1, 2006.

Harry Potter and the Half-Blood Prince

Page 189   "Book Six does what I wanted": www.jkrowling.com/textonly/en/faq_view, accessed April 8, 2006.

Page 189   "it's been about thirteen years": www.jkrowling.com/en, accessed April 8, 2006.

Page 189   the Pensieve re-creates a moment: www.mugglenet.com/jkrinterview3.shtml, accessed April 8, 2006.

Page 189   "the feasts at Hogwarts": www.quick-quote-quill.org/articles/2005/0705-edinburgh-ITVcubreporters.htm, accessed April 8, 2006.

Page 189   "I have always found it slightly sinister": Ibid.

Hoot

Page 218   **"a passion for wild places":** www.carlhiaasen.com, accessed March 14, 2006.

Page 218   **During Hiaasen's childhood, the owls:** www.bookreporter.com/authors/au-hiassen-carl.asp, accessed March 14, 2006.

Page 218   **"without worrying about the salty language":** www.carlhiaasen.com, accessed March 14, 2006.

Page 218   **His experiences being intimidated:** www.powells.com/authors/hiaasen.html, accessed March 14, 2006.

Out of the Dust

Page 224   **"The frugality of the life":** Newbery Medal acceptance speech, June 27, 1998, www.scholastic.com/titles/outofthedust/speech.htm, accessed January 8, 2006.

The View from Saturday

Page 247   **"more interested in what was going on":** Connie C. Rockman, ed., *Eighth Book of Junior Authors and Illustrators* (New York: H. W. Wilson, 2000), p. 276.

Page 248   **"When I write a book.":** Ibid., p. 277.

Page 248   **"A person must experience kindness":** Newbery Medal acceptance speech, 1997, Maria B. Salvadore, Roger Sutton, and Kathleen T. Horning, eds., *The Newbery & Caldecott Medal Books, 1986-2000: A Comprehensive Guide to the Winners* (Chicago and London: American Library Association, 2001), p. 273.

Walk Two Moons

Page 255   **became the fictional town of Bybanks:** Alice B. McGinty, *Sharon Creech* (New York: Rosen, 2006), p. 16.

Page 255   **trip that inspired Sal's cross-country journey:** Maria B. Salvadore, Roger Sutton, and Kathleen T. Horning, eds., *The Newbery & Caldecott Medal Books, 1986–2000: A Comprehensive Guide to the Winners* (Chicago and London: American Library Association, 2001), p. 231.

Page 255   **finding the name "Salamanca":** McGinty, *Sharon Creech*, p. 40.

Page 255   **a cousin told her she had:** Ibid., p. 17.

Page 255   **While struggling to strengthen:** Ibid., p. 38.

The House of the Scorpion

Page 262   **"My father took me to the American Legion hall":** *Something about the Author*, vol. 117 (Detroit: Gale, 2000), p. 57.

Eragon

Page 276   **Paolini says he had no intention:** www.teenreads.com/authors/au-paolini-christopher .asp, accessed October 12, 2005.

Page 276   **stepson of author Carl Hiaasen:** Ibid.

Page 277   **Paolini created three languages:** Ibid.

Page 277   **character of Angela the herbalist:** Ibid.

Al Capone Does My Shirts

Page 286   **"I interviewed people":** *Preview*, Spring 2004, www.choldenko.com/pages/interview .html, accessed January 10, 2006.

Ender's Game

Page 332   **Card wrote poetry, short stories, and plays; "on-again, off-again":** www.roanoke.com/ extra/wb/wb/xp-68705, accessed June 22, 2006.

Page 332   **more than forty novels:** www.hauntedcomputer.com/ghostwr22.htm, accessed November 29, 2005.

Page 332   **Mormon . . . two years in Brazil:** *Something about the Author*, vol. 127 (Detroit: Gale, 2002), p. 15.

Page 332   **"Without ever meaning to":** www.roanoke.com/extra/wb/wb/xp-68705, accessed June 22, 2006.

Page 332   **"Think about it":** www.hatrack.com/research/interviews/2004-endersgame.shtml, accessed April 6, 2006.

Page 333   **Space Peanut Butter and Jelly Wraps:** NASA, "Special Recipes Give Space Station Crew a Taste of Home," http://space.about.com/cs/iss/a/issholidaymeal.htm, accessed June 14, 2006.

Page 333   **crumbly food . . . can be hazardous:** Ibid.

Page 334   **Orange Space Drink:** www.NASAexplores.com, accessed June 14, 2006; as well as www.mariannedyson.com/spaceactivities.html, accessed April 6, 2006.

Page 334   **Space missions . . . minimize the weight; water, a by-product:** www.marianne dyson.com/spaceactivities.html, accessed April 6, 2006.

Page 334   **"can eat daily, forever":** http://www.hatrack.com/research/questions/q0102.shtml, accessed April 6, 2006.

The Giver

Page 341   **"I tried to make Jonas's world":** Newbery Medal acceptance speech, 1994, www.lois lowry.com/pdf/Newbery_Award.pdf, accessed February 8, 2006.

Page 341   "There's a right one": Ibid.

Page 341   landscape and still-life painter Carl Nelson: Ibid.

Page 341   "is a much more complicated book": "A Conversation with Lois Lowry," *The Giver: A Readers Guide: The Giver* (New York: Dell, 1993), p. 5.

The Sisterhood of the Traveling Pants

Page 355   The idea for the traveling pants: www.bookbrowse.com/author_interviews/, accessed March 22, 2006.

Page 355   "backstabbing and cruel social food chains": "Author Interview," *The Sisterhood of the Traveling Pants,* DVD (Warner Brothers, 2005).

Page 355   Brashares has never traveled: www.bookbrowse.com/author_interviews/, accessed March 22, 2006.

Stuck in Neutral

Page 363   "worst thing that ever happened" . . . "gave me insights": Kelly Milner Halls, "Terry Trueman: The Price of Honor," www.terrytrueman.com, accessed April 1, 2006.

The Curious Incident of the Dog in the Night-Time

Pages 372, "boring people with desperately limited lives" . . . "Austen writes": Mark Haddon, "B
373   Is for Bestseller," *The Guardian*, April 11, 2004, http://books.guardian.co.uk/departments/ childrenandteens/story/0,6000,1189538,00.html, accessed April 21, 2006.

Page 373   "because I wanted Christopher to work": www.randomhouse.co.uk/offthepage/ guide.htm, accessed April 21, 2006.

Page 373   "I realised that if you described": www.randomhouse.co.uk/readersgroup/qanda 0309.htm, accessed April 21, 2006.

Page 373   "straight out of my own head"; "If you enjoy": www.powells.com/authors/haddon .html, accessed April 21, 2006.

Page 374   "it was one of those glorious moments"; "the book could have worked": www .randomhouse.co.uk/readersgroup/qanda0309.htm, accessed April 21, 2006.

Speak

Page 397   "And so I had to write": Laurie Halse Anderson, "Speaking Out," *The ALAN Review*, Spring 2000, http://scholar.lib.vt.edu/ejournals/ALAN/spring00/anderson.htm, accessed January 18, 2006.

To Kill a Mockingbird

Page 403   **recluse named Sonny Boular:** Harold Bloom, *Bloom's Guides: Harper Lee's* To Kill a Mockingbird (Philadelphia: Chelsea House, 2004), p. 12.

Page 403   **Lee's trips . . . reawakened childhood memories:** Joyce Milton, *Barron's Book Notes: Harper Lee's* To Kill a Mockingbird (New York: Barron's Educational Series, 1984), p. 2.

Page 403   **the 1931 trial in Scottsboro, Alabama:** Bloom, *Bloom's Guides* . . . To Kill a Mockingbird, pp. 13–14.

Page 404   **in 1961 . . . working on a second novel:** Milton, *Barron's Book Notes* . . . To Kill a Mockingbird, p. 4.

Page 404   **a spirited girl who bullied boys:** Bloom, *Bloom's Guides* . . . To Kill a Mockingbird, p. 13.

Persepolis

Page 411   **she moved into a studio apartment in Paris:** www.asiasource.org/news/special_reports/satrapi.cfm, accessed April 3, 2006.

Page 411   **"thinking with images"; "From the second I made":** Ibid.

Page 411   **"If people are given the chance":** www.listeninglib.com/pantheon/graphicnovels/satrapi2.html, accessed March 2, 2006.

Page 411   **Satrapi was detained and questioned; Satrapi considers:** Edward Guthmann, "Weed, Sex, Paranoia—Iranian Graphic Novelist Marjane Satrapi Lets It All Out in 'Persepolis' Sequel," *San Francisco Chronicle*, October 2, 2004, www.sfgate.com/cgi-bin/article.cgi?f=/c/a/2004/10/02/DDG2J915OU1.DTL, accessed April 3, 2006.

Page 411   **"the most important thing":** www.listeninglib.com/pantheon/graphicnovels/satrapi2.html, accessed March 2, 2006.

Page 412   **In ancient times, the king of Persia:** Margaret Shaida, *The Legendary Cuisine of Persia* (New York: Interlink, 2002), p. 110.

Page 412   **Iranians of all social classes:** www.iranagrofood.com/mive/tree.htm, accessed May 11, 2006.

Page 413   **The prevalence of tea in Iranian society:** In *The Legendary Cuisine of Persia*, Margaret Shaida gives a concise and informative account of the history of coffeehouses (and later teahouses) in Iran, which we have summarized here.

Page 413   **combining Earl Grey and Darjeeling teas:** Ibid., p. 246.

Acknowledgments

Many people worked together to bring *The Kids' Book Club Book* to readers.

The Kids' Book Club Book could not have been written without the creativity and generosity of hundreds of youth book club members across the country. These parents, librarians, teachers, bookstore staff, students, program directors, and community leaders shared their stories, recipes, activity ideas, and suggestions for making the book club experience fulfilling and fun. Our thanks go to the many people who completed surveys, granted interviews, and in some cases, sent detailed information and updates on their clubs' activities over eighteen months, but who are not named in the book: Katy Colthart Abblett, Sylvia Anderle, Angela Arnold, Ruhama Kordatzky Bahr, Barb Ballou, Katina Barksdale, Gerald Benjamin, Laurie Benner, Jill Benson, Janet Bernardo, Paula Beswick, Linda Bethers, Miffie Blozvich, Alex Blum, Alison Boyer, Heidi Brown, Miriam Budin, Kris Buker, Vicky Burr, Marta Campbell, Marla Choslovsky, Cindy Christin, Paul Christopherson, Karen Clodfelter, Robin Cohen, Victoria Cohen, Helen Cordes, Aaron Coutu, Stacy Creel, Judy Cunningham, Frederick Daly, Janice Davoren, Jenna Davoren, Diane DeVore, Sherry DeWeerdt, Terrie Dorio, Sara Doyle, Jason Driver, Lindsey Dunn, Sandra Farrell, Lora Fegley, Sharon Feistner, Diana Fiske, Donna Fuell, Mary Garland, Alyse Goldman, Penny Gordon, Michele Gorman, Cynthia Grabke, Judi Greenberg, Danielle Greenburg, Jackie Gropman, Robin Gunter, Jennifer Haberkorn, JoAnn Hamm, Sharon Hamman, Debbie Hassi, Judy Hawkins, Karen Hebbert, Charity Hegna, Charlene Heinning, Stephanie Herlihy, Deb Hiett, Ned Hinman, Jim Huang, Elizabeth

Marsh Ide, Linda Israel, Courtney Jackson, Rachel Kamin, Paul Kaplan, Justin Keeler, Gaye Kulvete, Cathy Kyle, Nancy Lambert, Gabby Lavoie, Mary Lavoie, Lisa Lehman, Naomi Lerner, Sheila Levitan, Gail Liebhaber, Julia Lipman, Maria Lowe, Kitty Lyons, Jill MacKinnon, Terri MacRae, Deborah Madigan, Tirzah Maroun, Malavika Muralidharan, Cheryl McCurry, Carol McDaniel, Jerry McNally, Katherine Mellniek, Erin Miklauz, Sonja Milbourn, Amy Miller, Christian L. Miller, Jane Miller, Ryan Mohling, Deb Motley, Dianne Murray, Lisa Newfield, Michael Nolan, Lisa Ohman, Marian Ossman, Elizabeth Pata, Victoria Penny, Shawn Personke, Kathleen Pierce, Gary Pysznik, Marian Rafal, Jennifer Reichert, Peggy Rhoads, Linda Rice, Julie Roach, Mike Roberts, Lisa Rucinski, Frances Runnells, Cathy Russell, Cathy Ryne, Mary Sampson, Helen Sauter, Kimberly Schneider, Bernard Schum, Shawna Schwalb, Amy Shea, Amy Short, Jason Shinder, Char Sidell, Maya Spector, Angel Stafford, Joyce Steiner, Kim Stevens, Jennifer Strom, Sara Swenson, Christie Vilsack, Diane M. Walsh, Jennifer Weimann, Mindi Welton-Mitchell, Robin Willard, Karen Wise, Jennifer Worley, Robin Wright, Erin Wyatt, Deborah Yandell, Judith Zimmerman, and Deena Zuckerman

Our agent, Marianne Merola, offered her enthusiastic support of the project from its inception and gave us insightful comments and advice throughout. We're grateful for her patience and good humor. Thanks to our editor, Sara Carder, for shepherding the project ably from conception to completion.

We are grateful to our publisher, Joel Fotinos, for embracing our project, and to the talented Tarcher/Penguin staff and associates whose efforts smoothed the publication process from start to finish: assistant editor Kat Kimball, Laura Ingman, Lily Chin, Diane Hodges, Alex Gigante, Jennifer Ann Daddio, and Catherine Lau Hunt.

We are indebted to Peter Krupp for his eagle eye, and Peter Zheutlin for his sharp wit.

We are grateful to the authors who contributed comments, recipes, and activity suggestions, or simply offered guidance and direction. It was our pleasure to work with them: David Almond, Laurie Halse Anderson, Blue Balliett, Edward Bloor, Orson Scott Card, Gennifer Choldenko, Andrew Clements, Christopher Paul Curtis, Kate DiCamillo, Jeanne DuPrau, Deborah Ellis, Nancy Farmer, Sharon G. Flake, Margaret Haddix, Mark Haddon, Karen Hesse, S. E. Hinton, Kimberly Willis Holt, Angela Johnson, Norton Juster, Cynthia Kadohata, E. L. Konigsburg, Gordon Korman, Gail Carson Levine, Lois Lowry, Adeline Yen Mah, Walter Dean Myers, Christopher Paolini, Mary Rodgers, Pam Muñoz Ryan, Jerry Spinelli, Janet Tashjian, Stephanie Tolan, Terry Trueman, Wendelin Van Draanen, and Gloria Whelan.

Our volunteer recipe and activity testers gave their time (and ingredients) to test and help us perfect our recipes, and their suggestions improved each one. Our heartfelt thanks and appreciation go to: Cheryl Aglio-Girelli, Kay Allison, Steve Allison, Hannah Alpert, Ethan Bauer, Linda Bauer, Seth Bauer, Julia Blatt, Susan Bonaiuto, Heidi Brown, Annie Burgess, Laurie Burgess, Molly Burgess, Jim Case, Lars Gill Case, Lucia Gill Case, Karen Cheyney, Suzanne Church, Robin Cohen, Nomi Conway, Sharon Conway, Eden Diamond, Suzanne

Diamond, Mary Kate Dillon, Denise Dirocco, Rebecca Drill, John Evans, Anna Fassler, Eric Fassler, Molly Fassler, Andrew Gelman, Doris Gelman, Lois Gelman, Zoe Gelman, Aaron Aglio Girelli, Ian Aglio Girelli, Girl Scout Troop 1912 in Belmont, Massachusetts, Leslie Gordon, Kim Greenberg, Lynn Hamlin, Elizabeth Hefferon, Meg Hefferon, Louis Hutchins, Susan Katcher, Laura Katz, Jesse Kiel, Jeremy Klein, Stephanie Kornbleuth, Aaron Krupp, Ben Krupp, Joanna Krupp, Connie Leonard, Jane Levin, Barbara Matorin, Ceci Ogden, Ossian Pages, Carol Pankin, Debbie Pryor, Peg Raffa, Courtney Retsky, Julia Rifkin, Larni Rosenlev, Judy Safian, Joey Schindler, Abby Schwartz, Jacob Schwartz, Simon Schwartz, Anna Shuster, Carla Small, Debbie Squires, Sharon Walach-Gale, Danny Zheutlin, and Noah Zheutlin.

Many thanks to the following people, who provided advice, support, guidance, and other assistance: Heidi Brown; Lucia Gill Case; Denise DiRocco; Omoiye Kinney of Tasty Baking Company; Susan Krupp (for her fine artwork); Cathy McCoy of the Monroe County Heritage Museum in Monroeville, Alabama; Savala Nolan of the Studio Museum in Harlem; Elaine Ogden; Cheryl Perl of B.R. Guest Restaurants, Inc.; Tim Podell of Good Conversations!; and Evie Weinstein-Park.

We extend our appreciation to the restaurants and chefs who generously contributed recipes: Scott Drewno and Shawn Edelman, Ruby Foo's restaurants, New York City; Nur Kilic, Serenade Chocolatier, Brookline, Massachusetts; Mike Kostensky, Mike's Place, Kent, Ohio; Janet Sawyer, Courthouse Café, Monroeville, Alabama; and Ken Wada, Hana Restaurant, Seattle.

From Judy:

Thanks to my family—my husband, Peter, and sons, Danny and Noah—for their many contributions to this project, including counting chocolate chips, tying knots in ropes, tasting cookies, reading, and unloading the dishwasher. I am grateful to them for all the accommodations they made throughout the year that allowed us to create this book, and for their encouragement and support! And to the Ogden-Gelman and Gelman-Fassler families and my friends who were on call for testing, advice, and listening, I send many thanks.

From Vicki:

Thanks to my children, Aaron, Ben, and Joanna, who fed me book ideas, critiqued recipes and activities, and offered expert advice about what would, and would not, work for kids. Their joyful presence reminded me every day of why we embarked on this project. My husband, Peter, kept me sane and centered throughout a long process. I thank him for keeping the household running smoothly and working overtime to make crucial contributions to the flow and organization of the book. My family and friends tested recipes and offered all manner of advice and support. To all, I send my warm thanks!

Appendix A

TOP RECOMMENDED TITLES

These titles were recommended most frequently by book clubs we surveyed. An asterisk indicates a title featured in this book.

Fiction

YOUNGER READERS

Because of Winn-Dixie by Kate DiCamillo* (Candlewick Press, 2000)

The Boxcar Children by Gertrude Chandler Warner* (original: Rand McNally, 1924; revised: Scott Foresman, 1942)

Charlie and the Chocolate Factory by Roald Dahl* (Alfred A. Knopf, 1964)

Charlotte's Web by E. B. White (HarperCollins, 1952)

Ella Enchanted by Gail Carson Levine (Harper-Collins, 1997)

The Enormous Egg by Oliver Butterworth (Little, Brown, 1956)

Frindle by Andrew Clements* (Simon & Schuster, 1996)

From the Mixed-up Files of Mrs. Basil E. Frankweiler by E. L. Konigsburg (Atheneum, 1967)

Half Magic by Edward Eager* (Harcourt, 1954)

The Hundred Dresses by Eleanor Estes* (1944)

The Lion, the Witch and the Wardrobe by C. S. Lewis* (1950)

The Magic Tree House series by Mary Pope Osborne (Random House)

Maniac Magee by Jerry Spinelli* (Little, Brown, 1990)

The Phantom Tollbooth by Norton Juster* (Alfred A. Knopf, 1961)

Sarah, Plain and Tall by Patricia MacLachlan* (Joanna Cotler, 1985)

The Spiderwick Chronicles (1–5) by Holly Black (Simon & Schuster)

MIDDLE GRADE READERS

Among the Hidden by Margaret Peterson Haddix*
(Simon & Schuster, 1998)

The Amulet of Samarkand by Jonathan Stroud
(Miramax, 2003)

The Bad Beginning (A Series of Unfortunate
Events, Book 1), by Lemony Snicket
(HarperCollins,1999)

Bloomability by Sharon Creech (Joanna Cotler,
1998)

The Boy Who Saved Baseball by John H. Ritter
(Philomel, 2003)

The Breadwinner by Deborah Ellis* (Groundwood, 2001)

Bud, Not Buddy by Christopher Paul Curtis
(Delacorte, 1999)

The Call of the Wild by Jack London
(Macmillan, 1903)

Chasing Vermeer by Blue Balliett* (Scholastic,
2004)

Cirque Du Freak by Darren Shan (Little,
Brown, 2001)

The City of Ember by Jeanne DuPrau*
(Random House, 2003)

Coraline by Neil Gaiman (HarperCollins, 2002)

Dave at Night by Gail Carson Levine* (Harper-
Collins, 1999)

Define Normal by Julie Anne Peters (Megan
Tingley, 2000)

Eldest by Christopher Paolini (Alfred A. Knopf,
2005)

Eragon by Christopher Paolini* (Alfred A.
Knopf, 2003)

Esperanza Rising by Pam Muñoz Ryan*
(Scholastic, 2000)

Everything on a Waffle by Polly Horvath (Farrar,
Straus & Giroux, 2001)

Fair Weather by Richard Peck (Dial, 2001)

Faraway Summer by Johanna Hurwitz (William
Morrow, 1998)

Fever 1793 by Laurie Halse Anderson (Simon &
Schuster, 2000)

Freaky Friday by Mary Rodgers*
(HarperCollins, 1972)

Getting Near to Baby by Audrey Couloumbis
(Putnam, 1999)

The Girls by Amy Goldman Koss (Dial, 2000)

The Great Turkey Walk by Kathleen Karr
(Farrar, Straus & Giroux, 1998)

Gregor the Overlander by Suzanne Collins
(Scholastic, 2003)

Harry Potter and the Half-Blood Prince by J. K.
Rowling* (Scholastic, 2005)

Hatchet by Gary Paulsen* (Macmillan, 1987)

Here Today by Ann Martin (Scholastic, 2004)

Holes by Louis Sachar* (Farrar, Straus &
Giroux, 1998)

Homeless Bird by Gloria Whelan* (Harper-
Collins, 2000)

Hoot by Carl Hiaasen* (Alfred A. Knopf, 2002)

The House of the Scorpion by Nancy Farmer*
(Atheneum/Richard Jackson Books, 2002)

Joey Pigza Swallowed the Key by Jack Gantos
(Farrar, Straus & Giroux, 1998)

Keeper of the Doves by Betsy Byars (Viking,
2002)

The Landry News by Andrew Clements (Simon
& Schuster, 1999)

Lily's Crossing by Patricia Reilly Giff
(Delacorte, 1997)

Loser by Jerry Spinelli (Joanna Cotler, 2002)

Love Among the Walnuts by Jean Ferris
(Harcourt, 1998)

Love from Your Friend, Hannah by Mindy Warshaw Skolsky (Dorling Kindersley, 1998)

Love That Dog by Sharon Creech (Joanna
Cotler, 2001)

Matilda by Roald Dahl (Viking, 1988)

My Louisiana Sky by Kimberly Willis Holt*
(Henry Holt, 1998)

My Side of the Mountain by Jean Craighead George (Dutton, 1959)

No More Dead Dogs by Gordon Korman* (Hyperion, 2000)

Number the Stars by Lois Lowry (Houghton Mifflin, 1989)

Our Only May Amelia by Jennifer L. Holm (HarperCollins, 1999)

Out of the Dust by Karen Hesse* (Scholastic, 1997)

The Outcasts of 19 Schuyler Place by E. L. Konigsburg (Atheneum, 2004)

The People of Sparks by Jeanne DuPrau (Random House, 2004)

Pictures of Hollis Woods by Patricia Reilly Giff (Wendy Lamb, 2002)

The Ravenmaster's Secret by Elvira Woodruff (Scholastic, 2003)

Redwall by Brian Jacques (Ace, 1986)

Riding Freedom by Pam Muñoz Ryan (Scholastic, 1998)

Ruby Holler by Sharon Creech (Joanna Cotler, 2002)

Running Out of Time by Margaret Peterson Haddix (Simon & Schuster, 1995)

Sahara Special by Esmé Raji Codell (Hyperion, 2003)

Samantha's Story Collection by Susan S. Adler et al. (American Girl, 2004)

The Schwa Was Here by Neal Shusterman (Dutton, 2004)

The Secret of Platform 13 by Eva Ibbotson (Dutton, 1998)

Seedfolks by Paul Fleischman (Joanna Cotler, 1997)

The Sign of the Beaver by Elizabeth George Speare (Houghton Mifflin, 1983)

A Single Shard by Linda Sue Park (Clarion, 2001)

Skellig by David Almond* (Random House, 1998)

Surviving the Applewhites by Stephanie Tolan* (HarperCollins, 2002)

The Tale of Despereaux by Kate DiCamillo (Candlewick, 2003)

The Thief Lord by Cornelia Funke (Chicken House, 2002)

Things Not Seen by Andrew Clements (Philomel, 2002)

Tuck Everlasting by Natalie Babbitt (Farrar, Straus & Giroux, 1975)

The View from Saturday by E. L. Konigsburg* (Simon & Schuster, 1996)

Walk Two Moons by Sharon Creech* (Joanna Cotler, 1994)

The Watsons Go to Birmingham—1963 by Christopher Paul Curtis* (Delacorte, 1993)

The Westing Game by Ellen Raskin (Novel Units, 1998)

The Witch of Blackbird Pond by Elizabeth George Speare (Houghton Mifflin, 1958)

A Wrinkle in Time by Madeline L'Engle (Farrar, Straus & Giroux, 1962)

YOUNG TEEN READERS

Al Capone Does My Shirts by Gennifer Choldenko* (Putnam, 2004)

Alanna by Tamora Pierce (Peter Smith, 1999)

Big Mouth & Ugly Girl by Joyce Carol Oates (HarperTempest, 2002)

Bloody Jack by Louis Meyer (Harcourt, 2002)

A Break with Charity: A Story About the Salem Witch Trials by Ann Rinaldi (Gulliver, 1992)

Bronx Masquerade by Nikki Grimes (Dial, 2001)

The Chocolate War by Robert Cormier (Alfred A. Knopf, 1974)

Ender's Game by Orson Scott Card* (Tor, 1985)

Fat Chance by Leslea Newman (Putnam, 1994)

Fat Kid Rules the World by K. L. Going (Putnam, 2003)

Feed by M. T. Anderson (Candlewick, 2002)

Flipped by Wendelin Van Draanen* (Alfred A. Knopf, 2001)

The Giver by Lois Lowry* (Houghton Mifflin, 1993)

The Golden Compass by Philip Pullman (Alfred A. Knopf, 1996)

Hope Was Here by Joan Bauer (Putnam, 2000)

Kira-Kira by Cynthia Kadohata* (Atheneum, 2004)

Kissing Doorknobs by Terry Spencer Hesser (Delacorte, 1998)

Maus by Art Spiegelman (Pantheon, 1991)

Monster by Walter Dean Myers* (Amistad, 1999)

Nothing but the Truth by Avi (Scholastic, 1991)

The Other Side of Truth by Beverly Naidoo (Puffin, 2000)

The Outsiders by S. E. Hinton* (Viking, 1967)

Rules of the Road by Joan Bauer (Putnam, 1998)

Sabriel by Garth Nix (Eos, 1996)

Silent to the Bone by E. L. Konigsburg (Atheneum, 2000)

The Sisterhood of the Traveling Pants by Ann Brashares* (Delacorte, 2001)

The Skin I'm In by Sharon G. Flake* (Hyperion, 1998)

Snow in August by Pete Hamill (Little, Brown, 1997)

So B. It by Sarah Weeks (Laura Geringer, 2004)

Stargirl by Jerry Spinelli (Alfred A. Knopf, 2000)

Stormbreaker by Anthony Horowitz (Philomel, 2001)

Stuck in Neutral by Terry Trueman* (Harper-Collins, 2000)

Tangerine by Edward Bloor* (Harcourt, 1997)

That Summer by Sarah Dessen (Penguin, 1996)

Touching Spirit Bear by Ben Mikaelsen (Harper-Collins, 2001)

Twilight by Stephanie Meyer (Megan Tingley, 2005)

Uglies by Scott Westerfield (Simon Pulse, 2005)

Whale Talk by Cris Crutcher (Greenwillow, 2001)

OLDER TEEN READERS

Catch-22 by Joseph Heller (Simon & Schuster, 1961)

The Curious Incident of the Dog in the Night-Time by Mark Haddon* (Doubleday, 2003)

Cut by Patricia McCormick (Front Street, 2000)

Fahrenheit 451 by Ray Bradbury (Ballantine, 1953)

The First Part Last by Angela Johnson* (Simon & Schuster, 2003)

The Gospel According to Larry by Janet Tashjian* (Henry Holt, 2001)

How I Live Now by Meg Rosoff (Random House, 2004)

The Kite Runner by Khaled Hosseini (River-head, 2003)

Life of Pi by Yann Martel (Harcourt, 2002)

Looking for Alaska by John Green (Dutton, 2005)

The Lovely Bones by Alice Sebold (Little, Brown, 2002)

My Sister's Keeper by Jodi Picoult (Atria, 2004)

A Northern Light by Jennifer Donnelly (Harcourt, 2003)

The Perks of Being a Wallflower by Stephen Chbosky (MTV Books, 1999)

The Secret Life of Bees by Sue Monk Kidd (Viking, 2003)

Speak by Laurie Halse Anderson* (Farrar, Straus & Giroux, 1999)

To Kill a Mockingbird by Harper Lee* (1960)

Nonfiction

YOUNG TEEN READERS

Chinese Cinderella by Adeline Yen Mah*
    (Delacorte, 1999)
*Red Scarf Girl: A Memoir of the Cultural Revo-
    lution* by Ji Li Jiang (HarperCollins, 1997)

OLDER TEEN READERS

Nickel and Dimed by Barbara Ehrenreich
    (Metropolitan, 2001)
Persepolis by Marjane Satrapi* (Pantheon, 2003)

Classics

YOUNGER READERS

The Boxcar Children by Gertrude Chandler
    Warner*
Charlie and the Chocolate Factory by Roald
    Dahl*
Charlotte's Web by E. B. White
*From the Mixed-up Files of Mrs. Basil E.
    Frankweiler* by E. L. Konigsburg*
The Hundred Dresses by Eleanor Estes*
The Lion, the Witch and the Wardrobe
    by C. S. Lewis*
The Phantom Tollbooth by Norton Juster*

MIDDLE GRADE READERS

Freaky Friday by Mary Rodgers*
My Side of the Mountain by Jean Craighead
    George
Tuck Everlasting by Natalie Babbitt
The Westing Game by Ellen Raskin
The Witch of Blackbird Pond by Elizabeth
    George Speare
A Wrinkle in Time by Madeline L'Engle

YOUNG TEEN READERS

The Chocolate War by Robert Cormier

Ender's Game by Orson Scott Card*
The Outsiders by S. E. Hinton*

OLDER TEEN READERS

Catch-22 by Joseph Heller
Fahrenheit 451 by Ray Bradbury
To Kill a Mockingbird by Harper Lee*

Fantasy

YOUNGER READERS

Charlie and the Chocolate Factory
    by Roald Dahl*
Charlotte's Web by E. B. White
Ella Enchanted by Gail Carson Levine
The Enormous Egg by Oliver Butterworth
Half Magic by Edward Eager*
The Lion, the Witch and the Wardrobe
    by C. S. Lewis
The Magic Tree House series by Mary Pope
    Osborne
The Phantom Tollbooth by Norton Juster*
The Spiderwick Chronicles (1–5) by Holly Black

MIDDLE GRADE READERS

The Amulet of Samarkand by Jonathan Stroud
Cirque Du Freak by Darren Shan
Coraline by Neil Gaiman
Eldest by Christopher Paolini
Eragon by Christopher Paolini*
Freaky Friday by Mary Rodgers*
Harry Potter and the Half-Blood Prince
    by J. K. Rowling*
Gregor the Overlander by Suzanne Collins
Matilda by Roald Dahl
Redwall by Brian Jacques
The Secret of Platform 13 by Eva Ibbotson
The Thief Lord by Cornelia Funke
Things Not Seen by Andrew Clements
Tuck Everlasting by Natalie Babbitt

YOUNG TEEN READERS

Alanna by Tamora Pierce
The Golden Compass by Philip Pullman
Sabriel by Garth Nix
Skellig by David Almond*
Twilight by Stephanie Meyer

Historical Fiction

YOUNGER READERS

Sarah, Plain and Tall by Patricia MacLachlan*

MIDDLE GRADE READERS

The Breadwinner by Deborah Ellis*
Bud, Not Buddy by Christopher Paul Curtis
Dave at Night by Gail Carson Levine*
Esperanza Rising by Pam Muñoz Ryan*
Fair Weather by Richard Peck
Faraway Summer by Johanna Hurwitz
Fever 1793 by Laurie Halse Anderson
The Great Turkey Walk by Kathleen Karr
Keeper of the Doves by Betsy Byars
Lily's Crossing by Patricia Reilly Giff
Love from Your Friend, Hannah by Mindy Warshaw Skolsky
Number the Stars by Lois Lowry
Our Only May Amelia by Jennifer L. Holm
Out of the Dust by Karen Hesse*
The Ravenmaster's Secret by Elvira Woodruff
Riding Freedom by Pam Muñoz Ryan
Samantha's Story Collection by Susan S. Adler et al.
The Sign of the Beaver by Elizabeth George Speare
The Watsons Go to Birmingham—1963 by Christopher Paul Curtis*

YOUNG TEEN READERS

Al Capone Does My Shirts by Gennifer Choldenko*

Bloody Jack by Louis Meyer
A Break with Charity: A Story About the Salem Witch Trials by Ann Rinaldi
Snow in August by Pete Hamill

OLDER TEEN READERS

Catch-22 by Joseph Heller
A Northern Light by Jennifer Donnelly
The Secret Life of Bees by Sue Monk Kidd
To Kill a Mockingbird by Harper Lee*

Mystery/Suspense

YOUNGER READERS

The Boxcar Children by Gertrude Chandler Warner*
The Spiderwick Chronicles (1–5) by Holly Black

MIDDLE GRADE READERS

Among the Hidden by Margaret Peterson Haddix*
Chasing Vermeer by Blue Balliett*
Cirque Du Freak by Darren Shan
Coraline by Neil Gaiman
Hoot by Carl Hiaasen*
The Westing Game by Ellen Raskin

YOUNG TEEN READERS

Stormbreaker by Anthony Horowitz

OLDER TEEN READERS

The Curious Incident of the Dog in the Night-Time by Mark Haddon*

Outdoor Adventure

MIDDLE GRADE READERS

Call of the Wild by Jack London
Hatchet by Gary Paulsen*
My Side of the Mountain by Jean Craighead George

Science Fiction

MIDDLE GRADE READERS

Among the Hidden by Margaret Peterson Haddix*
The City of Ember by Jeanne DuPrau*
The House of the Scorpion by Nancy Farmer*
The People of Sparks by Jeanne DuPrau
A Wrinkle in Time by Madeline L'Engle

YOUNG TEEN READERS

Ender's Game by Orson Scott Card*
Feed by M. T. Anderson
The Giver by Lois Lowry*
Uglies by Scott Westerfield

OLDER TEEN READERS

Fahrenheit 451 by Ray Bradbury

African Themes

YOUNG ADULTS

The Other Side of Truth by Beverly Naidoo

African-American Themes

YOUNG READERS

Maniac Magee by Jerry Spinelli*

MIDDLE GRADE READERS

Bud, Not Buddy by Christopher Paul Curtis
Here Today by Ann Martin
Holes by Louis Sachar*
Sahara Special by Esmé Raji Codell
The Watsons Go to Birmingham—1963
    by Christopher Paul Curtis*

YOUNG TEEN READERS

Bronx Masquerade by Nikki Grimes
Monster by Walter Dean Myers*
The Skin I'm In by Sharon G. Flake*

OLDER TEEN READERS

The First Part Last by Angela Johnson*
The Secret Life of Bees by Sue Monk Kidd
To Kill a Mockingbird by Harper Lee*

Asian Themes

MIDDLE GRADE READERS

Chinese Cinderella by Adeline Yen Mah*
A Single Shard by Linda Sue Park

YOUNG TEEN READERS

Kira-Kira by Cynthia Kadohata*
Red Scarf Girl: A Memoir of the Cultural
    Revolution by Ji Li Jiang

Indian/Hindu Themes

MIDDLE GRADE READERS

Homeless Bird by Gloria Whelan*
The View from Saturday by E. L. Konigsburg*

OLDER TEEN READERS

Life of Pi by Yann Martel

Jewish Themes

MIDDLE GRADE READERS

Dave at Night by Gail Carson Levine
Faraway Summer by Johanna Hurwitz
Lily's Crossing by Patricia Reilly Giff
Number the Stars by Lois Lowry

YOUNG TEEN READERS

Maus by Art Spiegelman
Snow in August by Pete Hamill

Latin American/ Mexican Themes

MIDDLE GRADE READERS

The Boy Who Saved Baseball by John Ritter
Esperanza Rising by Pam Muñoz Ryan*
The House of the Scorpion by Nancy Farmer*

Multicultural Themes

MIDDLE GRADE READERS

Seedfolks by Paul Fleishman
The View from Saturday by E. L. Konigsburg*

YOUNG TEEN READERS

Whale Talk by Cris Crutcher

Native American Themes

MIDDLE GRADE READERS

The Sign of the Beaver by Elizabeth George
Speare

YOUNG TEEN READERS

Touching Spirit Bear by Ben Mikaelsen
Walk Two Moons by Sharon Creech*

Female Main Characters

YOUNGER READERS

Because of Winn-Dixie by Kate DiCamillo*
The Hundred Dresses by Eleanor Estes*
Sarah, Plain and Tall by Patricia MacLachlan*

MIDDLE GRADE READERS

Bloomability by Sharon Creech
The Breadwinner by Deborah Ellis*
Chinese Cinderella by Adeline Yen Mah*
Coraline by Neil Gaiman
Define Normal by Julie Anne Peters
Ella Enchanted by Gail Carson Levine

Esperanza Rising by Pam Muñoz Ryan*
Everything on a Waffle by Polly Horvath
Fair Weather by Richard Peck
Faraway Summer by Johanna Hurwitz
Fever 1793 by Laurie Halse Anderson
Freaky Friday by Mary Rodgers*
Getting Near to Baby by Audrey Couloumbis
The Girls by Amy Goldman Koss
Here Today by Ann Martin
Homeless Bird by Gloria Whelan*
Keeper of the Doves by Betsy Byars
The Landry News by Andrew Clements
Lily's Crossing by Patricia Reilly Giff
Love from Your Friend, Hannah by Mindy
Warshaw Skolsky
Matilda by Roald Dahl
My Louisiana Sky by Kimberly Willis Holt*
Number the Stars by Lois Lowry
Our Only May Amelia by Jennifer L. Holm
Out of the Dust by Karen Hesse
The Outcasts of 19 Schuyler Place by E. L.
Konigsburg
Pictures of Hollis Woods by Patricia Reilly Giff
Riding Freedom by Pam Muñoz Ryan
Running Out of Time by Margaret Peterson
Haddix
Sahara Special by Esmé Raji Codell
Samantha's Story Collection
by Susan S. Adler et al.
Tuck Everlasting by Natalie Babbitt
Walk Two Moons by Sharon Creech*
The Witch of Blackbird Pond by Elizabeth
George Speare

YOUNG TEEN READERS

Alanna by Tamora Pierce
Big Mouth & Ugly Girl by Joyce Carol Oates
Bloody Jack by Louis Meyer
*A Break with Charity: A Story About the Salem
Witch Trials* by Ann Rinaldi

Fat Chance by Leslea Newman
The Golden Compass by Philip Pullman
Hope Was Here by Joan Bauer
Kira-Kira by Cynthia Kadohata*
Kissing Doorknobs by Terry Hesser
The Other Side of Truth by Beverly Naidoo
Red Scarf Girl: A Memoir of the Cultural Revolution by Ji Li Jiang
Rules of the Road by Joan Bauer
Sisterhood of the Traveling Pants by Ann Brashares*
The Skin I'm In by Sharon G. Flake*
So B. It by Sarah Weeks
That Summer by Sarah Dessen
Twilight by Stephanie Meyer
Uglies by Scott Westerfield

OLDER TEEN READERS

Cut by Patricia McCormick
How I Live Now by Meg Rosoff
The Lovely Bones by Alice Sebold
My Sister's Keeper by Jodi Picoult
A Northern Light by Jennifer Donnelly
Persepolis by Marjane Satrapi*
The Secret Life of Bees by Sue Monk Kidd
Speak by Laurie Halse Anderson

Male Main Characters

YOUNGER READERS

Charlie and the Chocolate Factory by Roald Dahl*
The Enormous Egg by Oliver Butterworth
Frindle by Andrew Clements*
Maniac Magee by Jerry Spinelli*
The Phantom Tollbooth by Norton Juster*

MIDDLE GRADE READERS

Among the Hidden by Margaret Peterson Haddix*
The Amulet of Samarkand by Jonathan Stroud
The Boy Who Saved Baseball by John Ritter

Bud, Not Buddy by Christopher Paul Curtis
Cirque Du Freak by Darren Shan
Dave at Night by Gail Carson Levine*
Eragon by Christopher Paolini*
The Great Turkey Walk by Kathleen Karr
Gregor the Overlander by Suzanne Collins
Harry Potter and the Half-Blood Prince by J. K. Rowling*
Hatchet by Gary Paulsen*
Holes by Louis Sachar*
Hoot by Carl Hiaasen*
The House of the Scorpion by Nancy Farmer*
Joey Pigza Swallowed the Key by Jack Gantos
Loser by Jerry Spinelli
Love Among the Walnuts by Jean Ferris
Love That Dog by Sharon Creech
My Side of the Mountain by Jean Craighead George
No More Dead Dogs by Gordon Korman*
The Ravenmaster's Secret by Elvira Woodruff
The Schwa Was Here by Neal Shusterman
The Secret of Platform 13 by Eva Ibbotson
The Sign of the Beaver by Elizabeth George Speare
A Single Shard by Linda Sue Park
Surviving the Applewhites by Stephanie Tolan*
The Thief Lord by Cornelia Funke
Things Not Seen by Andrew Clements
The Watsons Go to Birmingham—1963 by Christopher Paul Curtis*

YOUNG TEEN READERS

Al Capone Does My Shirts by Gennifer Choldenko*
The Chocolate War by Robert Cormier
Ender's Game by Orson Scott Card*
Fat Kid Rules the World by K. L. Going
Feed by M. T. Anderson
The Giver by Lois Lowry*
Maus by Art Spiegelman

Monster by Walter Dean Myers*
Nothing but the Truth by Avi
The Outsiders by S. E. Hinton*
Sabriel by Garth Nix
Silent to the Bone by E. L. Konigsburg
Snow in August by Pete Hamill
Stormbreaker by Anthony Horowitz
Stuck in Neutral by Terry Trueman*
Tangerine by Edward Bloor*
Touching Spirit Bear by Ben Mikaelsen
Whale Talk by Cris Crutcher

OLDER TEEN READERS

Catch-22 by Joseph Heller
The Curious Incident of the Dog in the Night-Time by Mark Haddon*
The First Part Last by Angela Johnson*
The Gospel According to Larry by Janet Tashjian*
The Kite Runner by Khaled Hosseini
Life of Pi by Yann Martel
Looking for Alaska by John Green
The Perks of Being a Wallflower by Stephen Chbosky

Both Male and Female Main Characters

YOUNGER READERS

The Boxcar Children by Gertrude Chandler Warner*
From the Mixed-up Files of Mrs. Basil E. Frankweiler by E. L. Konigsburg
Half Magic by Edward Eager*
The Lion, the Witch and the Wardrobe by C. S. Lewis*
The Magic Tree House series by Mary Pope Osborne
The Spiderwick Chronicles (1–5) by Holly Black

MIDDLE GRADE READERS

The Bad Beginning (A Series of Unfortunate Events, Book 1) by Lemony Snicket
Chasing Vermeer by Blue Balliett*
The City of Ember by Jeanne DuPrau*
The People of Sparks by Jeanne DuPrau
Ruby Holler by Sharon Creech
Seedfolks by Paul Flesichman
The View from Saturday by E. L. Konigsburg*
The Westing Game by Ellen Raskin
A Wrinkle in Time by Madeline L'Engle

YOUNG TEEN READERS

Bronx Masquerade by Nikki Grimes
Flipped by Wendelin Van Draanen*
Stargirl by Jerry Spinelli

OLDER TEEN READERS

To Kill a Mockingbird by Harper Lee*

AWARDS FOR FEATURED BOOKS

Pura Belpré Award

Esperanza Rising by Pam Muñoz Ryan

Carnegie Medal

Skellig by David Almond

Coretta Scott King Book Award

The First Part Last by Angela Johnson

National Book Award

Holes by Louis Sachar
Homeless Bird by Gloria Whelan
The House of the Scorpion by Nancy Farmer

John Newbery Medal

The Giver by Lois Lowry
Holes by Louis Sachar
Kira-Kira by Cynthia Kadohata
Maniac Magee by Jerry Spinelli
Out of the Dust by Karen Hesse
Sarah, Plain and Tall by Patricia MacLachlan
The View from Saturday by E. L. Konigsburg
Walk Two Moons by Sharon Creech

Michael L. Printz Award

The First Part Last by Angela Johnson
The House of the Scorpion by Nancy Farmer
Monster by Walter Dean Myers

Pulitzer Prize for Fiction

To Kill a Mockingbird by Harper Lee

Whitbread Children's Book of the Year Award

Skellig by David Almond

Whitbread Book of the Year Award

The Curious Incident of the Dog in the Night-Time by Mark Haddon

Whitbread Novel Award

The Curious Incident of the Dog in the Night-Time by Mark Haddon

Appendix C

RESOURCES

Teen Reads
www.teenreads.com
Reading guides, contests, author interviews, and biographical information for teens.

AUTHOR INTERVIEWS
All About the Book
www.allaboutthebook.com
Videotapes and DVDs for purchase, featuring book discussions with children.

Good Conversations
www.goodconversations.com
Videotapes and DVDs featuring interviews with many contemporary children's authors (including authors featured in this book) for purchase.

Invite an Author Program
http://www.bookclubcookbook.com/invite.htm
List of authors willing to speak to your book club by phone.

Books

FOR AND ABOUT BOOK CLUBS
Deconstructing Penguins: Parents, Kids, and the Bond of Reading by Lawrence and Nancy Goldstone (Ballantine, 2005)
A guide to organizing and facilitating parent-child book groups.

The Mother-Daughter Book Club: How Ten Busy Mothers and Daughters Came Together to Talk, Laugh, and Learn Through Their Love of Reading by Shireen Dodson (HarperCollins, 1997)
Offers advice and inspiration to mother-daughter book clubs through the story of one such group.

The Read-Aloud Handbook by Jim Trelease (Penguin, 2001)
Ideas for books and for how to read aloud with children.

WITH RECOMMENDED TITLES
Book Sense Best Children's Books: 240 Favorites for All Ages Recommended by Independent Booksellers (Newmarket, 2005)
Great Books for Boys: More Than 600 Books for Boys 2 to 14 by Kathleen Odean (Ballantine, 1998)
Great Books for Girls: More Than 600 Books to Inspire Today's Girls and Tomorrow's Women by Kathleen Odean (Ballantine, 2002)
Great Books About Things Kids Love: More Than 750 Recommended Books for Children 3 to 14 by Kathleen Odean (Ballantine, 2001)
The New York Times Parent's Guide to the Best Books for Children: 3rd Edition by Eden Ross Lipson (Three Rivers Press, 2000)
100 Best Books for Children: A Parent's Guide to Making the Right Choices for Your Young Reader, Toddler to Preteen by Anita Silvey (Houghton Mifflin, 2004)
100 Books for Girls to Grow On by Shireen Dodson (HarperPerennial, 1998)

Community Reading

"The Big Read" (National Endowment for the Arts)
www.neabigread.org/communities.php

"One Book" Reading Promotion Projects (Center for the Book, Library of Congress)
www.loc.gov/loc/cfbook/one-book.html
Community reading programs listed by author and community.

General Index

Book and Author Index

Activity Index

Recipe and Food Index

Book Club Index

© Chip Fanelli

Judy Gelman (left) and Vicki Levy Krupp are book enthusiasts, cooks, and friends who came together to coauthor *The Book Club Cookbook: Recipes and Food for Thought from Your Book Club's Favorite Books and Authors* (Tarcher, 2004), featuring recipes and discussion ideas for adult book clubs.

They were motivated to write *The Kids' Book Club Book* after librarians, parents, and teachers who attended their talks asked for a similar book for the growing number of youth book clubs across the country. During their eighteen months of research and writing on this trend, they were inspired by the enthusiasm and ideas of youth book club members, and the insights of notable children's authors whom they contacted. They relished their journey into children's literature.

The authors continue to participate in many book clubs, with both adults and children. They enjoy speaking about book clubs, and appreciate their ongoing conversations with book and food enthusiasts across the country.

Judy Gelman and Vicki Levy Krupp live with their families in the Boston area.

To learn more, visit **www.kidsbookclubbook.com**.